Ocean to Outback

AUSTRALIAN LANDSCAPE PAINTING 1850–1950

Ron Radford

■ national gallery of **australia**

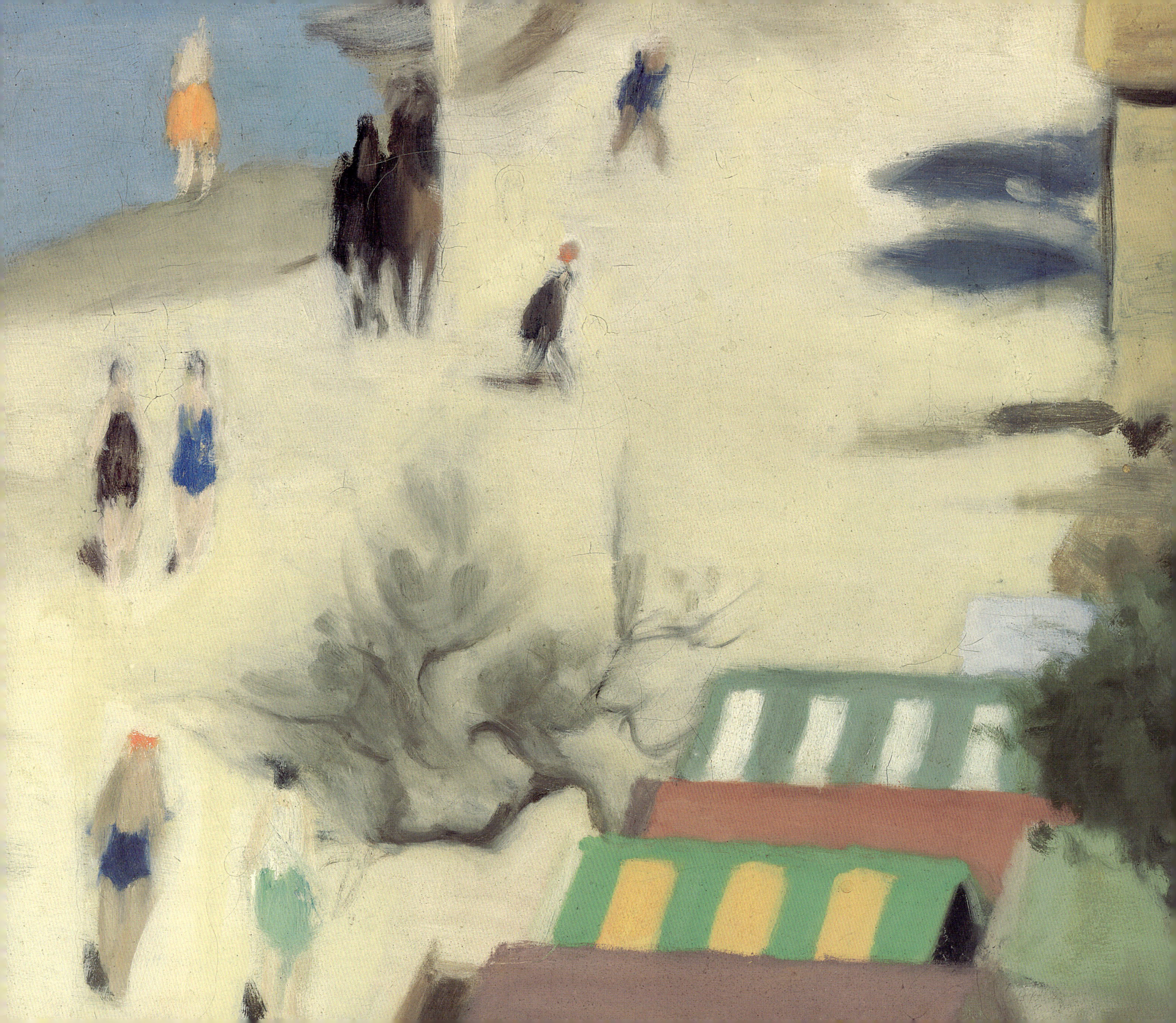

Contents

Clarice Beckett (1887–1935)
Sandringham Beach c. 1933 (detail)
oil on canvas 55.8 x 50.9 cm
Purchased 1971

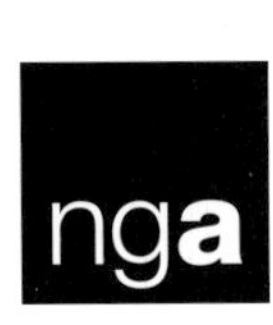

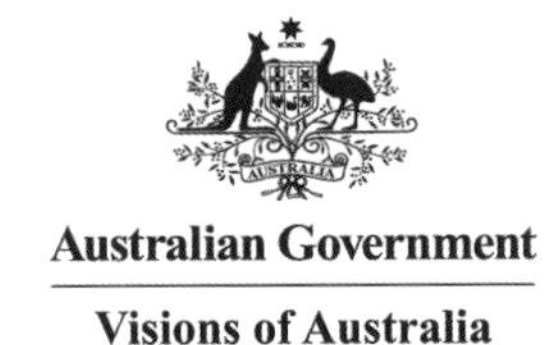

This exhibition and publication have been sponsored by the National Gallery of Australia Council Exhibitions Fund.

Ocean to Outback: Australian landscape painting 1850–1950 has been sponsored by the recently formed National Gallery of Australia Council Exhibitions Fund. This fund is a bold and generous 25th Anniversary initiative of the Gallery's Council and aims to ensure that people across Australia have access to the treasures of the National Collection in this case in the form of this Australian landscape exhibition and publication.

This exhibition is supported by Visions of Australia, an Australian Government Program supporting touring exhibitions by providing funding assistance for the development and touring of Australian cultural material across Australia.

A. E. Newbury (1891–1941)
Eltham 1919 (detail)
oil on academy board 30.8 x 23.2 cm
Purchased 1979

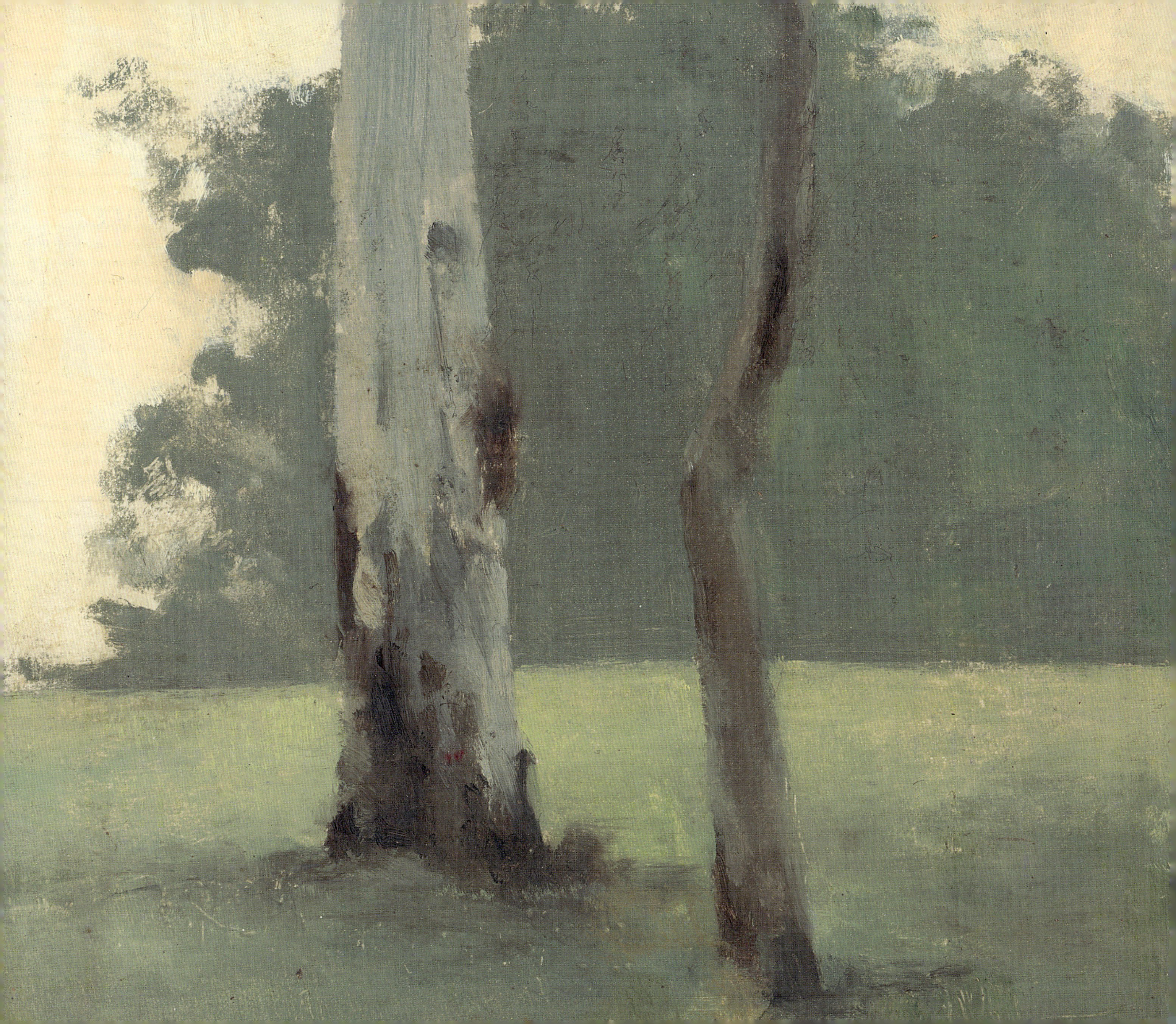

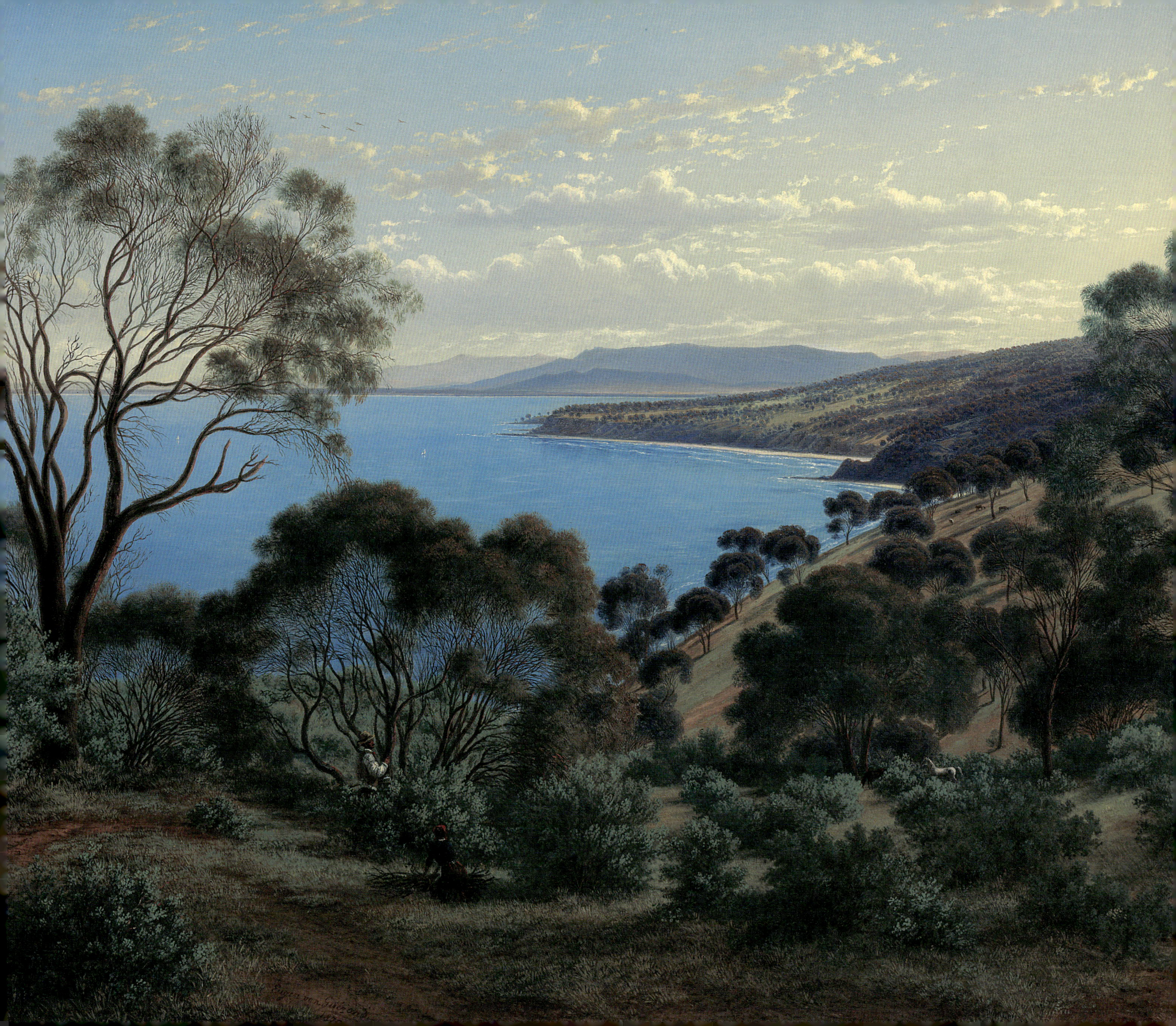

Director's foreword

The exhibition *Ocean to Outback: Australian landscape painting 1850–1950* and this supporting publication were undertaken as part of the twenty-fifth anniversary celebrations of the National Gallery of Australia. All the paintings in the exhibition are from the National Collection of art. *Ocean to Outback* was conceived in order to share these works with the smaller public galleries of the nation, in an extensive tour that embraces every state and territory. In selecting the paintings I have included famous masterpieces of Australian art that are usually on permanent display at the National Gallery. The selection also includes interesting little-known works that, because of their condition, out-of-period framing and insufficient hanging space at the National Gallery, have rarely or never been displayed in Canberra; all of these paintings have now been cleaned and restored and appropriately reframed in time for the tour. A few other landscapes have only just been acquired and will join the Gallery's permanent hang with many others from this show for the first time when the works return to the National Gallery. So a good number of the paintings in this survey are on public display for the first time.

All the paintings date from the great century of Australian landscape art, 1850 to 1950, and the artists include nearly all the major landscape painters of the period who worked in the medium of oil paint. Normally in such a survey landscapes in watercolour would be included too, but because they are fragile and light sensitive, watercolours have to be omitted from such an extensive exhibition tour. Colonial watercolour landscapes by Conrad Martens, S. T. Gill and Ludwig Becker, Federation watercolours by J. J. Hilder, Blamire Young and Hans Heysen, and the modernist Queensland landscapes of Kenneth Macqueen, are therefore absent. Regrettably, significant watercolours by the Indigenous artist Albert Namatjira, who worked in Central Australia from the mid-1930s, have also been omitted. So all the paintings chosen for the exhibition are painted in sturdier oil paint – or, as in the case of works by Ray Crooke, Arthur Boyd and Howard Taylor, in egg tempera.

The exhibition is truly national not only because of its tour to every Australian state and territory, but more importantly because it includes landscape images from every state and territory. The exhibition also reflects the strengths of the National Collection, with its large holdings of major landscapes by

Eugene von Guérard (1811–1901)
Schnapper Point from 'Beleura' 1870 (detail)
oil on canvas 66.1 x 104.2 cm
From the James Fairfax collection
Gift of Bridgestar Pty Ltd 1995

Eugene von Guérard, Tom Roberts, Arthur Streeton, Clarice Beckett, Russell Drysdale, Arthur Boyd and Sidney Nolan. Our Australian painting collection gains more depth towards the mid-twentieth century and consequently so does this exhibition. The wide-ranging scale of landscape art of the period is also captured, from a tiny 22-centimetre-wide panel by Charles Conder to a large 1.5-metre-wide painting by Sidney Nolan.

The following text is not a history of Australian art of the years 1850 to 1950. Although it affirms that landscape was definitely the most painted subject and the most artistically successful category in Australian art during that period, the text is not even a full outline of Australian landscape painting across the time span. That would require a much larger and wider selection than can be accommodated in any touring exhibition, and hence a much longer essay. It serves, however, as an introduction to the major landscape painters of the era and touches on the development of their subjects, themes and influences.

Finishing in the early 1950s, it is not surprising that only two of the artists in the exhibition, Jeffrey Smart and Ray Crooke, are still alive in 2007.

It has been a great joy to select the works for this exhibition, a special event for the nation from the National Gallery on the occasion of the Gallery's twenty-fifth anniversary. I hope that these exceptionally fine landscape paintings depicting all parts of our nation will also bring great joy to many, especially to Australians in regional areas.

Ron Radford AM
Director
National Gallery of Australia

Sidney Nolan (1917–1992)
Burke at Cooper's Creek 1950 (detail)
oil and enamel paint on composition board
121.5 x 152.0 cm
A gift to the people of Australia by Mr and Mrs Benno Schmidt of New York City and Esperance, Western Australia through the American Friends of the Australian National Gallery 1987

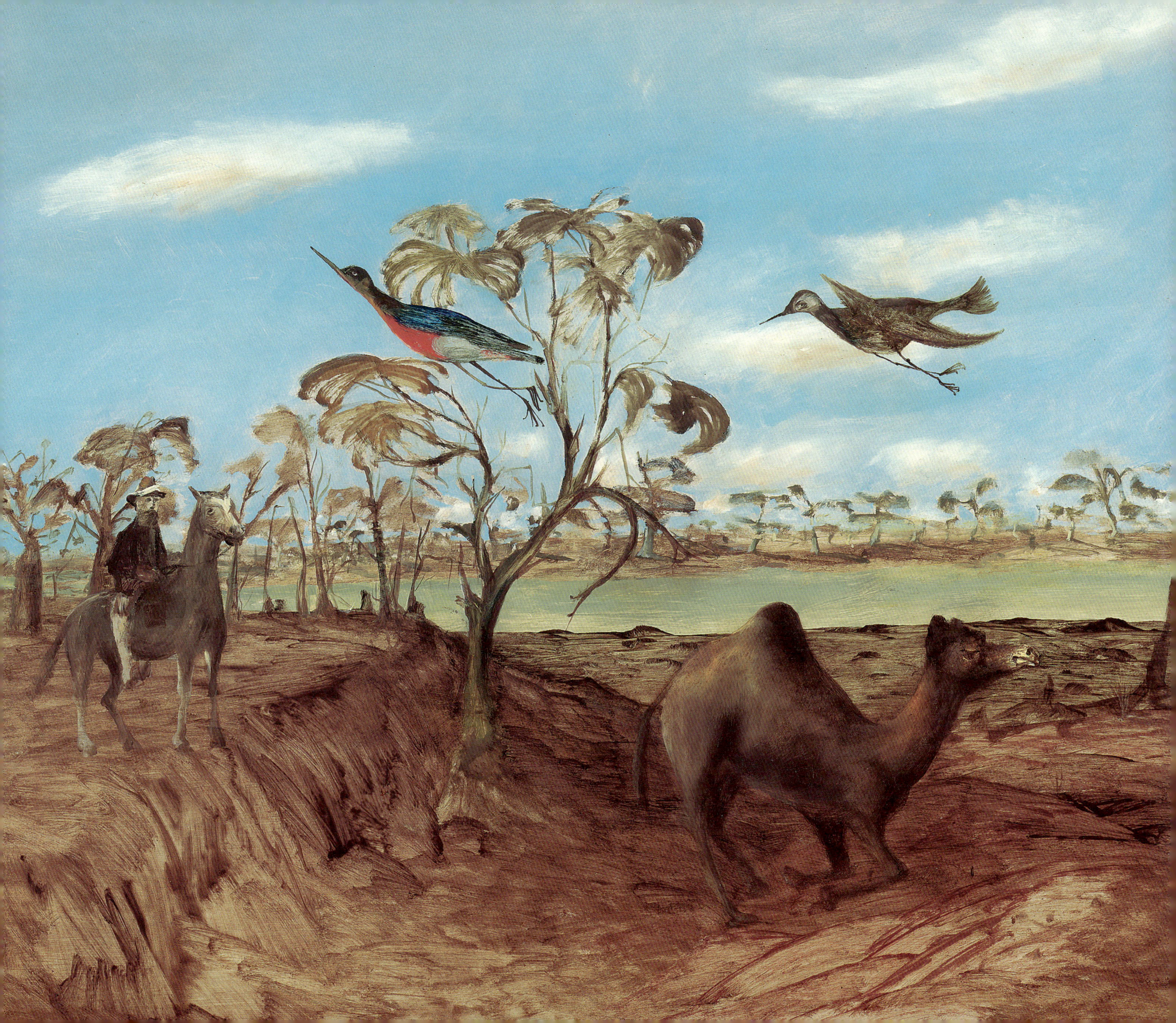

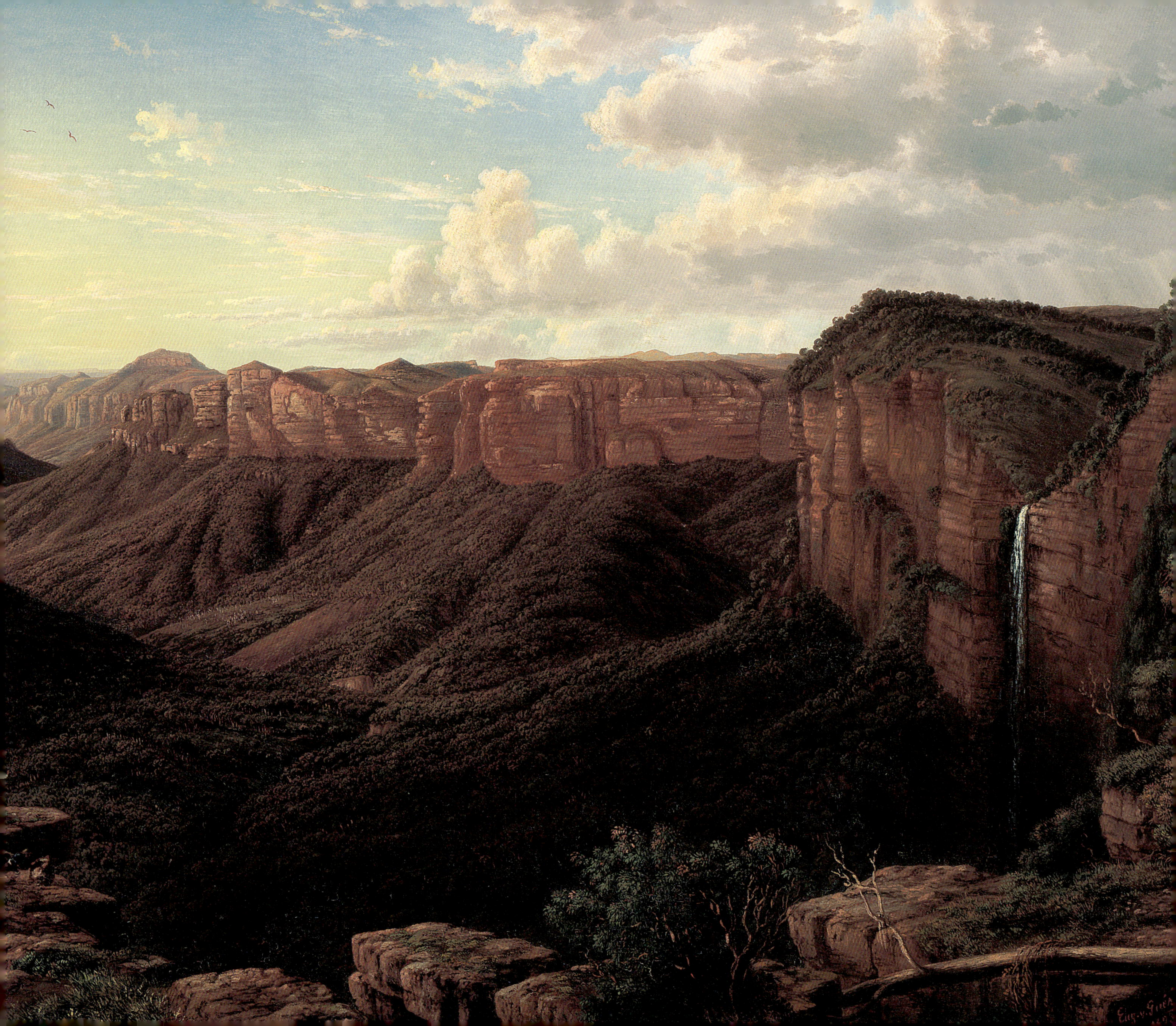

Ocean to Outback: Australian landscape painting 1850–1950

Ron Radford

Before the beginning

The ancient continent of Australia embraces extremes of glorious landscape, plunging cliffs and gentle coastal beaches, mountain ranges and vast plains, dense rainforests and arid deserts. This exhibition, *Ocean to Outback: Australian landscape painting 1850–1950,* embraces these natural extremes, the landscapes in between and the cultural landscapes created by human settlement.

For tens of thousands of years the Indigenous people of Australia adapted to the different environments across the continent. As nomadic people they took from the land what they needed and moved on. They learned how to touch the land lightly, without having to establish cities or destroy the environment that they, the first human arrivals, had no doubt modified. At the end of the eighteenth century and in the early nineteenth century, British settlers claimed and clung first to the south-east coast and coastal estuaries, building towns and clearing for farmland, thus dispossessing and displacing Indigenous people. It was only much later that the intruders gradually ventured further and settled inland.

When the British colonised the land which they soon named Australia, at the same time as they were establishing other colonies around the globe, the art of landscape painting was gaining ground in Britain. As the Empire expanded, British art increasingly moved away from figure and portrait painting to paintings of land and sea. Landscapes executed in watercolour became very popular in the first decades of the nineteenth century and Britain became known especially for its watercolour painting. Since watercolour was a portable and convenient medium it was also used to record new lands and species by artists included in voyages of discovery.

Portrait painting had dominated British art for three centuries, but by the 1820s it had lost its supremacy. Landscape became the dominant creative force in British art, in oil painting as well as watercolour. The landscape artists who led the way were J. M. W. Turner and John Constable, but they were only two of many. Their fresh but different approaches to nature influenced much Continental and American art, as well as landscape painting in Britain's own colonies.

Eugene von Guérard (1811–1901)
Govett's Leap and Grose River Valley, Blue Mountains, New South Wales 1873 (detail)
oil on canvas 68.5 x 106.4 cm
Purchased 2000

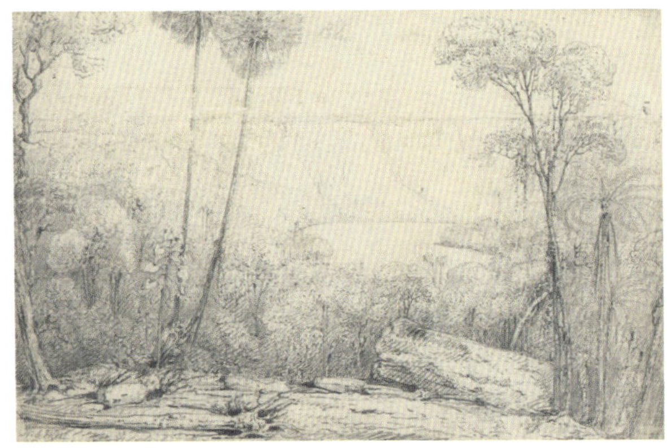

William Westall (1781–1850)
Hawkesbury River (View no. 6) 1802
pencil on paper
18.3 x 27.4 cm
National Library of Australia, Canberra
Federal Government Funds 1959

OPPOSITE
Knut Bull (1811–1889)
The wreck of the 'George the Third' 1850 (detail)
oil on canvas 84.5 x 123.0 cm
Purchased with funds from the Nerissa Johnson Bequest 2001

Given this trend in British art, and given the compelling natural landscape and distinctive light of her Australian colonies, landscape painting would emerge as the major force in Australia's European culture.

The beginning

The European landscape tradition in Australian art began with William Westall's coastal views in pencil and watercolour. These were executed when Westall was employed to record coastal profiles, landscapes and native figures on Matthew Flinders's voyage of cartographic exploration, which in 1801–03 was the first circumnavigation of Australia. In the first decade of the nineteenth century the resident artists who followed and produced a number of Australian watercolour landscapes were G. W. Evans, John Eyre and John Lewin. The convict artist Joseph Lycett who arrived in the next decade, and the itinerant Augustus Earle in the decade after that, also produced landscapes in watercolour, and occasionally in oils. It was not until the 1830s, with the arrival of John Glover in Tasmania and Conrad Martens in New South Wales, that Australia received its first long-term-resident professional landscape painters. By the 1840s the watercolourist John Skinner Prout had joined Martens in Sydney before moving to Tasmania. At the same time in Adelaide, capital of the infant colony of South Australia, S. T. Gill and George French Angas were producing local landscapes in watercolour.

Yet in the first half of the nineteenth century the Australian colonies saw more natural-history painters and professional portrait painters than professional landscape painters. And views of the developing coastal settlements and of homesteads were preferred to inland landscapes. The still unfamiliar Australian wilderness had not been fully conquered and pictures of it were not yet especially desired.

In the 1850s landscape painting became the sustaining motivation within Australian art, a status it retained for more than a century. *Ocean to Outback* therefore focuses on the great century of Australian landscape painting from 1850 to 1950. This was a nation-building century. It saw self-government in the 1850s and Federation of the separate colonies in 1901; it saw the great gold rushes of the 1850s; two great depressions in the early 1890s and early 1930s; and two great world wars in 1914–18 and 1939–45, to which Australia was vitally committed. All this is reflected in the nation's art.

The exhibition draws on the strength of the National Collection, with its rich holdings of work by landscape artists such as Eugene von Guérard, Tom Roberts, Arthur Streeton, Clarice Beckett, Russell Drysdale, Arthur Boyd and Sidney Nolan.

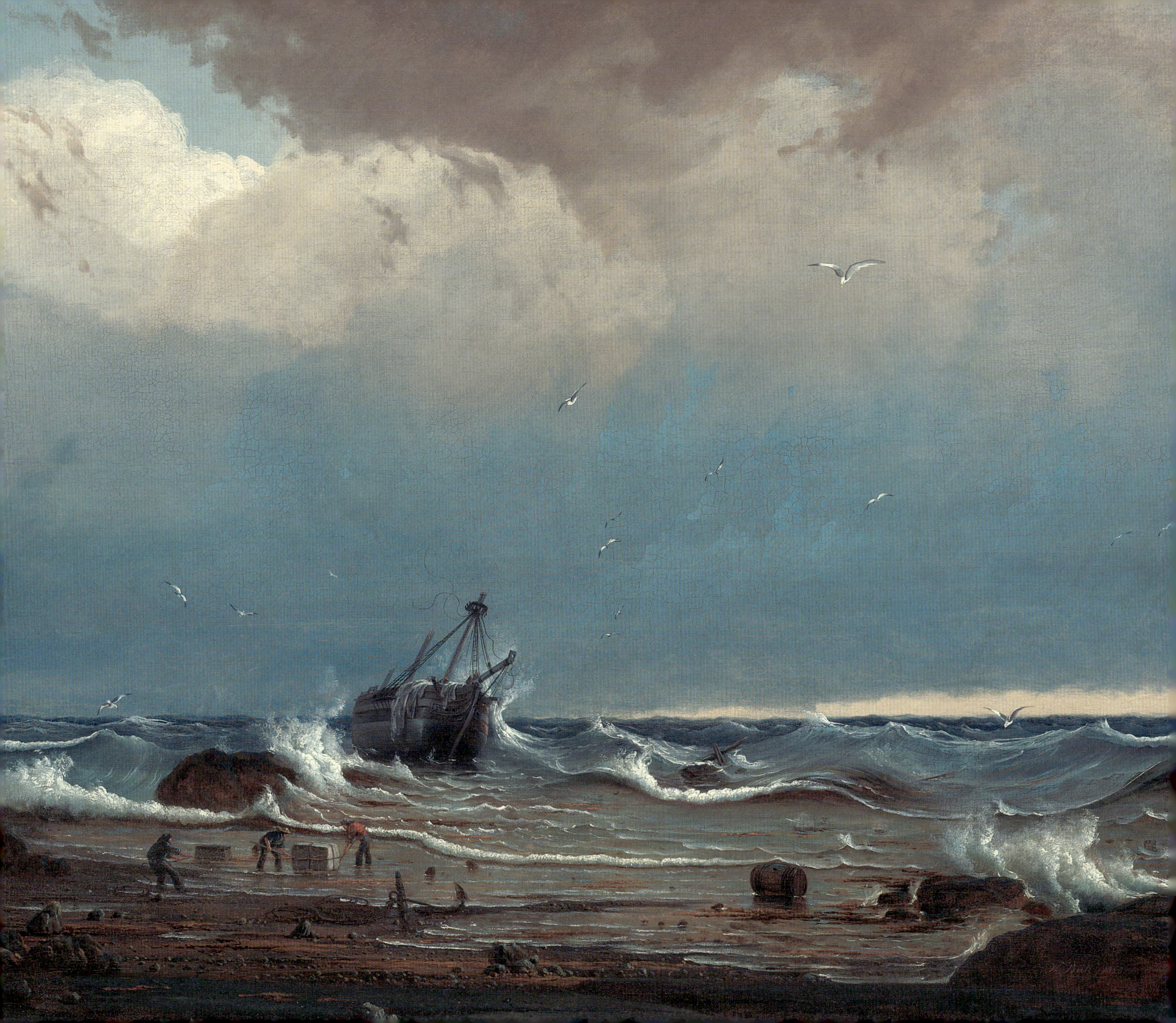

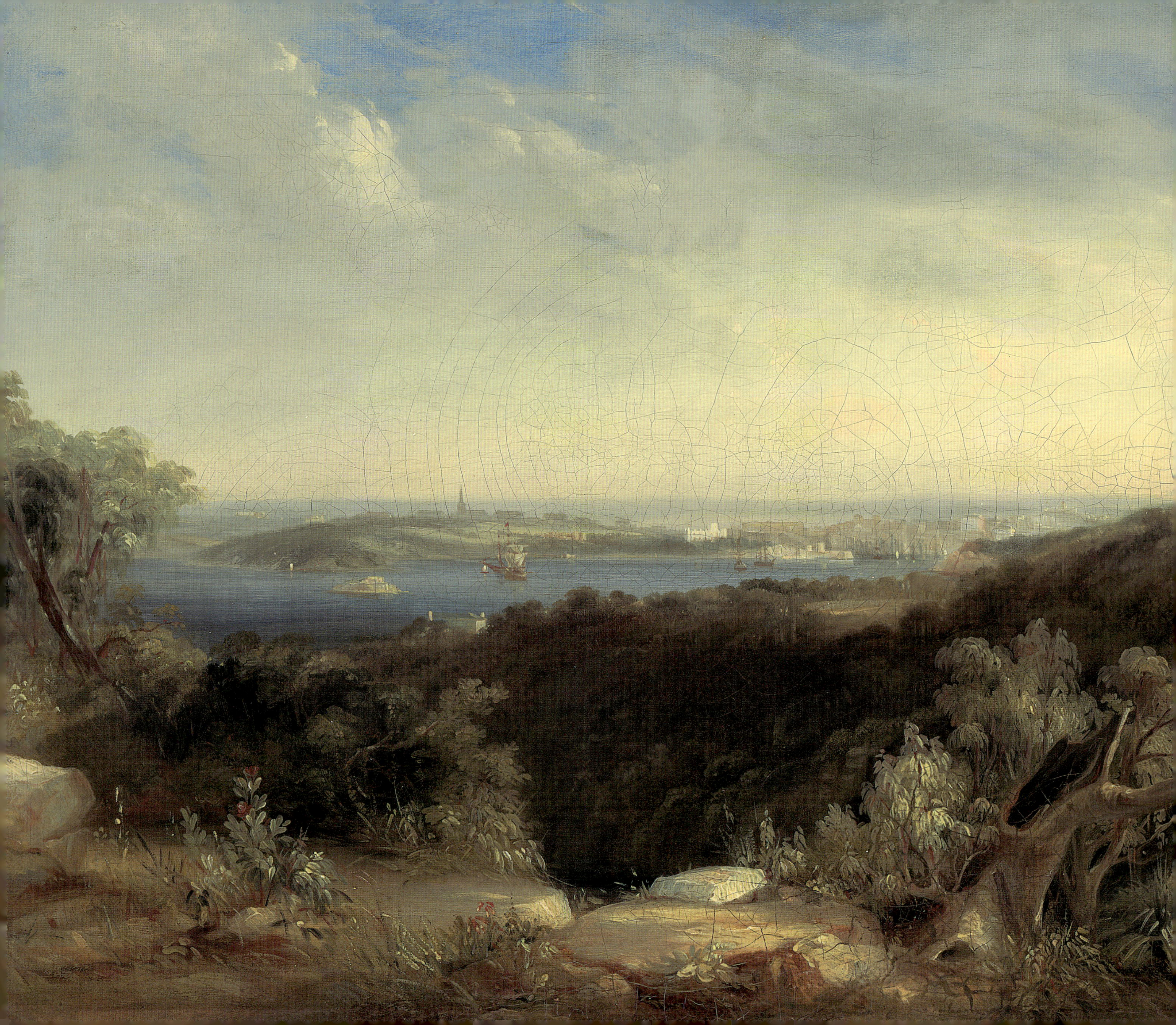

Later colonial landscapes 1850–80

Ocean to Outback fittingly begins with an ocean subject, a shipwreck seen from the coast. Settlers crossed the great oceans in small vessels to venture to Australia. It was the world's longest of all voyages and a risky one. Deaths on board were common and shipwrecks were not unusual. This tragic scene of wild seas, *The wreck of the 'George the Third'*, painted in 1850 in Hobart by the convict artist Knut Bull, shows a re-creation of the breaking up in 1835 of the convict-transport ship *'George the Third'* at the entrance to the D'Entrecasteaux Channel in the south of Tasmania. Of the cargo of 220 prisoners, 127 perished, half of them trapped in the ship's hospital suffering scurvy, most of the others restrained by the military guard from coming on deck, and two shot. Fifteen years after the disaster it was a scandal still vividly remembered. Knut Bull, a Norwegian artist trained in the northern Romantic landscape tradition, had been convicted of fraud soon after arriving in London and was transported to Australia in 1846. He was the last of the convict artists. One can imagine Bull's particular sympathy for the convict victims, but shipwrecks were potent images for all our early settlers. This bleak reconstruction of the aftermath of the wreck would also have been a chilling reminder of the potential hazards for those who might wish to return 'home'.

The earliest painting of Australian land in this exhibition is aptly a view of Sydney Harbour, the birthplace of European Australia. It was painted by Conrad Martens, a British-born and trained artist who arrived in Sydney in 1835 and remained until his death in 1878. For more than four decades Martens was the undisputed leader of landscape art in New South Wales. Like almost all the landscape painters who arrived before 1850 he had trained and preferred to work as a watercolour painter; it was only later, in the colony, that he taught himself oil painting, executing in that medium only a small number of landscapes from the beginning of the 1840s to the beginning of the 1850s.[1]

Martens's oil, *View of Sydney Harbour showing Sydney Cove* (c. 1850), is from Cremorne looking across the harbour to the centre of the growing mercantile city of Sydney. From 1840 Sydney was proudly no longer a place to which convicts were transported. One can see the island of Fort Denison and also the promontory Fort Macquarie at the entrance to Sydney Cove, the spire of St James's Church on the hill, and below it the newly finished grand Government House. These buildings are extant today, except for Fort Macquarie which was demolished in 1901. Although the exact date of the painting is unknown it was probably painted around 1850 after the completion of Government House in 1845. This was just before the separation of Victoria from New South Wales in 1851 and before the Australian gold rushes that began later in the same year. The gold rushes, first in Bathurst in New South Wales and then much more vigorously in a number of places in Victoria, disrupted the orderly settlement of Australia, causing a flood of unregulated immigration.

1 The major exception to this is John Glover, who had made his fortune in Britain as a watercolourist, but in Tasmania largely painted in oil.

Conrad Martens (1801–1878)
View of Sydney Harbour showing Sydney Cove
c. 1850 (detail)
oil on canvas on composition board 46.5 x 65.0 cm
Rex Nan Kivell Collection: National Library of Australia and the National Gallery of Australia, Canberra

The view by Martens shows colonial Sydney at a peak moment. It was convict-free by this time and the best established and largest city in Australia. It was the capital of an expansive New South Wales, which then included the whole of eastern and northern Australia. (In 1859 Queensland would follow Victoria and separate from the first colony.) But the massive gold rush to Victoria challenged Sydney's supremacy. In the 1850s and 1860s Victoria's capital, Melbourne, quickly grew to become the largest and most prosperous city in Australia. Sydney in comparison became a backwater and its population did not surpass Melbourne's again until the early twentieth century.

Melbourne by the mid-1850s had become the art centre of Australia. The gold rushes attracted many artists from Europe, particularly a number of landscape painters of German and Swiss origin. Unlike the earlier arrivals from Britain, who preferred to work in watercolour, these artists mainly painted in oil. They came for the gold of the land but stayed to make art of the land. Eugene von Guérard was one of the first and the finest of these artists, having trained in the German Romantic tradition. He arrived in 1852 and tramped to the Ballarat goldfields, but soon established himself as an artist in Melbourne, beginning his full-scale romantic landscapes of Australia in 1856. By then Australian settlers felt more comfortable with the natural untouched landscape and could happily live with pictures of it.

In 1857 von Guérard painted his large and ambitious masterpiece *Ferntree Gully in the Dandenong Ranges,* one of Australia's first grand landscapes in oil and a key work in this exhibition. It depicts a damp and dark secluded valley where 'exotic' primeval tree-ferns flourish. The luxuriant growth of the temperate rainforest contrasts with the fallen ferns and the remains of stark truncated eucalypts. Death and regeneration is a theme of the painting. The open foreground provides a stage for the mating dance of Australia's unique lyrebirds, thus extending the idea of cyclical regeneration.

OPPOSITE
Eugene von Guérard (1811–1901)
Ferntree Gully in the Dandenong Ranges 1857 (detail)
oil on canvas 92.0 x 138.0 cm
Gift of Dr Joseph Brown AO OBE 1975

The dense growth of the enclosed forest valley in *Ferntree Gully in the Dandenong Ranges* contrasts with von Guérard's more expansive coastal view of Mornington Peninsula on Port Phillip Bay, *Schnapper Point from 'Beleura'* (1870), with its sparser vegetation of wind-blown trees and shrubs. Even more expansive is von Guérard's panoramic view with a waterfall, *Govett's Leap and Grose River Valley, Blue Mountains, New South Wales* (1873). From a view over a precipice, von Guérard reveals the ancient weathered escarpments of the formidable Blue Mountains which half a century earlier had presented a barrier to inland settlement.

Eugene von Guérard (1811–1901)
North-east view from the northern top of Mount Kosciusko 1863
oil on canvas 66.5 x 116.8 cm
National Gallery of Australia, Canberra
Purchased 1973

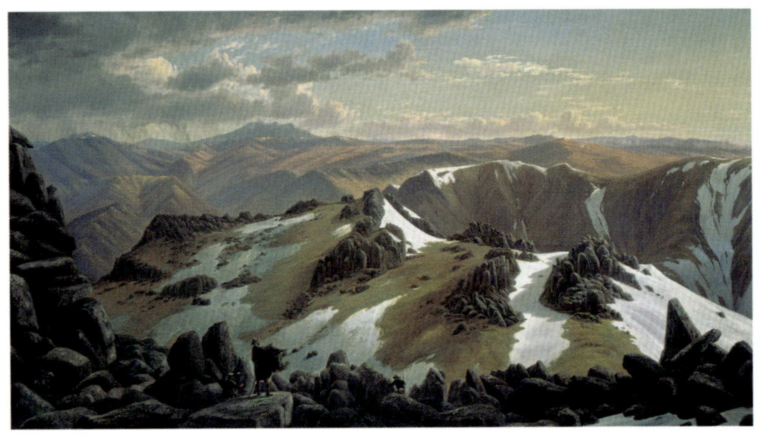

By the time he painted the Blue Mountains, von Guérard had travelled and explored much of south-eastern Australia, including the island of Tasmania, and also New Zealand. Travelling to record already well-known beauty spots not far from the major cities, he also reached more remote alpine regions. He brought to Australasia a heightened sense of wonderment in its natural landscapes, an approach inherent in the German landscape tradition. In his

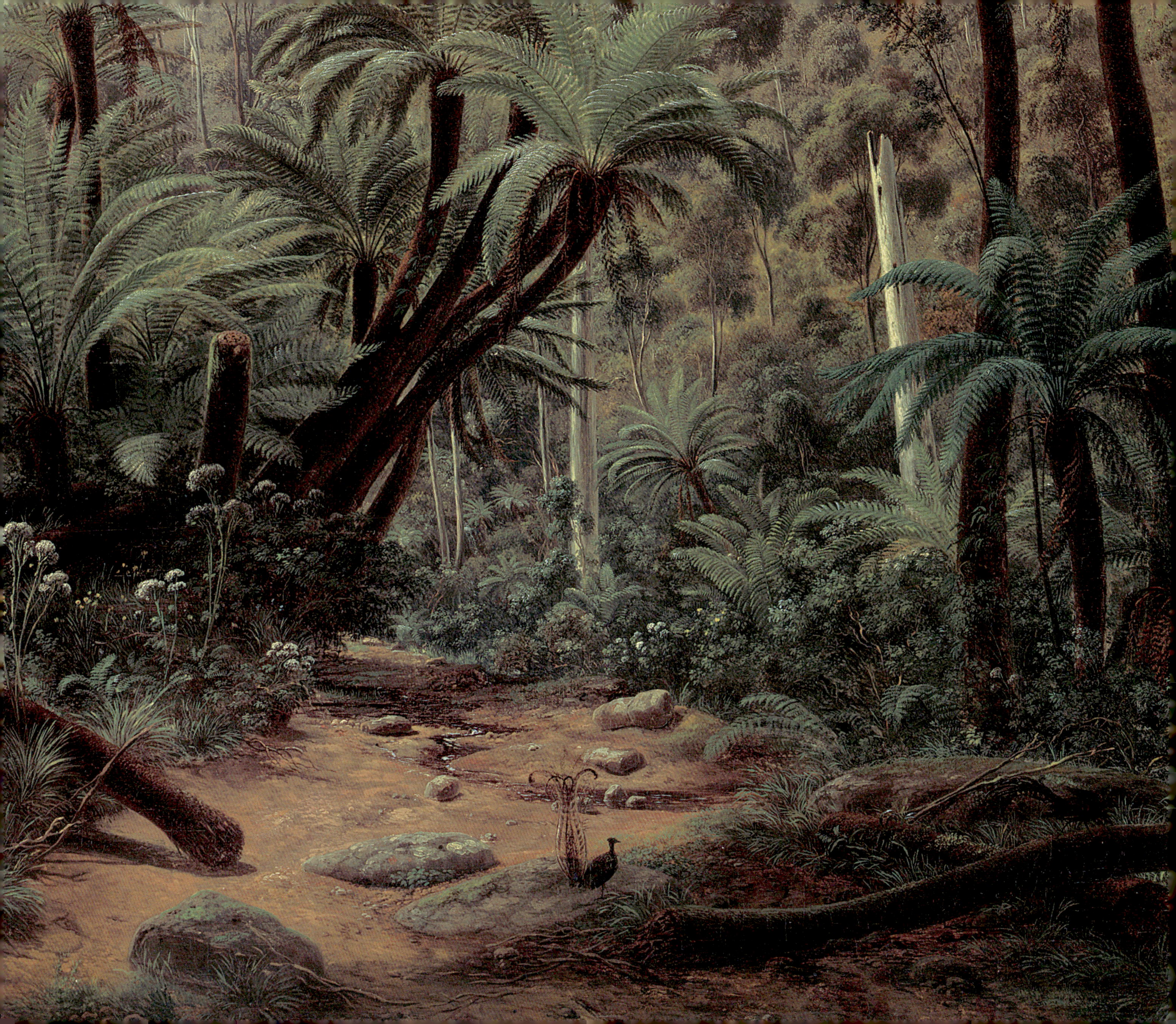

often spectacular views, von Guérard simplified the basic natural structures of the land and then embroidered onto them a love of nature's detail. All God's creations, great and small, were to be worthy of clear and specific depiction. His pictures, however, are never merely descriptive but are unified by an enveloping sense of awe.

A follower of von Guérard, the Swiss artist Nicholas Chevalier arrived in Melbourne at the end of 1854. His popular oil paintings of dramatic mountains and waterfalls, and tranquil rivers, are more illustrative than von Guérard's, but have something of the same northern European romantic mood and insistent detail. His large canvas, *Studley Park at sunrise* (1861), shows a peaceful and glassy Yarra River, the banks of which were then still covered by native bush. Morning mist hovers over the water while the punts cross where a bridge would eventually be built between Collingwood and Kew.

A more dramatically romantic river scene is W. C. Piguenit's *On the Nepean, New South Wales* (1881), showing the Nepean River flanked by plunging cliffs. The single rowing boat on the river is dwarfed by the rocky, tree-covered escarpments. Piguenit was born in 1836 in convict Hobart where he took up art, but moved to Sydney in 1880, the year before he painted this river view. He was Australia's first locally born and trained landscape painter. Well into the Federation period of the early twentieth century he adhered to the earlier romantic rivers-and-mountains conventions favoured by the European-trained artists Knut Bull, Eugene von Guérard and Nicholas Chevalier.

In a sense von Guérard, Chevalier and Piguenit, each of who travelled extensively, were the last of the explorer artists; they could trace a lineage back to William Westall on Matthew Flinders's circumnavigational voyage of discovery. But in the mid-nineteenth century the most professional

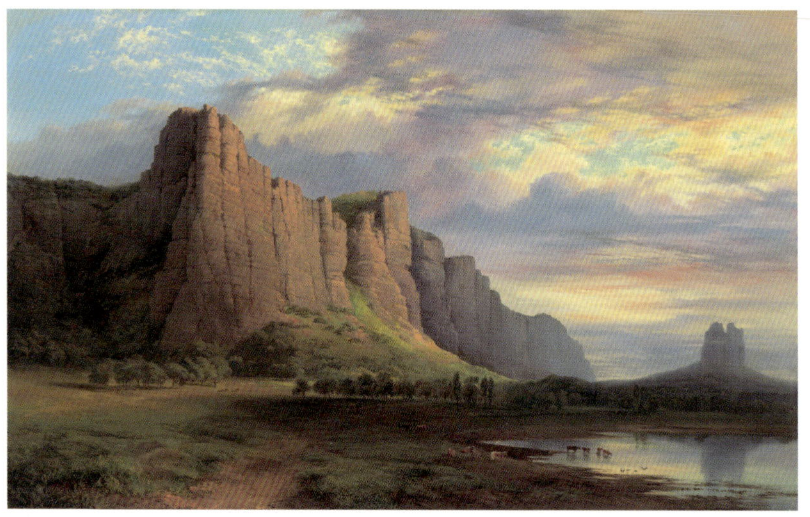

Nicholas Chevalier (1828–1902)
Mount Arapiles and the Mitre Rock 1863
oil on canvas 77.5 x 120.6 cm
National Gallery of Australia, Canberra
Gift of Dr Joseph Brown AO OBE 1979

explorer-artist was Thomas Baines. British-born, he had worked in South Africa before arriving in Australia in 1855 to accompany Augustus Gregory's inland expedition through what is now the Northern Territory. No-one hitherto had visually documented the inland north. The National Gallery owns four of Baines's paintings, based on field sketches he made on Gregory's expedition but worked up in oil twelve years later in 1868. *Gouty stem tree, Adansonia Gregorii, 58 feet circumference, near a creek south-east of Stokes Range, Victoria River* is perhaps the most interesting of them. It features the strange bottle-like baobab tree of immense girth, a great curiosity to these Englishmen. The foreground shows the explorers' supplies lined-up, the responsibility for which had been assigned to the artist. Baines illustrates the oddities peculiar to this northern Australian landscape, but also documents the complex organisation required for survival of Europeans on a long expedition. For them it was a hazardous place, although Indigenous Australians had successfully lived there for thousands of years.

This exotic, scenic approach to Australian landscape, captured in great detail, was soon to end. It was carried on in Tasmania well into the twentieth century by the immensely productive Haughton Forrest, as seen in his somewhat earlier painting *Mount Wellington from Cascades* (c.1885). However, Forrest's work, which was often based on photographs, was an isolated late exception.

The Swiss artist Louis Buvelot, influenced by the Barbizon School of French outdoor painting, led Australia's shift from drama and adventure, and the spectacle of high mountains, big rivers and gullies, to a love of gentler landforms and the domesticated 'inside' country familiar to city-dwellers. Living in prosperous Melbourne from 1865, Buvelot had earlier spent twelve years in Brazil where he no doubt learnt to appreciate unfamiliar, non-European landscapes. His painting *Near Lilydale* (1874) is an approachable rural landscape with typical Australian vegetation of shabby gums and native shrubs. This is not a majestic vista of the kind favoured by Bull, von Guérard, Chevalier and Piguenit, and Conrad Martens in his late works, or a landscape of exploration like Baines's, but a tamed pastoral landscape of cattle lazily grazing by a trickling creek in the late afternoon sun. The scene is further domesticated by the inclusion of two women strolling along a track, followed by a pet lamb. The basket the women carry may suggest they will collect blackberries in the cooler late afternoon.

Buvelot was often commissioned to paint homesteads, as were Martens, von Guérard and Chevalier before him. Homestead pictures documented landholders' proud progress in claiming and working their land. Buvelot's approach was more informal than homestead commissions painted by earlier artists. In his *'Mount Fyans' homestead* (1869) the herd of cattle and flock of sheep in the foreground play a role equal to the centrally placed homestead with its classically columned veranda, while the reeds and pampas grass growing wildly by the creek in the left foreground have even more prominence. Nonetheless, Buvelot records the successful development of good sheep and cattle country, as required by his patron in the Western District of Victoria, a region first described by Thomas Mitchell as 'Australia Felix', meaning 'fortunate Australia'.

Henry Rielly, a follower of Buvelot, painted the undeveloped bushland closer to Melbourne. *Woodland, vale and hill* (1874) is probably a subject to the north-east of the city. Like Buvelot's paintings the view is not formidable, however despite the inclusion of horses the landscape does appear uninhabited and there is no evidence of the domestication we usually see in Buvelot's landscapes. Nor is Rielly's untamed landscape traditionally composed, as are many of Buvelot's compositions, including *Near Lilydale*, painted in the same year.

Australian Impressionism 1885–1900

Louis Buvelot's more familiar approach to the Australian scene and his use of looser, more painterly brushwork were qualities that inspired a new generation of landscape painters. Tom Roberts was a leader of the younger artists who admired Buvelot; among the others were Frederick McCubbin, Arthur Streeton, Charles Conder and Walter Withers. In 1885 Roberts had returned to Australia from Europe where he saw at first hand both modern French outdoor landscape paintings and the Japanese-inspired compositions of James McNeill Whistler. One of the first works executed on his return to Melbourne was *A quiet day on Darebin Creek* (1885). Painted on an excursion to the outskirts of Melbourne with Frederick McCubbin and probably Llewellyn Jones – two artist companions are seen in the painting – it demonstrates a new intimate and even more informal approach than Buvelot's. It depicts an unremarkable snatch of nature – a small creek and pond in the foreground, a treeless hill above, and a suggestion of a scrubby valley to the left, below a high skyline. It is given scale, focus and interest by the inclusion of the two fellow artists. Painted on the spot to capture the exact atmosphere of the moist overcast morning, the strength of this small painting lies in its fresh veracity and immediacy instead of overly self-conscious compositional devices.

Roberts's *A Sunday afternoon* (c. 1886) was probably painted the following year, at Box Hill, where he and his friends established the first of their Melbourne outer-suburban artists' camps for open-air landscape painting. Here the intimate snapshot observation of nature seen in Roberts's *A quiet day on Darebin Creek* is brought even closer by the absence of a skyline. It is as if we are amidst the native saplings and long grasses, spying on the young couple's holiday picnic. The Australian bush is now completely familiar and approachable; it is a private refuge for the couple's leisurely reading, refreshment and tobacco. This small patch of local bush is portrayed with a fresh sketch-like application that encapsulates the dappled sunlight falling on saplings, shrubs and spring grasses.

Young Arthur Streeton joined Roberts and McCubbin at their painting camps by the sea and in the bush not long after Roberts painted this Box Hill subject. Together they aimed for 'truth to nature' (Roberts's favourite phrase) in Australian landscape and light. By the time of the centenary celebrations of European settlement in Australia in 1888 we see daringly bright paintings of high noon, celebrating

OPPOSITE
Tom Roberts (1856–1931)
A Sunday afternoon c. 1886 (detail)
oil on canvas 41.0 x 30.8 cm
Purchased 1984

FOLLOWING PAGE
Charles Conder (1868–1909)
Ricketts Point, Beaumaris 1890 (detail)
oil on wood panel 12.0 x 21.5 cm
Purchased 1973

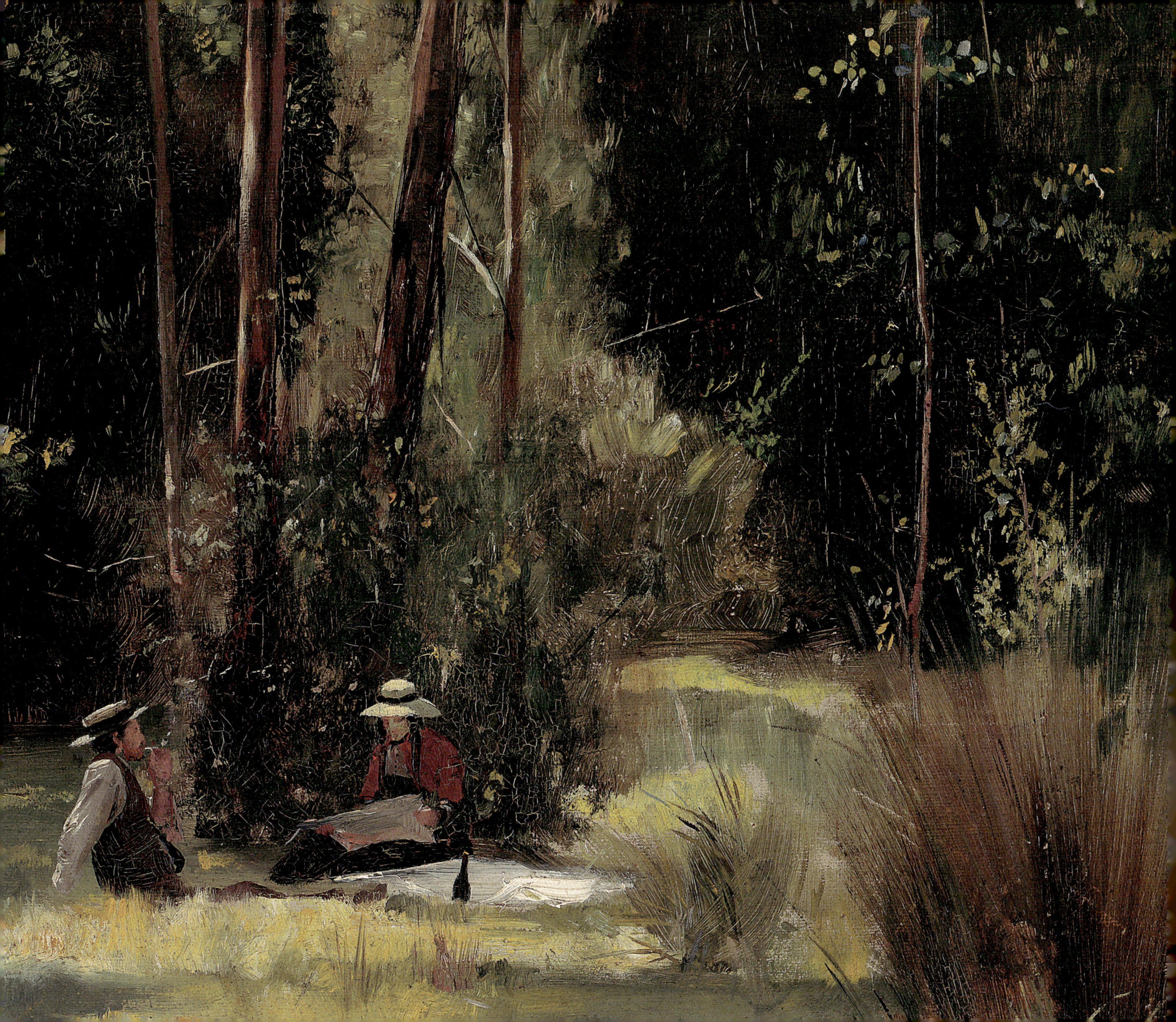

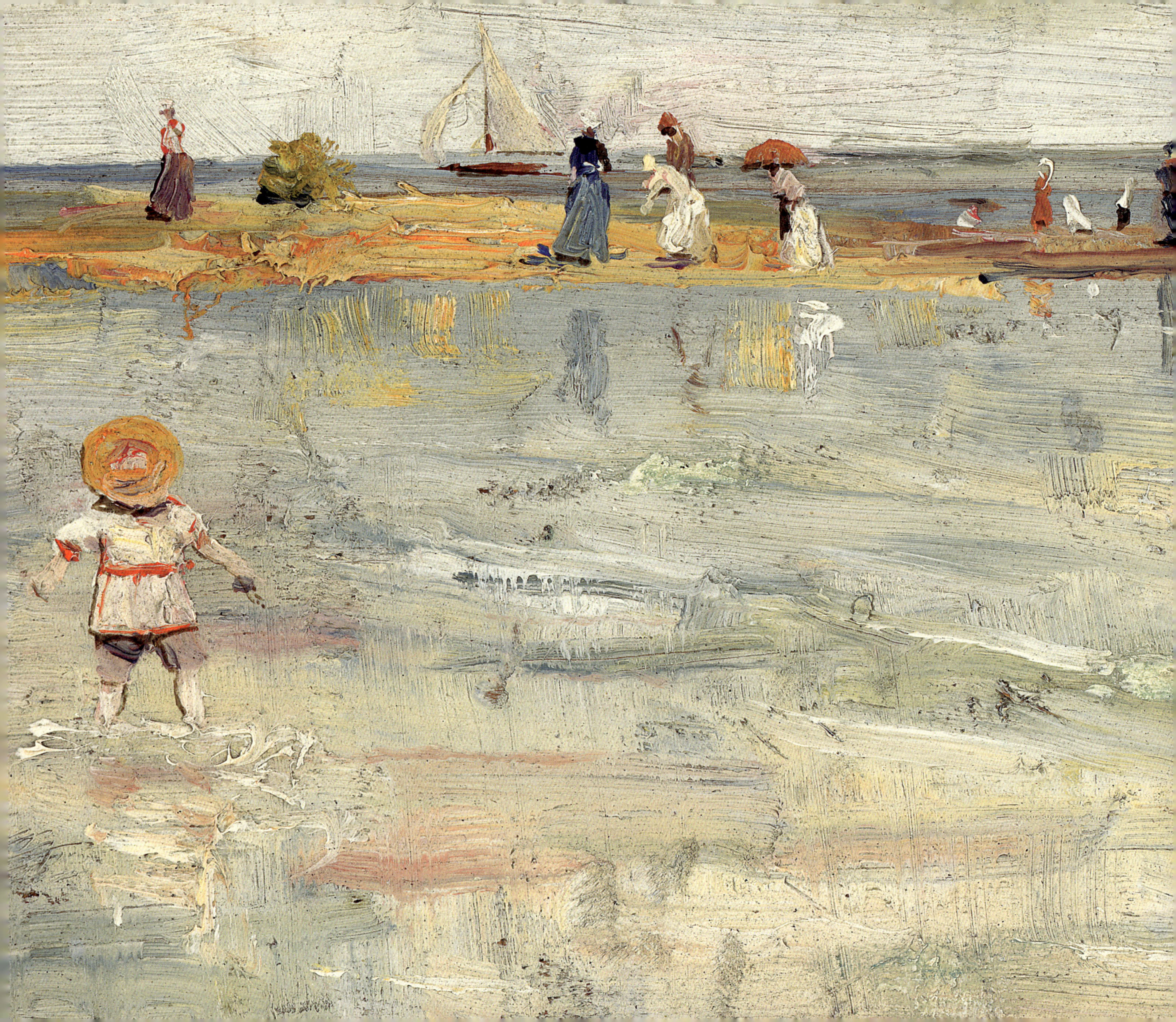

the intensity of Australian light. Streeton's *The selector's hut (Whelan on the log)* (1890), painted shortly after the centenary, records the intense midday sun while a woodchopper takes a 'smoko' seated on the tree he has felled. Whelan's rest from hard labour is a contrast to the middle-class leisure seekers in Roberts's painting of a picnic. Although he in fact painted Whelan near outer-suburban Heidelberg, which had been settled for half a century, Streeton suggests that the axeman is a pioneer clearing the land. At a time when most Australians were safely established in large coastal cities, subjects of noble bush-workers and pioneers, especially the kind painted by Roberts and McCubbin, became celebrated not only in painting but also in literature. It was a growing response to Australian nationalism as settler generations of Australians from Europe began to feel very much at home and sought reassurance from art. They wanted art that understood and appreciated their own immediate landscape and history.

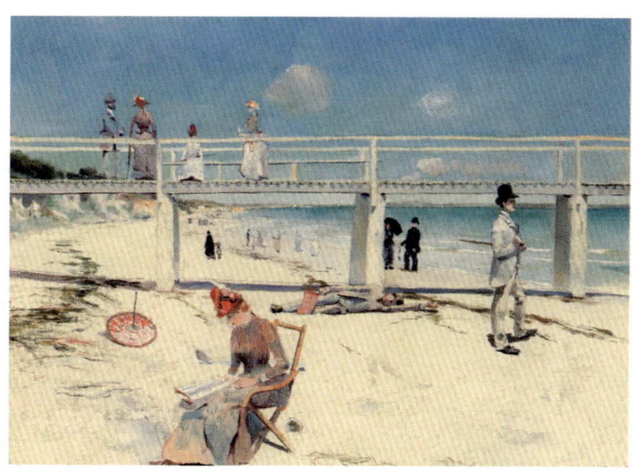

Charles Conder (1868–1909)
A holiday at Mentone 1888
oil on canvas 46.2 x 60.8 cm
Art Gallery of South Australia, Adelaide
South Australian Government Grant with the assistance of Bond Corporation Holdings Limited through the Art Gallery of South Australia Foundation to mark the Gallery's Centenary 1981

At the same time as the bush subjects, some of which were rather mythologised, there was delight in clear sunlight that flooded a new subject – the Australian beach. Although there had been coastal paintings in the colonial period it was not until the mid-1880s that beach leisure and sun worship became a crucial part of Australian life and art. Tom Roberts, a pioneer of Australian seaside painting, met up with a young Charles Conder during an eventful visit to Sydney and during Easter 1888 together they painted memorable coastal pictures at Coogee.

Conder soon left Sydney to join Roberts and Streeton in the more advanced art scene of Melbourne and there continued to paint beach scenes. One of them, *A holiday at Mentone* (1888) (Art Gallery of South Australia, Adelaide), a sparkling springtime promenade of fashionable young people, is one of Australia's most famous images. In his tiny and wonderfully fresh late-summer oil sketch of *Ricketts Point, Beaumaris* (1890) Conder shows a reef of golden rock and shallow water sprinkled with decoratively placed children at play and women strolling.

Tom Roberts (1856–1931)
A break away! 1891
oil on canvas 137.3 x 167.8 cm
Art Gallery of South Australia, Adelaide
Elder Bequest Fund 1899

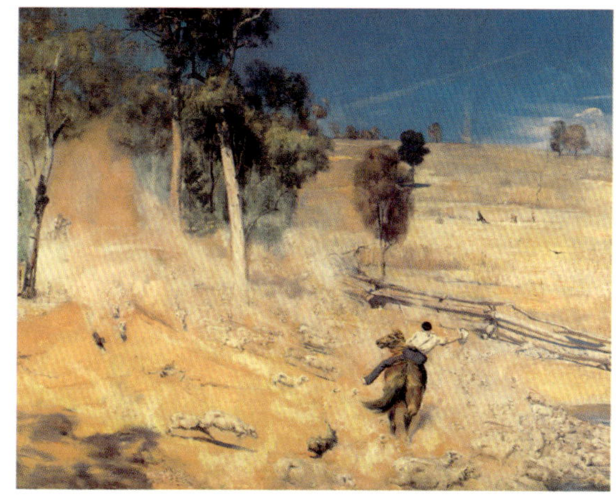

Around the time of Australia's centennial, the extremes of coastal beaches and inland bush were celebrated in paint and pen as part of a new national consciousness. Bush workers, and bush and beach leisure-seekers became common themes. As well as little paintings for private homes, such as Conder's *Ricketts Point, Beaumaris*, large canvases were consciously painted for public display. Examples of the latter include Roberts's *A break away!* (1891) (Art Gallery of South Australia) and *In a corner on the Macintyre* (1895) (National Gallery of Australia); McCubbin's *On the wallaby track* (1896) (Art Gallery of New South Wales, Sydney) and *Down on his luck* (1889) (Art Gallery of Western Australia, Perth); and Streeton's *Golden summer, Eaglemont* (1889) (National Gallery of Australia). These works are all now in public collections, for which they were intended, and they remain the most iconic and popular paintings in Australian culture.

Other artists took up similar themes and approaches. The Melbourne artist Walter Withers painted non-agricultural rural workers in *The fossickers* (1893). Two of the last of the

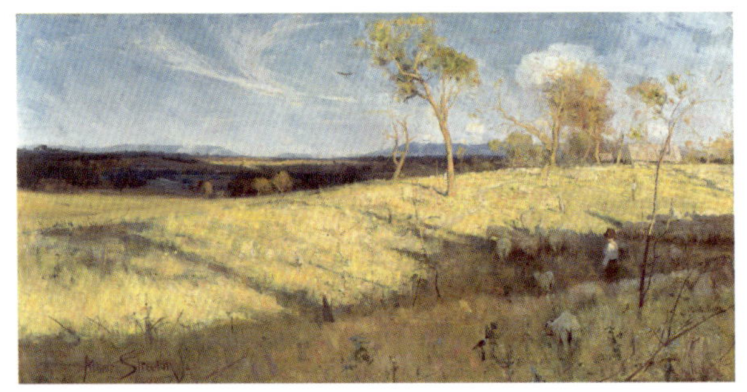

alluvial gold miners in Creswick, near Ballarat, take a break, smoking and yarning in the midday Australian sun. Withers later preferred softer mornings or evenings or even storms, for which he is better known. In this high-keyed early painting Withers emphasises the unique appearance of a eucalyptus tree in much more detail than Roberts or Streeton ever did. The double-trunked young gum is more prominent than the figures. Gum trees in nineteenth-century Australian impressionist paintings are much more generic than specific, but here in Withers's stone and gravel landscape the trees' peeling bark and gnarled trunks are carefully and specifically rendered. There is more than a hint of what was to become a convention in the slightly later Federation period, when Hans Heysen and others made the Australian gum tree the central heroic subject of the Australian landscape.

Arthur Streeton (1867–1943)
Golden summer, Eaglemont 1889
oil on canvas 81.3 x 152.6 cm
National Gallery of Australia, Canberra
Purchased 1995

OPPOSITE
Walter Withers (1854–1914)
The fossickers 1893 (detail)
oil on canvas 67.7 x 49.0 cm
Gift of Mrs Alec de Bretteville 1969

Withers, in Creswick, taught landscape painting to local resident Percy Lindsay, the eldest of what became the famous Lindsay family of five artists: Percy, Lionel, Norman, Ruby and Daryl. Percy Lindsay's impressionist approach was a tribute to his teacher Withers but also to Streeton, whose work he would have seen in Melbourne. The bright light of Lindsay's alluvial mining scene, *Miners and cradle, Creswick* (c. 1893), contemporary with Withers's fossickers, is captured with a broad brush and one gets a lively sense of the miners' rhythmic movement and energy. Percy Lindsay was one of the few artists born and trained in a country town in nineteenth-century Australia, and the only country-based Impressionist. Although he later moved to Melbourne and then Sydney, he did his finest impressionist landscapes in the 1890s, at home in the sleepy mining-town of Creswick.

Tom Roberts (1856–1931)
In a corner on the Macintyre 1895
oil on canvas 71.1 x 86.4 cm
National Gallery of Australia, Canberra
Purchased 1971

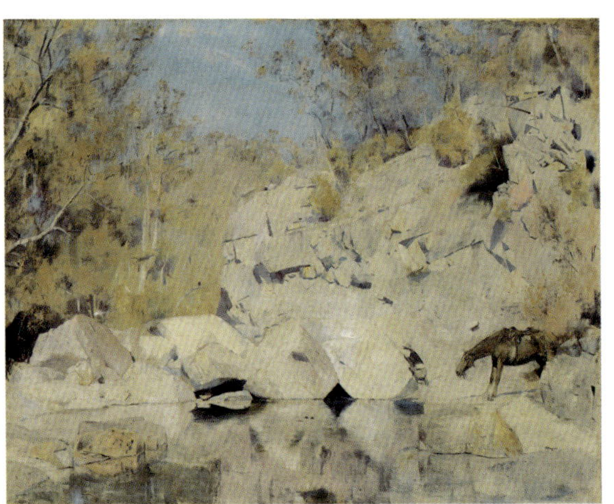

Australia's leading Impressionist painters, Roberts and Streeton, moved from Melbourne to Sydney in 1891 and 1892 respectively. Conder had left for Europe in 1890. Sydney suffered less from the widespread depression in the early 1890s that followed the disastrous collapse of Melbourne's land boom, and it promised better sales for Australian paintings. Artists could live cheaply in tented harbourside camps at Mosman and elsewhere. Streeton, partly for economy, often painted on cast-off drapers' boards and the eccentric proportions of these narrow panels encouraged Japanese-style landscape compositions, orientated either vertically or horizontally. Decorative Japanese art was fashionable in Sydney in the 1890s and one of Streeton's most successful examples of Japonisme is *Sirius Cove* (c. 1895). Painted vertically on a draper's panel, it is like a calligraphic Japanese or Chinese landscape on a hanging scroll and is a highly original depiction of the rocky shore near his camp at Mosman. Only the tiny steamer at the top right of the painting and the minute rowing boat at the top left hint at the scale of the massive cliffs and give realism to the almost abstract-expressionist brushwork down the panel. Bold dark brushstrokes indicating the cliffs contrast with the white 'negative' light on the suggestion of the sea. Near the bottom left a spray of gum-leaves strays in Japanese fashion into the composition. This is a brilliantly stylish merging of the spontaneity of western Impressionism with eastern calligraphic landscape.

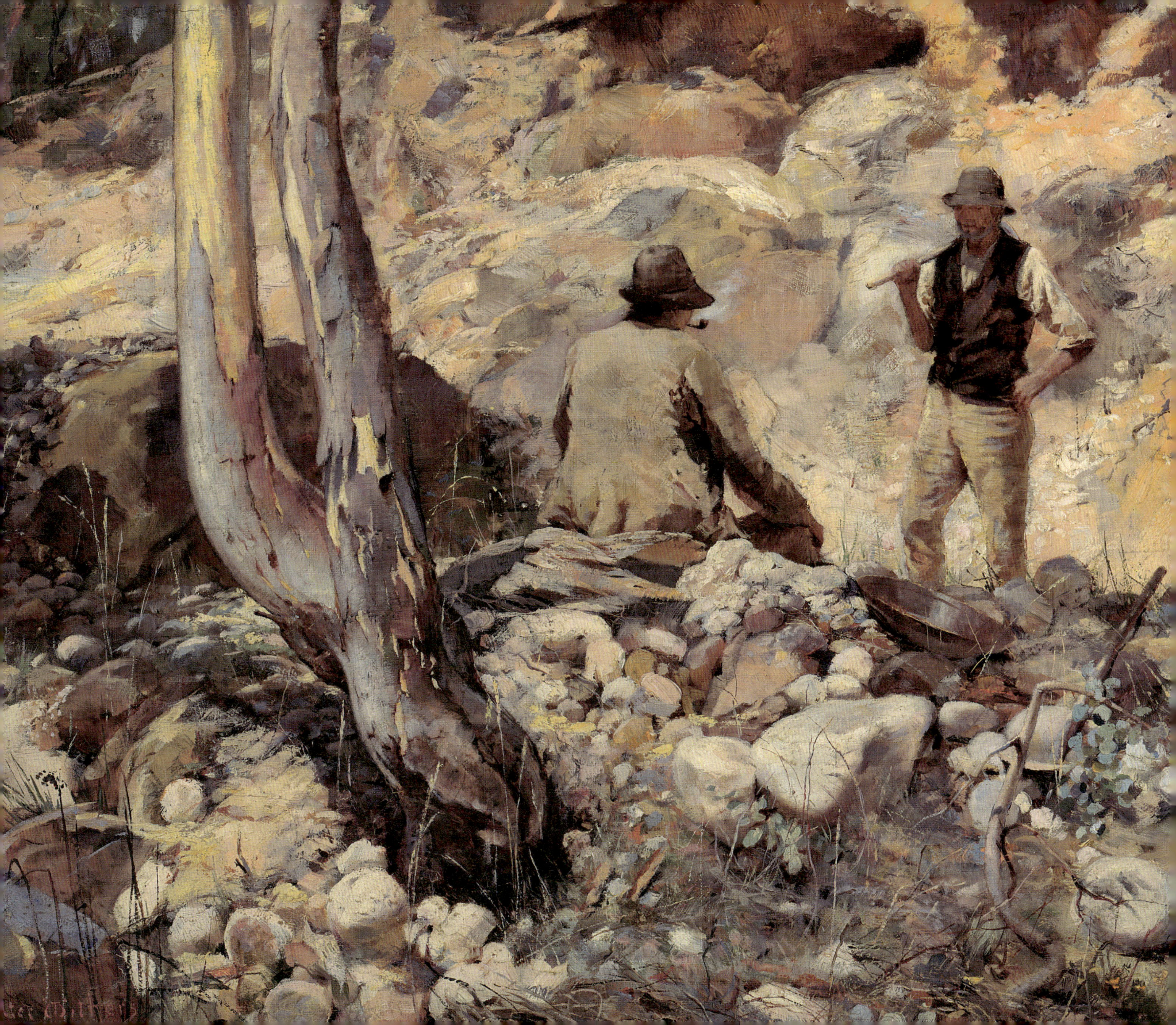

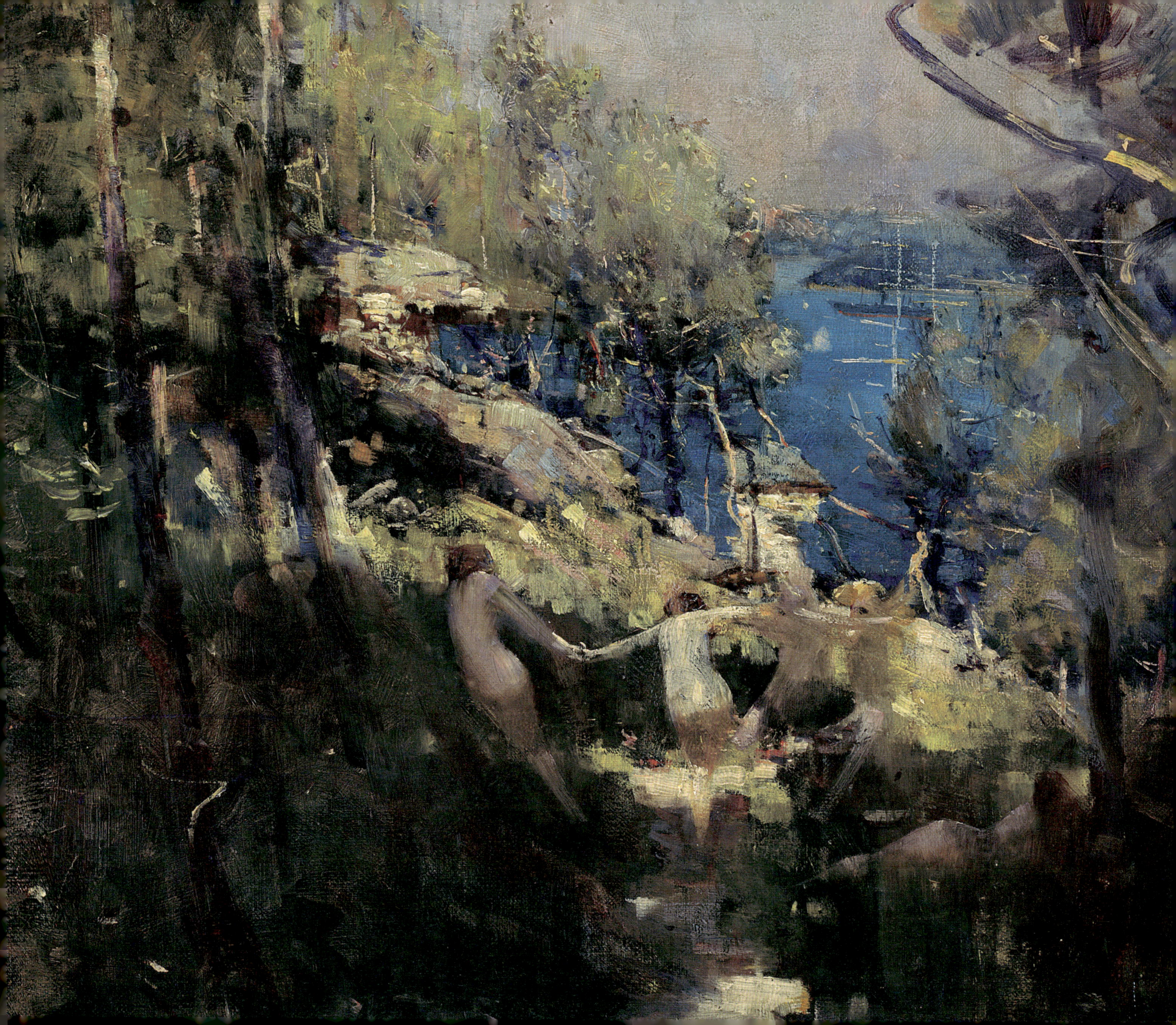

Streeton's similarly vertical, less Asian-inspired, but nonetheless mannered and decorative *Sydney Harbour: A souvenir* (c. 1897) is a poeticised memory of Mosman. It shows a harbour view framed by native trees wilfully spiralling, tossed as if by a gust of wind. It suggests a willy-willy wind uplifting dust that morphs into a ring of insubstantial naked figures swirling above the cliff edge. In the late 1890s Streeton, then Sydney Long, introduced mythical spirit-figures of this kind into the Australian bush. Streeton's 'streakers' are a romantic and nostalgic attempt to populate the Australian bush with local bush sprites, an equivalent to classical Mediterranean nymphs and dryads.

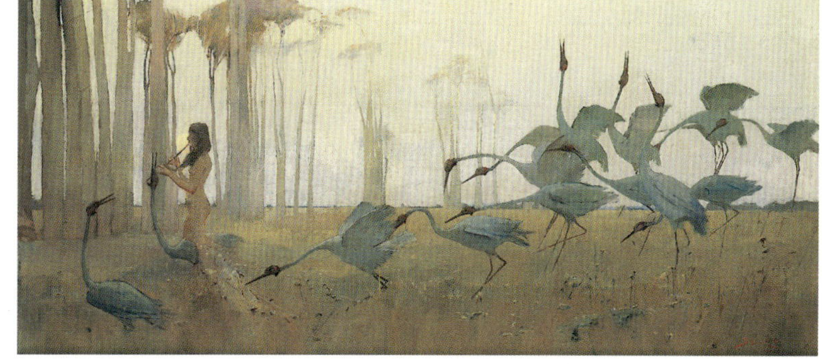

Sydney Long (1871–1955)
The Spirit of the Plains 1897
oil on canvas on wood 62 x 131.4 cm
Queensland Art Gallery, Brisbane
Gift of William Howard-Smith in memory of his grandfather, Ormond Charles Smith, 1940.
Reproduced with the kind permission of the Ophthalmic Research Institute of Australia

OPPOSITE
Arthur Streeton (1867–1943)
Sydney Harbour: A souvenir c. 1897 (detail)
oil on canvas mounted on cardboard 64.9 x 40.3 cm
Gift of S. H. Ervin 1962

Sydney Long's most famous later-1890s picture with a bush nymph is his *The Spirit of the Plains* (1897) (Queensland Art Gallery, Brisbane), in which a naked figure leads and enchants native birds in an art-nouveau dance, gliding through gum trees. In this exhibition Long's *Feeding time* (1896), painted a year earlier, is a more prosaic farm scene – no imaginary nature spirit here but a down-to-earth maiden feeding her domestic poultry and calves in clear winter-morning sunlight. This study of natural light and life was painted at Griffiths's farm near the Hawkesbury River at Richmond; a rustic site favoured by the leading Sydney art teacher Julian Ashton and many of his students.

Federation landscapes and the Federation tradition 1900–40

Frederick McCubbin, a few years later than Sydney Long but in the same spirit of national sentiment, introduced bush fairies into some of his Australian forest landscapes. McCubbin, unlike Tom Roberts and Walter Withers, but like the younger Arthur Streeton and Long, had been born in Australia. These locally-born artists tried to introduce a local spiritual mythology into the ancient Australian landscape, not yet quite aware of the thousands of years of spiritual understanding by the Aboriginal people. McCubbin's fairy forests were also partly painted to amuse his children. He loved children and from the mid-1880s regularly featured them as key motifs in his landscapes – gathering wildflowers, getting lost or watching fairies. Many of these works were painted near his retreat at Mount Macedon, about an hour by train from Melbourne. He named the place 'Fontainebleau' after the forest in France where the Barbizon painters of outdoor landscapes had come together.

A late landscape by McCubbin, *Girl in forest, Mount Macedon* (1913), shows a small child in a forest clearing, with a basket for wildflowers. It is executed in his mature style of flickering broken colours applied largely by a palette knife, and captures the effect of patches of bright spring light within a forest. McCubbin changed his more conservative nineteenth-century tonal style after his one momentous visit to Europe in 1907. He saw French Impressionist paintings in Paris but was even more inspired by the late works of J. M. W. Turner that he saw in London. Using the influence of Turner's unifying light, he painted *The coming of spring* (1912) from near his garden in suburban Kensington Road, South Yarra, looking across the river to industrial Richmond. He has integrated the rural appearance of the foreground – a cow, spring blossoms and grasses – with the distant factories and smoke beyond the river. The light and his opalescent palette unite the almost irreconcilable industrial and rural landscapes. McCubbin was one of the first Australian artists to embrace industrial landscape subjects. He cherished the idea of work and progress in brutal man-made constructions softened by smoke, dust and light, giving industry a sense of noble poetry.

McCubbin and Hans Heysen were the leading landscape artists in Australia after Federation in 1901. Many other artists of the period, particularly figure and portrait painters, had left for better training and the bigger artistic forum of Europe. Streeton left in 1897, Max Meldrum, George W. Lambert, Hugh Ramsay and Agnes Goodsir in 1900, E. Phillips Fox in 1901, Tom Roberts in 1903, and there were many others. The artists who stayed at home painted patriotic landscapes, often on a large scale for public display within the newly Federated Commonwealth of Australia. Besides McCubbin and Heysen, the major landscape artists included Sydney Long, Clara Southern, Walter Withers, W. Lister Lister and the senior painter W. C. Piguenit, as well as the watercolourists Blamire Young and J. J. Hilder.

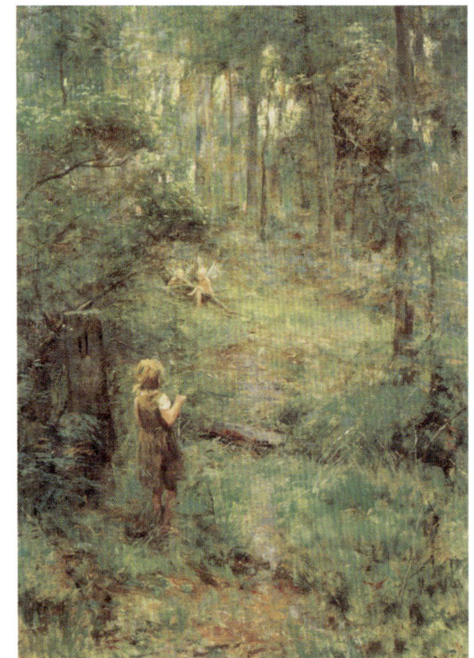

OPPOSITE
Frederick McCubbin (1855–1917)
Girl in forest, Mount Macedon 1913 (detail)
oil on canvas 50.8 x 76.2 cm
Purchased 1962

Frederick McCubbin (1855–1917)
What the little girl saw in the bush 1904
oil on canvas 96.5 x 66.0 cm
Private collection

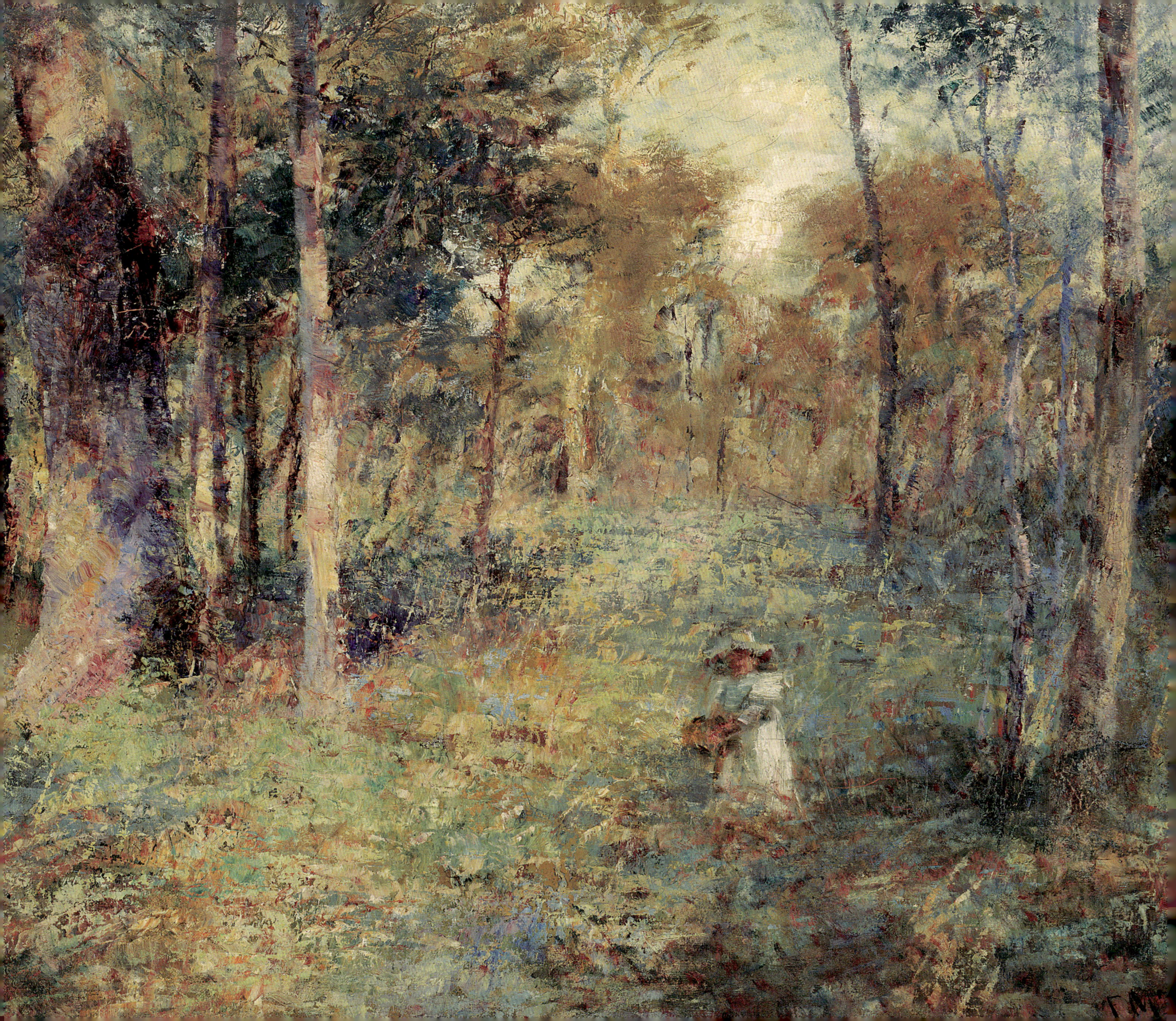

A lesser known painter and illustrator of the time, Harry Garlick, captured a less optimistic subject than most other Federation landscape painters: the long-lasting 'Federation drought', which lasted from 1895 to 1902. His stark Australian sheep-scape, *The drover* (1906), showing a mob forced on the road by drought, was possibly painted near his western New South Wales hometown of Orange. A lone horseman drives sheep across a parched sun-drenched plain. Distant mauve hills are visible but there are no trees for shade. The work could illustrate some of the lines from the famous and popular Federation poem by Dorothea Mackellar, *My country*, written in New South Wales in 1904:

I love a sunburnt country, A land of sweeping plains,
Of ragged mountain ranges, Of droughts and flooding rains.
I love her far horizons, I love her jewel-sea,
Her beauty and her terror – The wide brown land for me!

Other single lines in the poem – 'The hot gold hush of noon …', 'Her pitiless blue sky …', 'Over the thirsty paddocks …' – also seem very relevant to this painting of drought-stricken livestock.

In the period between Federation and the First World War, and indeed beyond, national sentiment was even more keenly expressed in literature and landscape painting than it had been in the 1880s and 1890s. Australian landscapes were privately purchased in greater numbers, and art museums and exhibitions were well attended, usually for people to admire the iconic examples of local landscape then prominently displayed. It was the beginning of Australians' lasting love of their art museums: Australians per capita are arguably the greatest art-museum visitors in the world. Although curious about different cultures, Australians still love their own art best, especially their landscapes.

The Sydney painter Elioth Gruner continued the landscape tradition of the Federation period well into the modernist period of the 1920s and 1930s. His conservative landscapes of soft light combine some of the elements of Hans Heysen and the more lyrical watercolours of J. J. Hilder. Rural scenes bathed in the gentle light of mornings and late afternoons were Gruner's speciality, as can be seen in his small landscape gem *Autumn morning* (c. 1916). The spreading tree in this picture is silhouetted against the misty light of an early morning sky. The fan-like branches and the cows beneath them cast radiating foreground shadows across the green pasture. Gruner's later and larger summertime landscape, *Murrumbidgee Ranges, Canberra* (1934), shows the rolling pastoral hills and forested ranges to the west of the nation's capital. This ideal reality of golden pastures, misty blue distances and clear blue sky had come to be popularly viewed as the typical Australian landscape. Roberts and particularly Streeton had pioneered this 'blue-and-gold' pastoral tradition in the late 1880s. It was launched triumphantly in Streeton's *Golden summer, Eaglemont* and, in the present exhibition, mentioned earlier, his *The selector's hut (Whelan on the log)*. Streeton himself, Heysen, Gruner and a host of lesser artists continued the tradition into the 1930s and beyond. A younger generation of Australian modernist artists eventually rebelled against these reactionary landscapes. Streeton had returned to Australia in 1920 determined to reinforce the pastoral

Harry Garlick (1878–1910)
The drover 1906 (detail)
oil on canvas board 60.8 x 45.4 cm
Purchased 1972

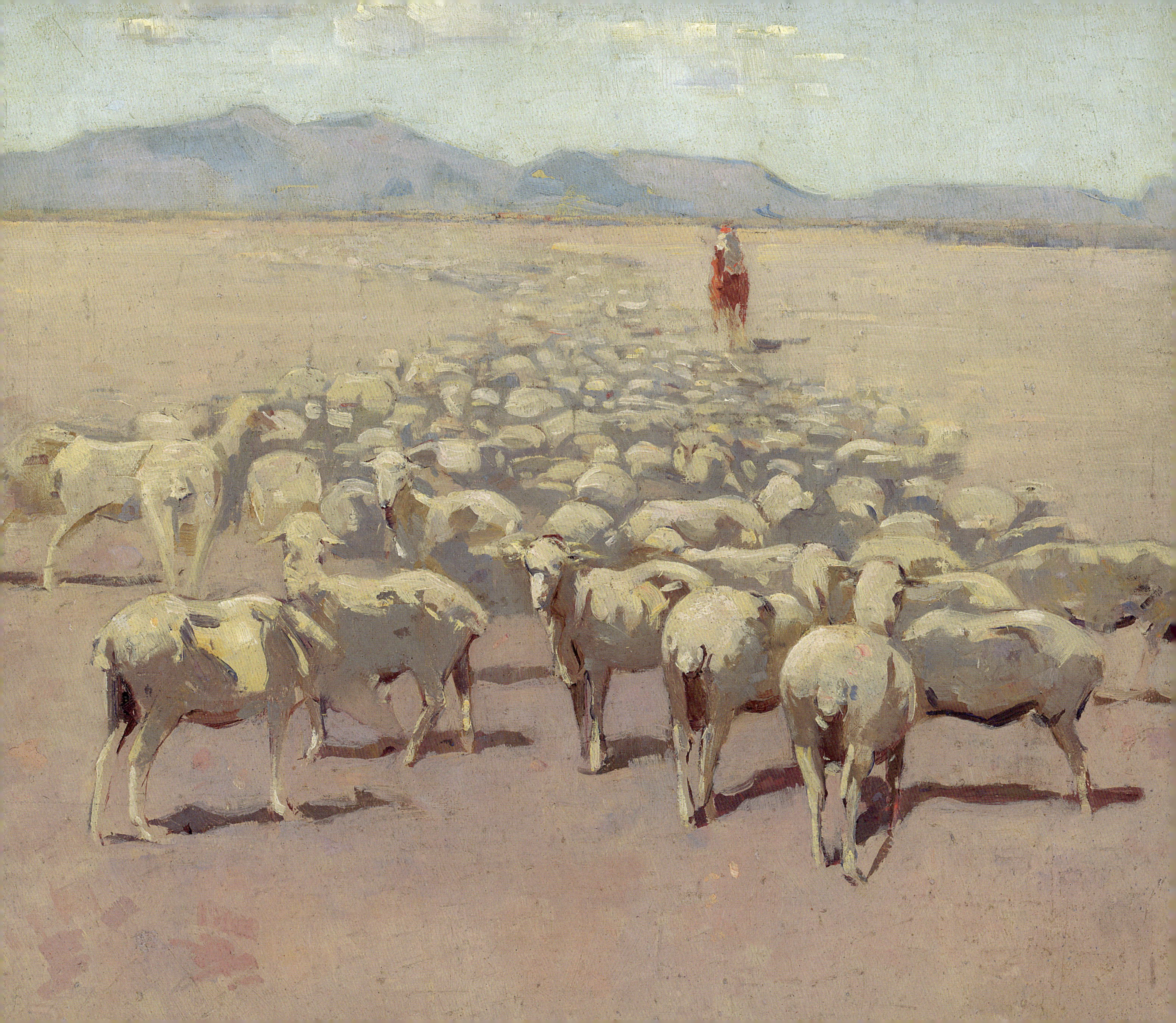

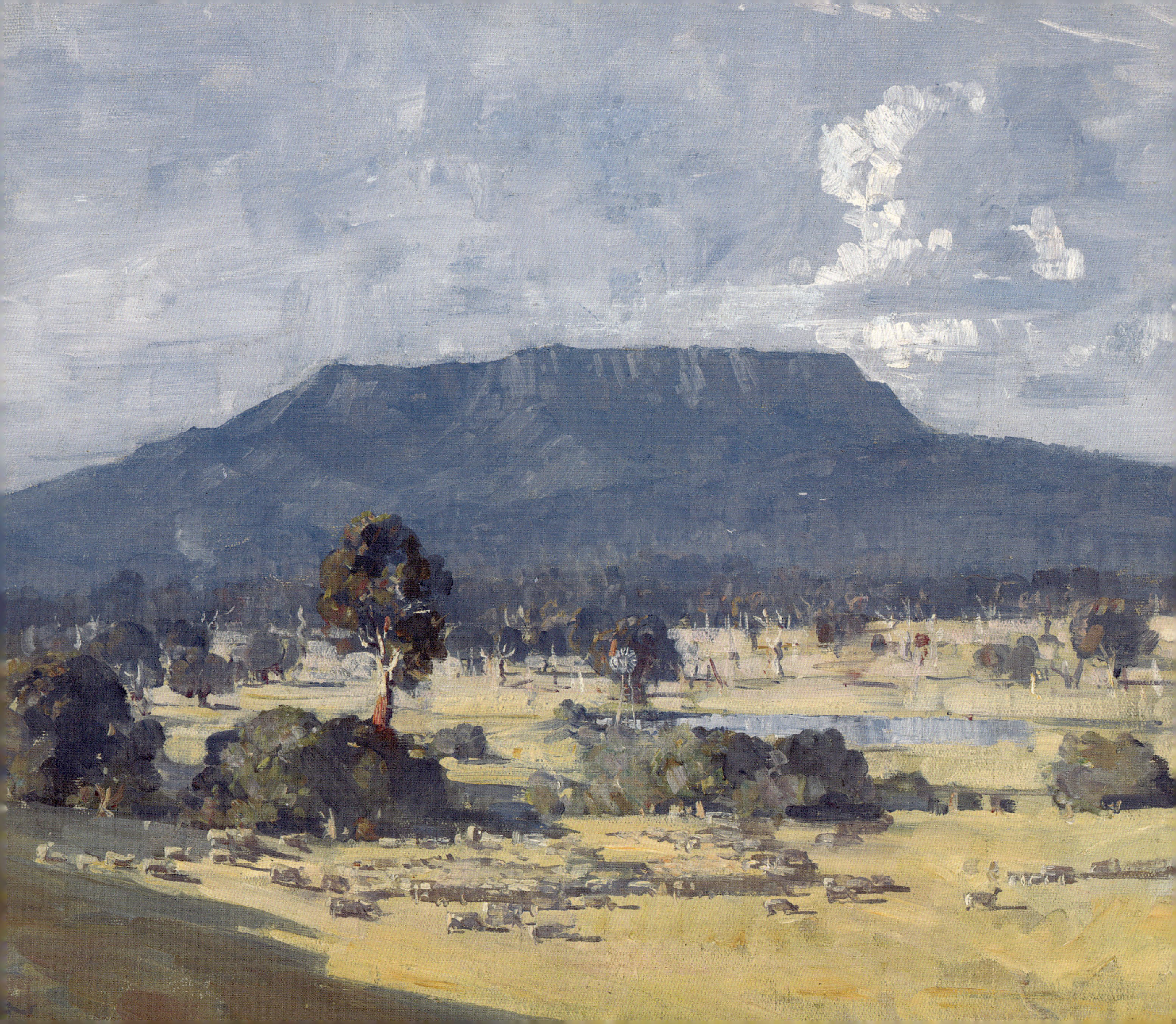

tradition against the 'corruption' of European modernism. He reaped the reward of conservative nationalistic patronage with paintings such as his late iconic work *Land of the Golden Fleece* (1926), of which he painted three profitable versions. The composition emphasises Australia as an open and peaceful pastoral paradise turning its back on over-populated and war-damaged Europe. The clear expanse of warm gold and blue spoke of ease and calm for Australians still traumatised by the memory of the European war.

The blue-and-gold convention of this period takes on a very different dynamism with Streeton's former mentor, Tom Roberts, in his small work *The quarry, Maria Island* (1926). Roberts frequently painted in Tasmania, where he had marital relatives, and this late Tasmanian subject exemplifies the modest scale and ambitions of the work produced after he returned permanently to Australia in 1923. Although the unpretentious landscape is a far cry from his large and consciously nationalistic works of the 1880s and 1890s, it nonetheless has more vitality and sense of place than Streeton's famous *Land of the Golden Fleece*, painted in the same year. Roberts's daring triangle of bright blue sky above red-gold rocky cliffs and man-broken limestone is a dynamic sign for the productive labour that supplied a cement works. Eight toiling quarrymen, hardly distinguishable from the fossil-rich rocks themselves, are embedded in the scene. The work is reminiscent of Percy Lindsay's more intimate mining scene of the 1890s, but has much greater intellectual complexity. Streeton's tranquil pastoral landscape, on the other hand, suggests an abundant land where sheep look after themselves. Roberts, like McCubbin, never abandoned the subject of Australian workers in the landscape.

Hans Heysen painted many pastoral blue-and-gold landscapes in both watercolour and oil during the period between Federation and the First World War, and for some years beyond. But unlike Streeton and Roberts, or for that matter almost any of the other Australian Impressionists, Heysen made the monumental Australian gum tree the hero of his nationalistic Federation-period pictures. In 1926, however, caught in an artistic rut, his painting was revitalised by the first of his many trips to the rocky region of the central Flinders Ranges, more than 500 kilometres north of Adelaide. Heysen's Flinders Ranges subjects suddenly added a new dry and sculptural style, in reds and amber, to the Australian landscape repertory. This was before colour photography and film revealed the red heart of Australia. To his many patrons in Sydney and Melbourne who were unfamiliar with the exact location of the Flinders Ranges, Heysen's work represented an exotic dead heart of Australia where white men had scarcely ventured. This geographical confusion was not helped by some of Heysen's titles, for example the title of the painting in this exhibition, *In the Flinders – Far North* (1951). The Flinders Ranges are in fact marginal pastoral land far south of the red centre of the continent, and not much further north than Port Macquarie in New South Wales. In some of Heysen's Flinders pictures he included monumental gums (which had been the focus of his earlier Federation landscapes) as ancient symbols of survival in this semi-arid Arcadia. *In the Flinders – Far North* was painted as a tribute to Australia's jubilee of Federation in 1951 and, for the unusually large canvas he used at this late date, Heysen aptly chose a landscape that combined

Arthur Streeton (1867–1943)
Land of the Golden Fleece 1926 (detail)
oil on canvas 50.7 x 75.5 cm
The Oscar Paul Collection, Gift of Henriette von Dallwitz and of Richard Paul in honour of his father 1965

rugged red and purple ranges with a stand of giant gums whose clawing roots hold on against adversity. By the mid-twentieth century, Heysen's landscapes, though still magnificent, were anachronistic survivors from an earlier phase of Australian landscape. He painted on in this fashion until his death in 1968.

Another artist who painted on, but differently, in a somewhat reactionary fashion was Max Meldrum. He had originally trained in Melbourne in the 1890s under Bernard Hall's academic realism. After a long period in Europe where he studied the art of Velázquez, Corot and Whistler, Meldrum returned to Melbourne in 1911. He developed a narrow theory that painting should only be about tone, that there are no lines in nature, and therefore that drawing in painting, or in preparation for painting, should be dispensed with. His dogmatic essay, 'The invariable truths of depictive art', written in 1917 and published two years later, was intended to help with his missionary teaching in a school attended by many devoted Melbourne followers. His own paintings – far more convincing than his theory – take on a reductive tonal quality with floating patches of flat thin colour. His earlier French landscapes and his usually smaller Australian landscapes add attractively to Australia's landscape tradition. *Shadows, landscape with trees* (c. 1925), a subject from Eltham, upriver from Melbourne, shows dappled gum-tree trunks, cut off at the top of the picture, on a grassy slope bathed in sunlight. Although reduced to simplified tonal blocks and a restricted palette, Meldrum has captured much atmosphere in such a small bushland patch, and has created a great deal of art in an emphatically formalist arrangement of vertical tree-trunks, horizontal shadows and a single curved slope. (Fred Williams, whose landscapes are outside the scope of this exhibition, enjoyed structuring gum-tree landscapes in a similar way.)

Following Meldrum's method, his one-time disciple A. E. Newbury had earlier painted a similar small but beautiful aspect of nature at Eltham. Showing a decapitated tree-trunk and an accompanying sapling in a paddock with silhouetted background bush, the flattened shapes and misty atmosphere in Newbury's *Eltham* (1919) are more descriptive and more lyrical – more sentimental even – than Meldrum's tougher, more objective landscape exercise.

The most lyrical Meldrumite, however, was Clarice Beckett. Of all Meldrum's many followers, she is the one who made the most original contribution to Australian landscape painting. Her small works are often so tonally reduced that they verge on the abstract. *Beaumaris seascape* (c. 1925) is an essay in Whistlerian reduction. The cliff and its trees, distant coastline and reflective sea are only suggested. With soft waxy paint that seems to glide onto the surface, Beckett has created an intriguing coastal landscape filled with misty, foggy light. More descriptive yet still evocative is her later *Sandringham Beach* (c. 1933), showing the beach from a cliff above the sand. Captured in full Australian sunlight, Beckett has brushed in the beach walkers, relishing their colourful bathing togs and the brightly coloured striped roofs of the beach boxes. Her original, unexpected subjects such as moving trams, cars and motorcycles, or petrol pumps and electric-light poles, combined with her reductive shapes of tone and colour, have prompted some art historians to classify Beckett in recent years as a major modernist

Hans Heysen (1877–1968)
In the Flinders – Far North 1951 (detail)
oil on canvas 102.0 x 141.0 cm
Purchased 1959

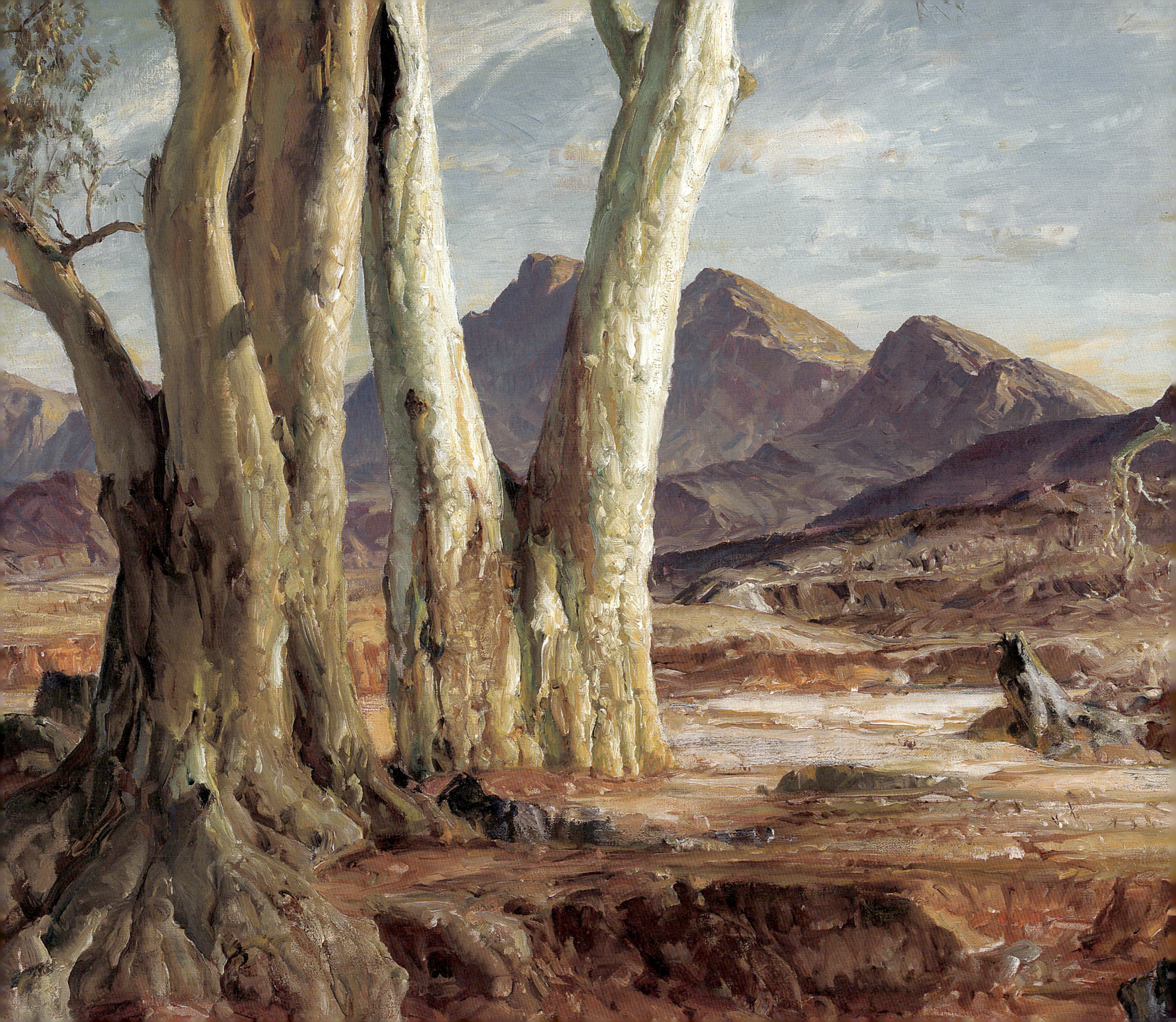

painter. She would probably have rejected such a label, but her original and very personal interpretation of Meldrum's theory makes her the major Melbourne landscape painter between the wars.

The modernist landscape 1920–40

Melbourne maintained a much more conservative art scene than Sydney. Between the wars, with the ageing and conservative Bernard Hall still in control of the National Gallery of Victoria and its influential art school, with the towering presence of the now reactionary Arthur Streeton, who was also a prominent art critic, and with the pugnacious Max Meldrum and his followers, modernism struggled. However, by the 1930s Melbourne did have its share of moderate modernist painters and influential teachers such as Eric Thake, George Bell, Arnold Shore, William Frater and Sam Atyeo. Atyeo was the most adventurous of the first Melbourne modernists and his *Norfolk Island pine, Metung* (1933) is a close-up of a South Pacific native conifer and a Gippsland Lakes beach beyond. It is painted with influences from Post-Impressionism, especially the analytic approach of Cézanne, but also with some of the vigour and rhythms of van Gogh. This was as progressive as any Melbourne landscape painting at the time. A year later Atyeo went on to paint Melbourne's first abstract composition *Organised line to yellow* (c. 1933) (National Gallery of Australia), an arabesque as a visual equivalent to the rise and fall of sound patterns in keyboard music, astonishing for its time and place but an isolated exercise for which there was no follow-up. Melbourne's Eric Thake painted a panoramic *Kosciusko and the Murray Flats at Towong* (1932), an undramatic distant view of Australia's highest mountain and snowfield, but while it shows a simplified objective landscape, it is barely modernist. Nevertheless, Thake soon became Melbourne's leading Surrealist painter.

By the time of the First World War Sydney had turned into the largest and fastest-growing city in Australia. It was seen as more progressive in art – and in everything else: the massive engineering of the Sydney Harbour Bridge from the late 1920s symbolised the city's embrace of progress and modernity. The progression of the bridge building was itself a favourite subject of modernist art, particularly by women painters and printmakers.

A group of Sydney artists who emerged from a late-Impressionist style during the First World War to become more radically modernist soon afterwards included Roy de Maistre, Roland Wakelin and Grace Cossington Smith. The Adelaide artist Margaret Preston returned from overseas, married, and settled in Sydney in 1920. The Adelaide-born Dorrit Black and the New South Wales pastoralist's daughter Grace Crowley returned to Sydney in 1929 and 1930 respectively, after studying Cubism in Europe, and offered classes at Dorrit Black's Modern Art Centre. In 1932, the year after Rah Fizelle returned to Sydney from Europe and became a close friend of Grace Crowley, they set up their own longer-lived Crowley-Fizelle School. To some extent modernist painters saw landscape painting itself as a conservative subject and the preserve of businessman-painters. Women modernists regularly chose other subjects, such as still lifes, interiors and figure compositions, or city and industrial subjects.

OPPOSITE
Roy de Maistre (1894–1968)
Forest landscape c. 1920
oil on cardboard 35.4 x 40.6 cm
Purchased 1971

Sam Atyeo (1910–1990)
Organised line to yellow c. 1933 (detail)
oil on canvas 68.0 x 54.2 cm
National Gallery of Australia, Canberra
Purchased 1970

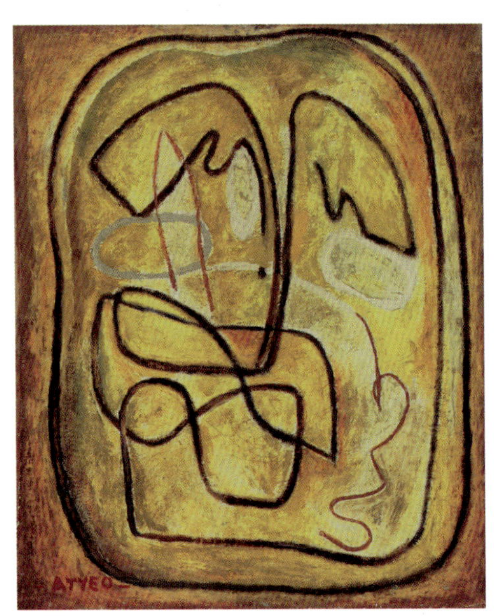

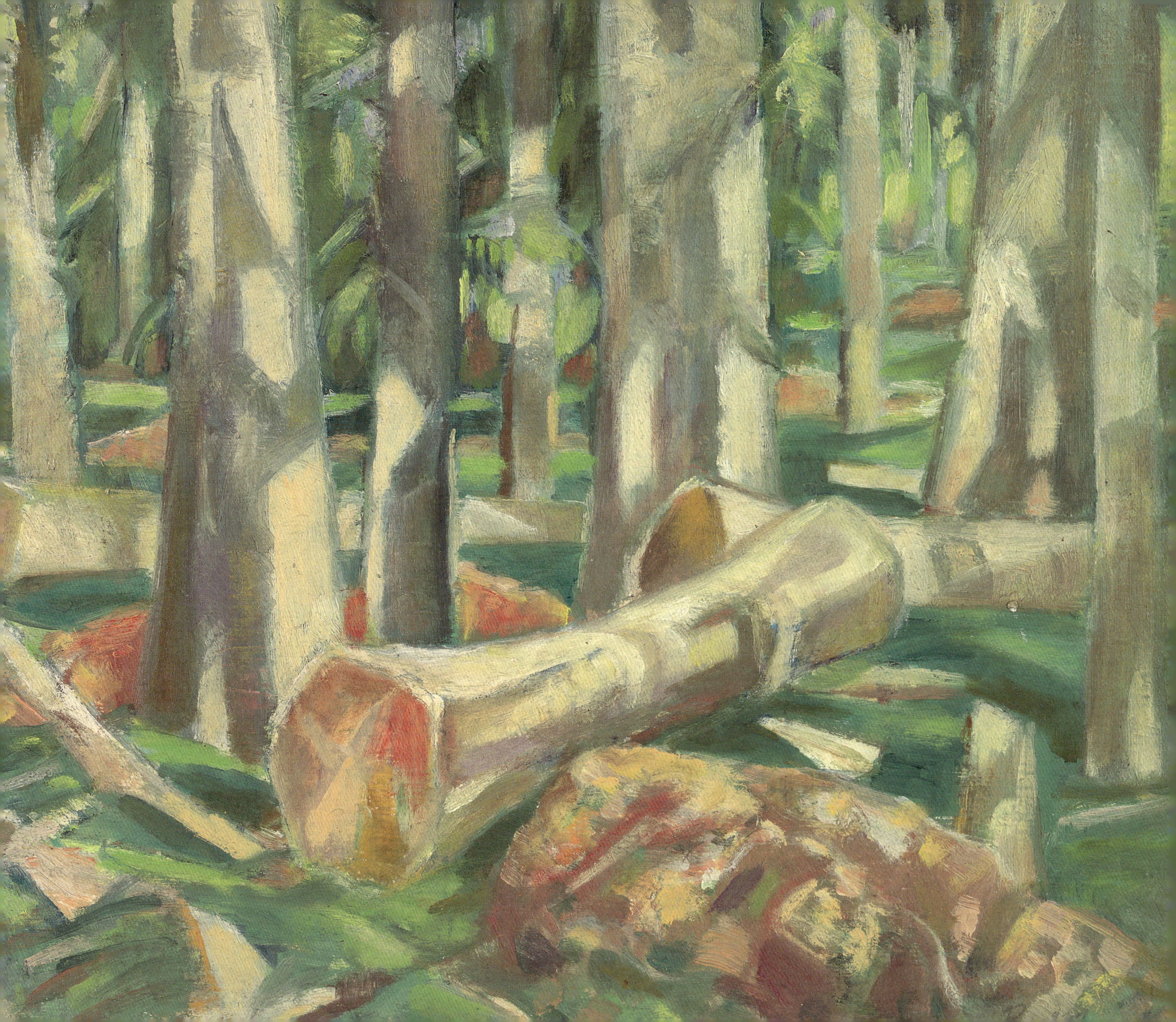

The leading modernist men, de Maistre and Wakelin, continued to paint suburban landscapes after an experimental phase in which de Maistre in particular worked on a theory of colour scales that related musical sounds to coloured forms. In 1919 they showed abstract and near-abstract work in a controversial exhibition in Sydney. One of the small landscapes that could have been in that 'colour-music' exhibition was Wakelin's freshly coloured *Barn near Tuggerah* (1919), where trees, sheds and path are reduced to simplified colour forms. De Maistre's abstracted *Forest landscape* (c. 1920), probably painted in Australia around this time, shows the influence of Cézanne. Forest stands with felled trees had been a frequent subject for landscape during the Federation period, honouring a rural industry but also expressing nostalgia for the loss of native forest. But de Maistre's painting, apparently a partly felled plantation, is an objective exercise in reduced forms and the play of warm advancing and cool receding colours. The tonal reduction we observe in Meldrum's landscapes of trees is here replaced by clean bright colour – and it is significant that both de Maistre and Wakelin flirted for a short time in the early 1920s with Meldrum's stepped dark and light tones.

The most dynamic of the Sydney modernists in the 1920s and early 1930s was Grace Cossington Smith. She did paint landscapes, but they were unconventional, and she painted many other subjects as well, including an extraordinary series of industrial landscape paintings and drawings of the Sydney Harbour Bridge under construction. Other women artists, including Dorrit Black and printmakers Jessie Traill and Adelaide Perry, also celebrated the construction of the bridge and enjoyed the opportunity it provided for modernist angularities and abstracted lines. Many conservative menfolk stuck to pastures and gum trees, but in extreme contrast to such art is Cossington Smith's *The Bridge in building* (1929–30), the most daring of all the paintings of the bridge. Can this near-abstract picture of complex engineering, of traversing, towering and reaching girders and cranes, really be called a landscape at all? It is a high-energy industrial landscape, the ultimate painting of a construction site, but there is still a glimpse of Sydney's harbourside buildings through the cranes, and concentric quadrants of radiant energy from the sun fill the sky above the steelwork.

Cossington Smith's hard angles and her strident oranges and complementary purples are emphasised rather than softened, whereas McCubbin nearly twenty years earlier had taken the soft option in his industrial landscapes. Likewise Rah Fizelle's *Pyrmont Power Station from Darling Harbour* (c. 1935) is a subject that McCubbin could have chosen but would have made more lyrical, with softened angularities. Here Fizelle has sharpened and accentuated the angles of the industrial wharfs, roofs and chimneys. Even the smoke and the clouds counteract in a pattern of stripes across the sky.

High-rise apartments had become common in inner Sydney neighbourhoods such as Kings Cross and Elizabeth Bay. As a modernist, Fizelle embraced such developments, living in a flat himself at the time, and he used them as modern subject matter. In his *Elizabeth Bay* (1931 or 1932) sharp diagonals of buildings and roofs are again emphasised, although he dispensed with a sky and instead closed

Grace Cossington Smith (1892–1984)
The Bridge in building 1929–30 (detail)
oil on pulpboard 75.0 x 53.0 cm
Gift of Ellen Waugh 2005

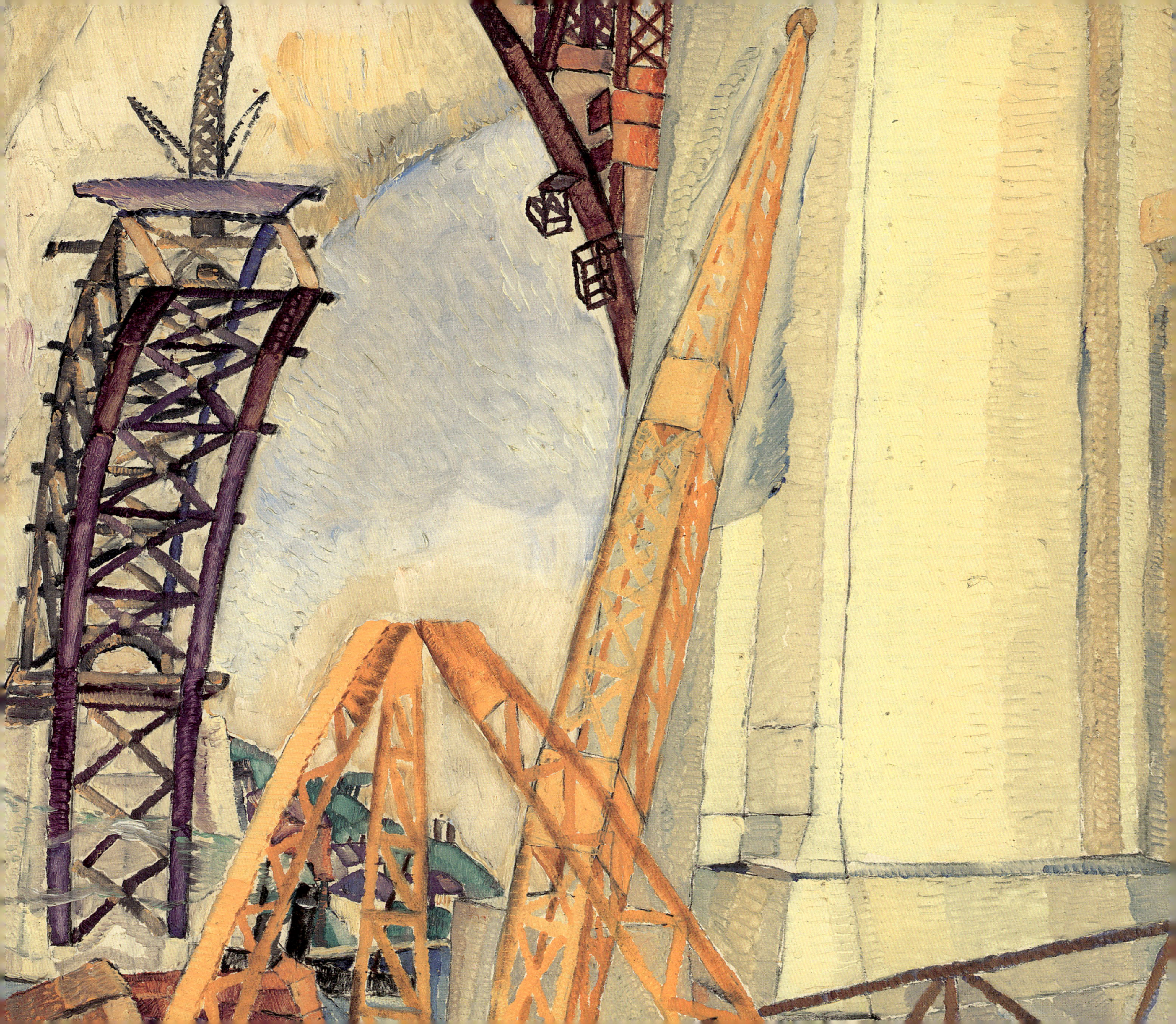

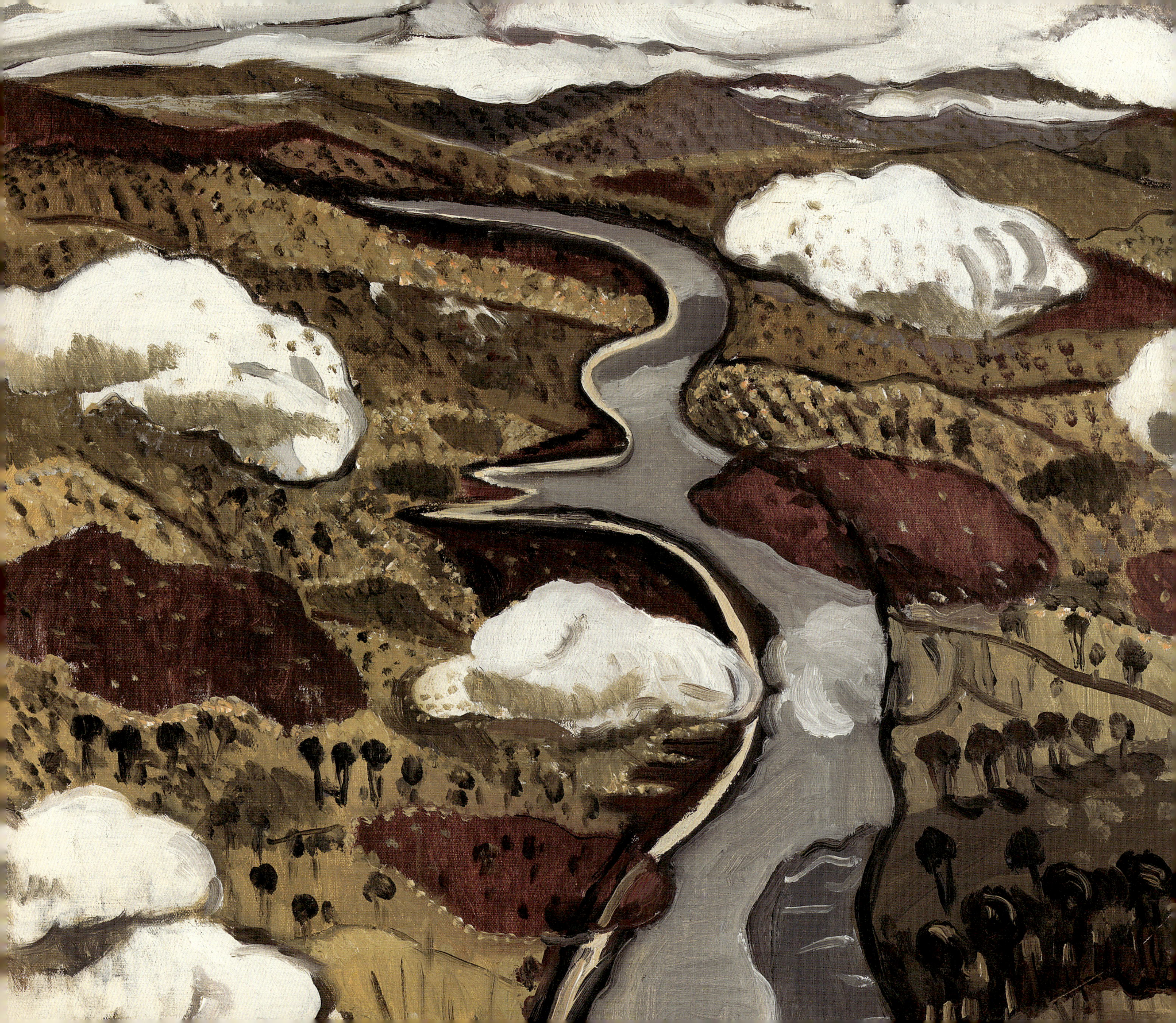

the composition by looking down to a quadrant of shoreline at neighbouring Rushcutters Bay. The warm orange of the modern apartment masonry is a counterpoint to the cool green of the vegetation and blue-green of the bay.

The Second World War and beyond 1940–50

The most visible and vociferous exponent of modernism in Sydney was Margaret Preston. In the 1920s and 1930s she had concentrated on flat, simplified still-life designs in both her paintings and hand-coloured woodblock prints. In the 1940s she turned to Australian landscape in both painting and monotype printmaking. She had begun to promote Aboriginal art and strongly believed that its example was what all truly Australian works of art should follow: 'Australia', she wrote, 'has ignored a fine simple art that exists at her own back door. It has to learn what this art could do to help clear up the minds of our people and give them a national culture'.[2] In the same year in which she drew attention to the intellectual clarity of Aboriginal art, Preston painted her outstanding *Flying over the Shoalhaven River* (1942). This work translates the Australian landscape from a European into an 'Aboriginal' visual language by means of quasi-Indigenous designs and dottings, and by limiting colour to the colours of the earth – yellow and red ochres, white clay and charcoal black. The view from an aeroplane flattens the river motif and the landscape itself, and the intervening white clouds with dark red-ochre shadows further flatten the surface design into something that resembles a map-like Indigenous representation of country.

Preston was the most travelled of all her artist contemporaries, having toured extensively in Asia, the Pacific and Europe. She also travelled in central and northern Australia. Her worldly view on the one hand, and her isolation because of the Second World War on the other, reinforced her sense of Australian nationalism and her idea of adapting Aboriginal art for her 'Australian' paintings and prints. Her 'Aboriginal landscapes' of the 1940s and early 1950s are a remarkable and unique contribution to Australian landscape art.

Lloyd Rees also painted outstanding landscapes in New South Wales in the 1940s, by which time his individual style had fully matured. It had evolved from immaculate, carefully detailed landscape drawings, executed in the early 1930s, into broadly handled oil paintings that concentrated on the sculptural qualities of landforms and emphasised them with exaggerated lighting effects. *A South Coast road* (1951) shows country near Werri Beach, on the south coast of New South Wales, where Rees had a holiday house. He expresses his strong sensations about the geological rhythms and structures beneath a landscape. He disregarded the local green surfaces and instead emphasised earthy tones and masses, bringing, as he said, 'the warmth to it'. He was probably influenced by the hot, arid earth colours in Russell Drysdale's landscapes.

Margaret Preston (1875–1963)
Flying over the Shoalhaven River 1942 (detail)
oil on canvas 50.6 x 50.6 cm
Purchased 1973
© Margaret Preston Licensed by VISCOPY, Australia, 2007

2 Margaret Preston, 'Influence of Aboriginal art', *The Studio* (London), vol. 124 (1942), p. 122.

Drysdale, a pupil of Melbourne's semi-modernist George Bell School, moved to Sydney in 1940. In Melbourne and Europe he had experimented with French modernism, but in New South Wales during the war he, like Preston, wrestled with the idea of what he should paint that was uniquely Australian but different from what had been portrayed previously. He turned away from international modernism and the sophistication of the large cities, and also from Australia's fertile coastal regions, to the less productive inland country, though not what we call the outback. At the time, his outback subjects came from a late-1944 campaign in the far west of New South Wales, to which he was sent by the *Sydney Morning Herald* to illustrate the effects of a drought. Some then-forgotten colonial explorer artists like S. T. Gill, Ludwig Becker and Thomas Baines had ventured far into Australia's remote inland, and Hans Heysen had painted the arid red country of the middle-distance Flinders Ranges from the late 1920s, but Drysdale was the first to shift into a general reddening of Australian landscape art. He specially embraced inland New South Wales and north Queensland, noting the melancholy of their semi-deserted towns, broken-down farms, erosion, stony ground and abandoned mines. His dried-up earth suggested that man had lost control of the land – nature had fought back and taken back. The theme is still poignant today. *Golden Gully* (1949) shows the almost deserted mining town of Hill End in the background and in the foreground the eroded, pitted and scarred remains of an abandoned gold mine. In *Emus in a landscape* (1950), a composition based on sketches from Drysdale's drought tour to Lake Mungo and thereabouts six years earlier, only the flightless native birds remain to witness the tragic ruins of a burnt-out sheep station. In the desert a stark, contorted pile of flame-shaped and emu-shaped sheets of iron remains to suggest a surreal memorial to the departed, and a reversion to the local forms of nature. By 1950 Drysdale, like Preston but rather later, was emphasising an Indigenous Australian presence in the landscape. In *Boy running, Cooktown* (c. 1952) he isolates the lone central figure of an Indigenous boy fleeing in a town named to commemorate Captain Cook's seven-week stay at the site in 1770 – the voyage on which Cook claimed the east coast of New Holland for the British and named it New South Wales, thus dispossessing the Indigenous people. In this ominously deserted street in Far North Queensland, from what is the boy running? Is it from white civilisation itself?

Drysdale left Melbourne just before a new constellation of slightly younger artists began to cluster there, a group that would search for another new and personal way to express as yet unsaid ideas and feelings about Australian life and landscape. The young artists Arthur Boyd, Sidney Nolan and Albert Tucker had urgent things to say.

Boyd, a third-generation artist from a family of painters, potters, writers and architects, began his career in the 1930s, painting traditional pastoral subjects while staying at seaside Rosebud with his artist grandfather, Arthur Boyd Senior, who by then mainly painted watercolour landscapes. His blond *Landscape with grazing sheep* (1937) may owe something to his grandfather's and Streeton's late landscapes, but his early grassland scenes are too stark and simplified to be a celebration of the pastoral industry; they are chiefly exercises in aesthetic layout and the rendering of Australian light and colour.

Russell Drysdale (1912–1981)
Emus in a landscape 1950 (detail)
oil on canvas 101.6 x 127.0 cm
Purchased 1970

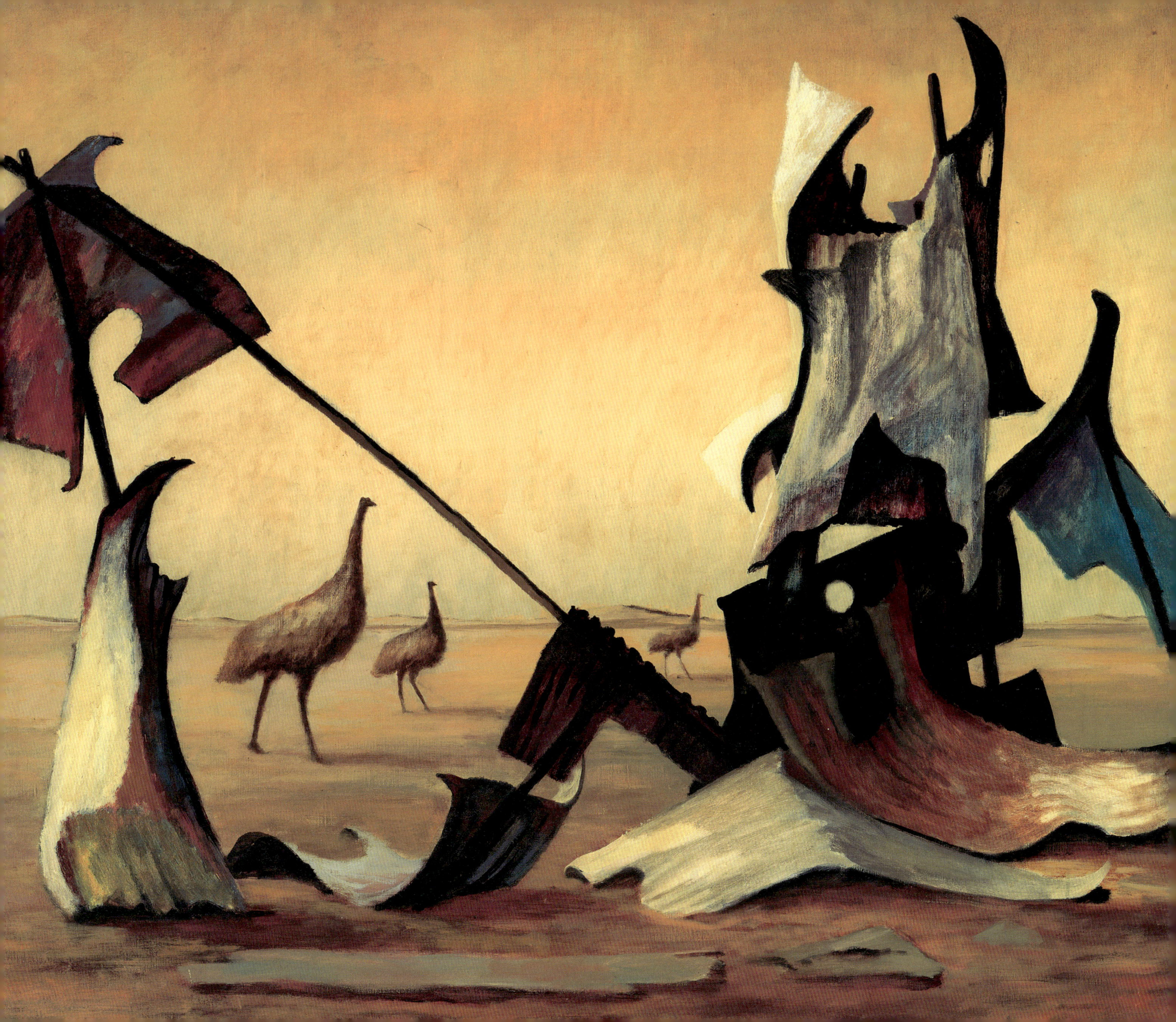

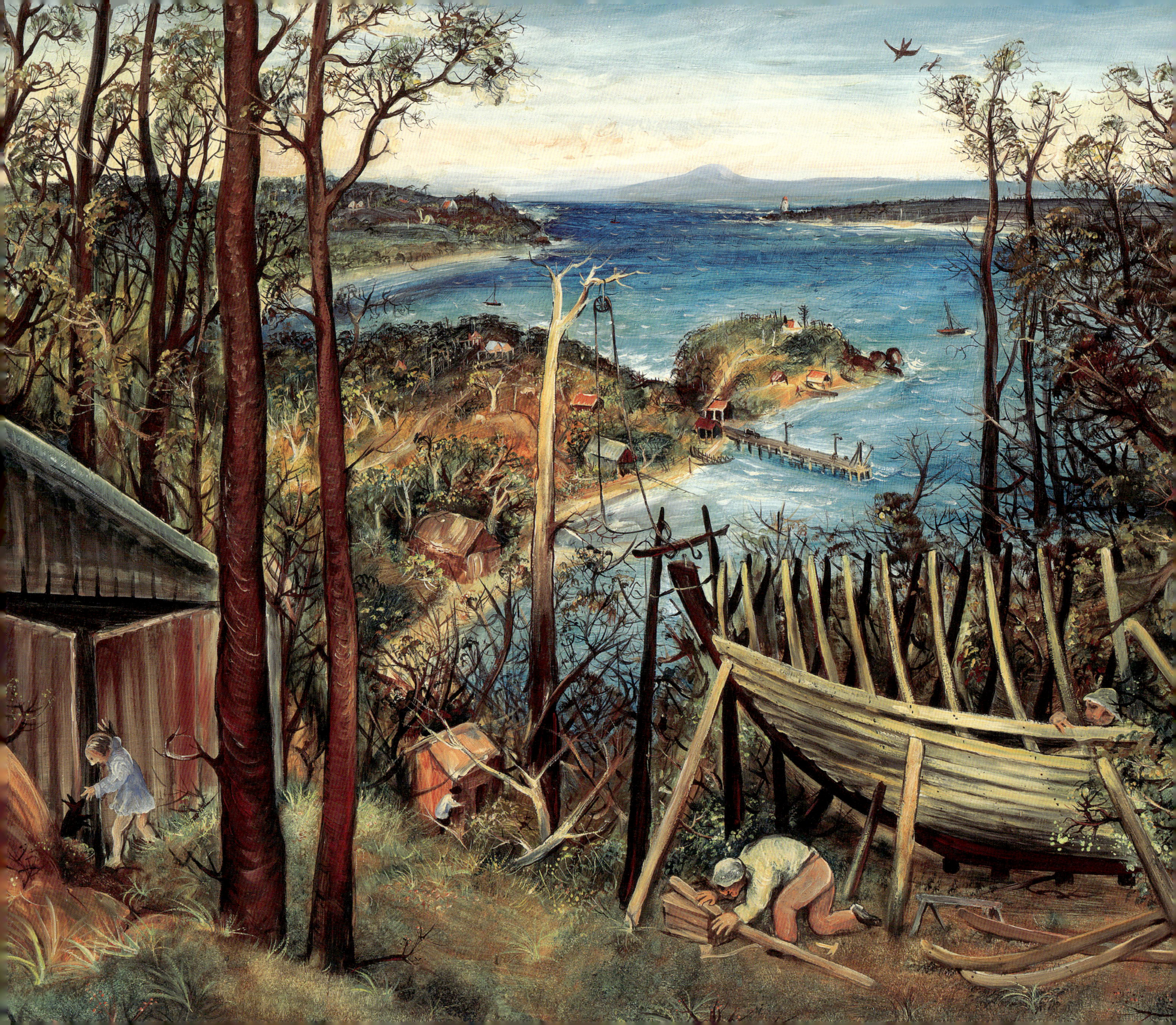

During the trauma of the war years Boyd's art took on a more personal, haunting expressiveness. His potter father, Merric Boyd, filled endless notebooks with psychotic colour drawings of people and strange distorted landscapes. That example and further exposure at home to reproductions of the greatest Old Master paintings by Bruegel, Rembrandt and Ruisdael profoundly affected the young painter. Boyd's dark Ruisdael-like forest in *The hunter I* (1944) expresses savage feelings new to Australian art. The white hunter and his non-native livestock intrude aggressively into Yarra Valley native bush. He is hunting anything that is native to Australia.

Boyd's masterpiece from the late 1940s, *Boat builders, Eden* (1948), records an actual view through bushland down to the southern New South Wales fishing-industry town of Eden, but it is seen through the influence of Bruegel's paintings, and it reminds us of the biblical building of Noah's Ark. In Boyd's Australian landscapes there are often hints of biblical sin, retribution and redemption.

Boyd's friend Sidney Nolan was to become one of the most imaginative and compelling painters of the Australian landscape and its stories. He began as an abstract painter and a poet at the end of the 1930s, but in 1942, after a war posting to the Wimmera district in inland western Victoria, he was struck by the vivid landscape and its possibilities. He stated: 'This [is a] very bright country, glittering in fact, and we might have lived in a studio in Paris or Berlin, for the amount of good it has done us. We all took the policy of Paris on, there was nothing else to do, but always [there] was the thought we would learn to tell our own story.'[3] This is certainly what he did with the now iconic Ned Kelly series completed in the mid-1940s and which is now one of the best-loved treasures of the National Collection. But he embraced other tragic heroes, for example the ill-fated nineteenth-century explorers Burke and Wills. A major work from this series is *Burke at Cooper's Creek* (1950). The diminished figure on his horse, and the awkward foreground camel, look ill at ease in this remotest of inland landscapes. Carefree native birds inspect the intruders and seem to own the place. The land is about to take Burke's life.

Nolan also undertook a series of pure landscapes seen in Central Australia. As in Margaret Preston's *Flying over the Shoalhaven River*, he painted airman's-eye views of the red heart of the continent. His *Inland Australia* (1950) turns sculptured rocky ranges into a dimly glowering and translucent ocean of heaving redness, whereas the sharp-edged plane of vivid blue sky hovers solid and opaque. No-one had hitherto painted our desert interior as if it were an organism of flesh, blood and skin, an uneasy place, to be classified as frighteningly Sublime, not calmly Beautiful or conventionally Picturesque. Heysen had painted the semi-arid Arcadia of the Flinders Ranges down south with classic stability and solid structure. Albert Namatjira's watercolours of his own Central Australian country show land where rocks and trees are guardian personages. Nolan's aerial views are formidable, alien. They could be of the moon's surface, or Mars.

3 Sidney Nolan, letter to Sunday Reed, October 1942, Dimboola, Reed papers, La Trobe Library, State Library of Victoria, Melbourne.

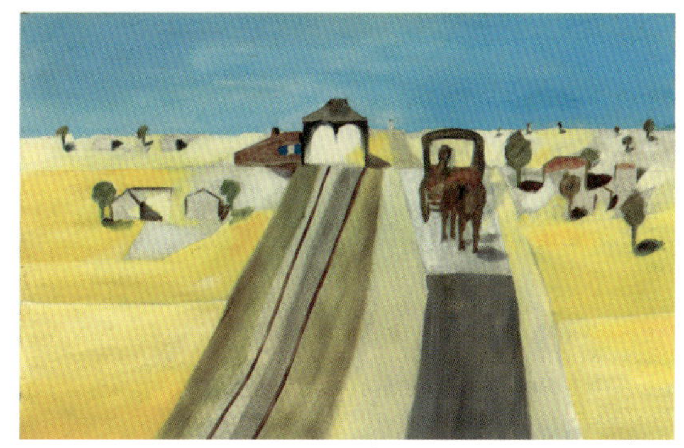

Sidney Nolan (1917–1992)
Kiata c. 1943
enamel on composition board 60.9 x 91.7 cm
National Gallery of Australia, Canberra
Purchased 1973

OPPOSITE
Arthur Boyd (1920–1999)
Boat builders, Eden 1948 (detail)
oil and egg tempera on composition board
85.6 x 101.7 cm
Purchased 1977

Sidney Nolan (1917–1992)
Ned Kelly 1946
enamel on composition board 90.8 x 121.5 cm
National Gallery of Australia, Canberra
Gift of Sunday Reed 1977

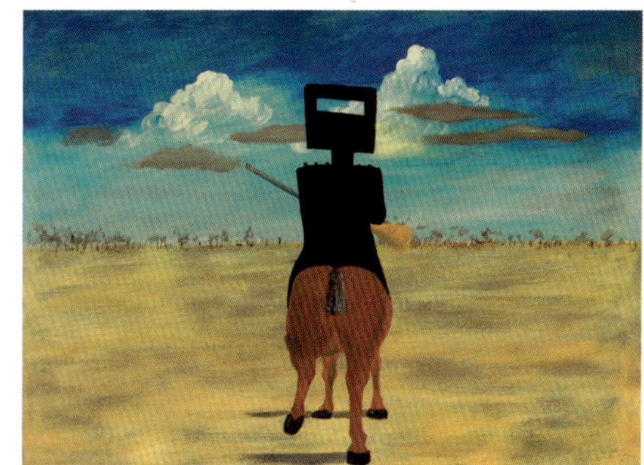

One of Nolan's most striking landscapes of this period is a one-of-a-kind bushfire, not part of any series. Bushfires bring fear and horror to the hearts of all Australians. Nolan experienced one close at hand when he was living beside a national park at Wahroonga on the northern bushland fringe of Sydney. His ensuing painting, *Ku-ring-gai Chase* (1948), shows the intense poetic beauty that accompanies the terror. We can almost hear the whoosh and crackling of the fire's explosive combustion. This is no mere description of a bushfire; we are made to feel the onslaught of radiating heat and to smell the burning.

Albert Tucker was fixed in a darker, angrier view of the world than either Boyd or Nolan. Influenced by Picasso and the German Expressionists, he developed a series of powerful drawings and paintings from 1943 to 1947 and called them *Images of modern evil.* Tucker was deeply affected by the war, which he felt brought out the worst in human behaviour. Melbourne's wartime blackouts seemed to him to create a city of darkness, menace and predatory lust. For Tucker even the day was dark and in his *Sunbathers* (1944) we see bands of hot dark sky and sea hanging over two bodies on an over-heated shore. Tucker strikes out against the notion of cheerful optimism in Australian beach culture. Nothing could be further from Conder's or Beckett's celebrations of Australian light and leisure. The dangerously exposed sunbakers are brutally depersonalised, lumps of meat thrown down to sizzle on a glowing barbecue.

The 1940s were a dynamic and creative decade for Australian art, including landscape painting. The real threat of war and the isolation forced upon Australia caused tensions that were compatible with the new languages of modernism, especially Surrealism, Expressionism and reductive abstraction. The situation galvanised the mainly younger painters to express themselves with a new force. After more than one-and-a-half centuries of European settlement, artists were seeing beyond landscape's superficial surface. They used the lessons of modernism to express deeper feelings about the land and its people during a time of national trauma.

This new artistic firmament of the 1940s was not confined to Melbourne and Sydney, but was also found in the smaller capitals. Adelaide in particular had a lively contemporary scene influenced by Cubist formalism, Surrealism and Expressionism and epitomised by the work of Dorrit Black, Ivor Francis and Douglas Roberts respectively. Here is not the place to talk about the various art scenes in each state and the contemporary art societies that sprang up around Australia, or to mention each artist's contribution. Suffice to mention a few artists. Jeffrey Smart, whose art evolved from the modernist formalism of his teacher Dorrit Black, and to some extent from Surrealism, was a central figure in the art world of Adelaide. *Wallaroo* (1951), a South Australian subject, was painted just after he left Adelaide for Sydney. At the former copper-mining town of Wallaroo on the Spencer Gulf, its abandoned industrial structures and debris, heavy sky and sombre figures remind us of Drysdale's quiet country towns. Smart is always a more sculptured, formalist artist, however, and his austere compositions avoid pathos and sentimentality. We are not meant to identify with the two figures in dwindling Wallaroo; they are there merely as compositional elements, forms to lead in from the sea to the interesting tower

Albert Tucker (1914–1999)
Sunbathers 1944 (detail)
oil on cardboard 59.2 x 86.0 cm
Purchased 1981

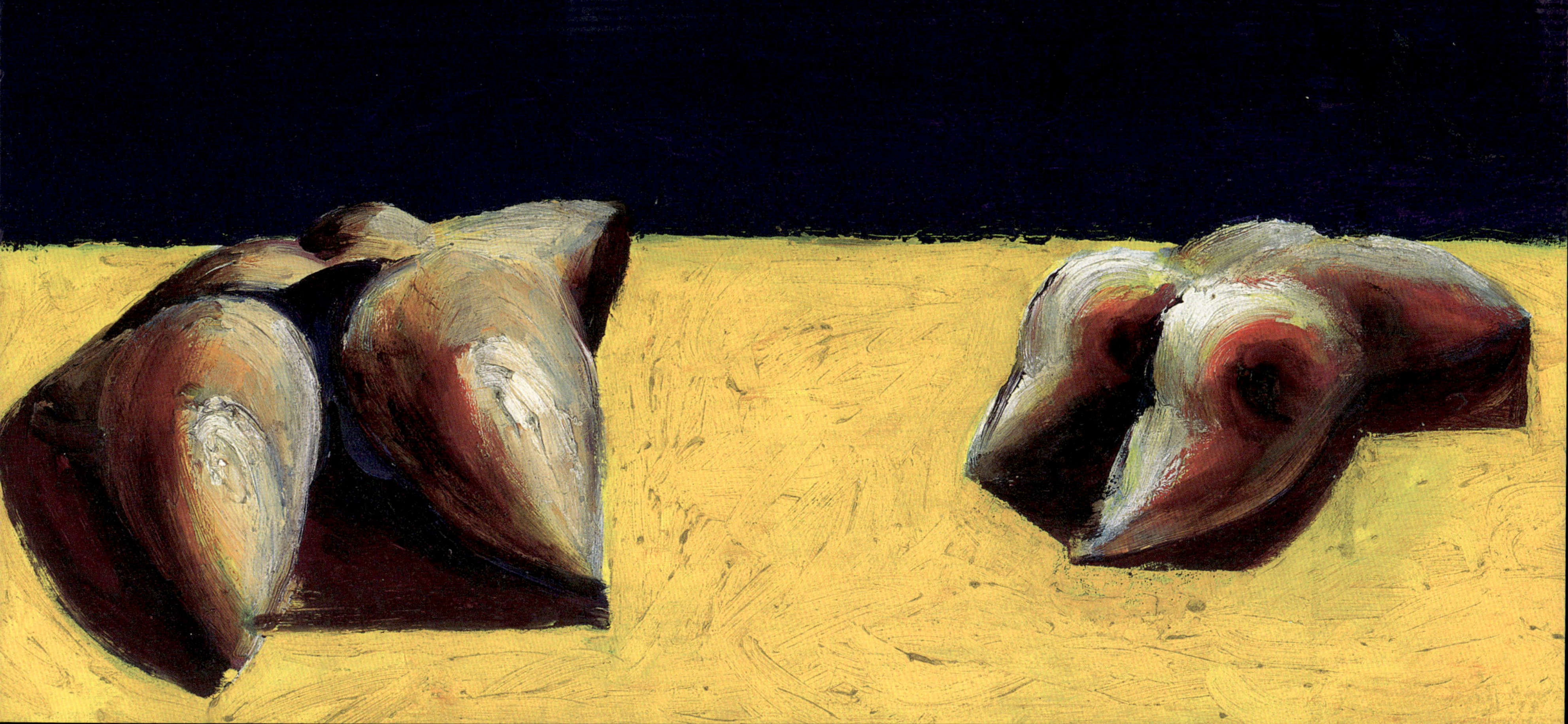

and mullock heaps that had generated the idea of making a picture. Yet there is a pervasive and undeniable haunting atmosphere.

The South Australian landscape painter Horace Trenerry had begun his career in the late 1920s, much influenced by the local artist Hans Heysen and the Sydney artist Elioth Gruner. Except for one visit to Sydney he never left South Australia, although he was later probably influenced by English paintings, by the Camden Town School of modernist artists, which in the late 1930s were entering the Art Gallery of South Australia and private collections in Adelaide. In the later 1930s and the 1940s Trenerry's rather traditional approach to landscape evolved into more abstracted calligraphic brush drawing on the canvas. With chalky colours he brushed dynamic compositions in warm and cool blues, mauves and pale yellow and red ochres. His typically sketchy *The ploughed field* (1947) was painted near his home at Port Willunga in the McLaren Vale district south of Adelaide.

Perth had modernist artists who evolved in the 1940s. Although they painted the local landscape, their ideas and experience derived from Europe, independent of what was happening elsewhere in Australia. Elise Blumann, one of the leaders, was born and trained in Germany from whence she had arrived in Australia in 1938 as a refugee. Much influenced by Matisse and French Expressionism, in Perth her work appeared bold and wild. Her *Storm on the Swan* (1946) has great expressive energy. We feel the full strength of nature's forces as trees bend to breaking point under strong wind off the Indian Ocean, and as winter rain falls in great sheets around her home on the banks of the Swan River estuary. She inhabits the storm. In the late 1940s in Perth Guy Grey-Smith developed abstracted landscapes that took Cézanne as a starting point but used the high-key colour of French Fauvism. His *Perth from Kings Park* (1949) expresses the bright optimism of this city of the west. Perth's great twentieth-century artist, Howard Taylor, also began his highly individual landscapes at this time. His *Trees* (1950) shows a stand of gums in a reductive modernist form using the medium of egg tempera with colour carefully applied in fine lines like coloured pencil. The centrally placed gums are formalised into a resemblance of a modernist sculpture, illuminated by radiant natural light. An intense interest in optical experience, of light and colour, remained a feature of Taylor's subsequent paintings and sculptures.

Moving from the far west of our continent to the opposite extremity of Far North Queensland we conclude with Ray Crooke's evocative *'Kingfisher', Thursday Island* (1950), a Torres Strait scene in the dry season. This exhibition *Ocean to Outback* opens with an ocean view of a shipwreck off the south-east coast of the island state of Tasmania, painted in 1850, and finishes with an abandoned wooden lugger in the harbour of Thursday Island painted exactly 100 years later, in 1950. The two paintings, both featuring abandoned vessels on island coasts off the continental mainland, represent not only the extremes of distance and geography across Australia but also the 100-year time span of the exhibition. Happily, Ray Crooke is still alive and painting in North Queensland in 2007.

Although this exhibition ends around 1950, having covered the greatest century of Australian landscape painting, landscape art in Australia by no means vanished in the mid-twentieth century.

Ray Crooke (b. 1922)
'Kingfisher', Thursday Island 1950 (detail)
egg tempera and oil on composition board
25.0 x 35.6 cm
Purchased 2006

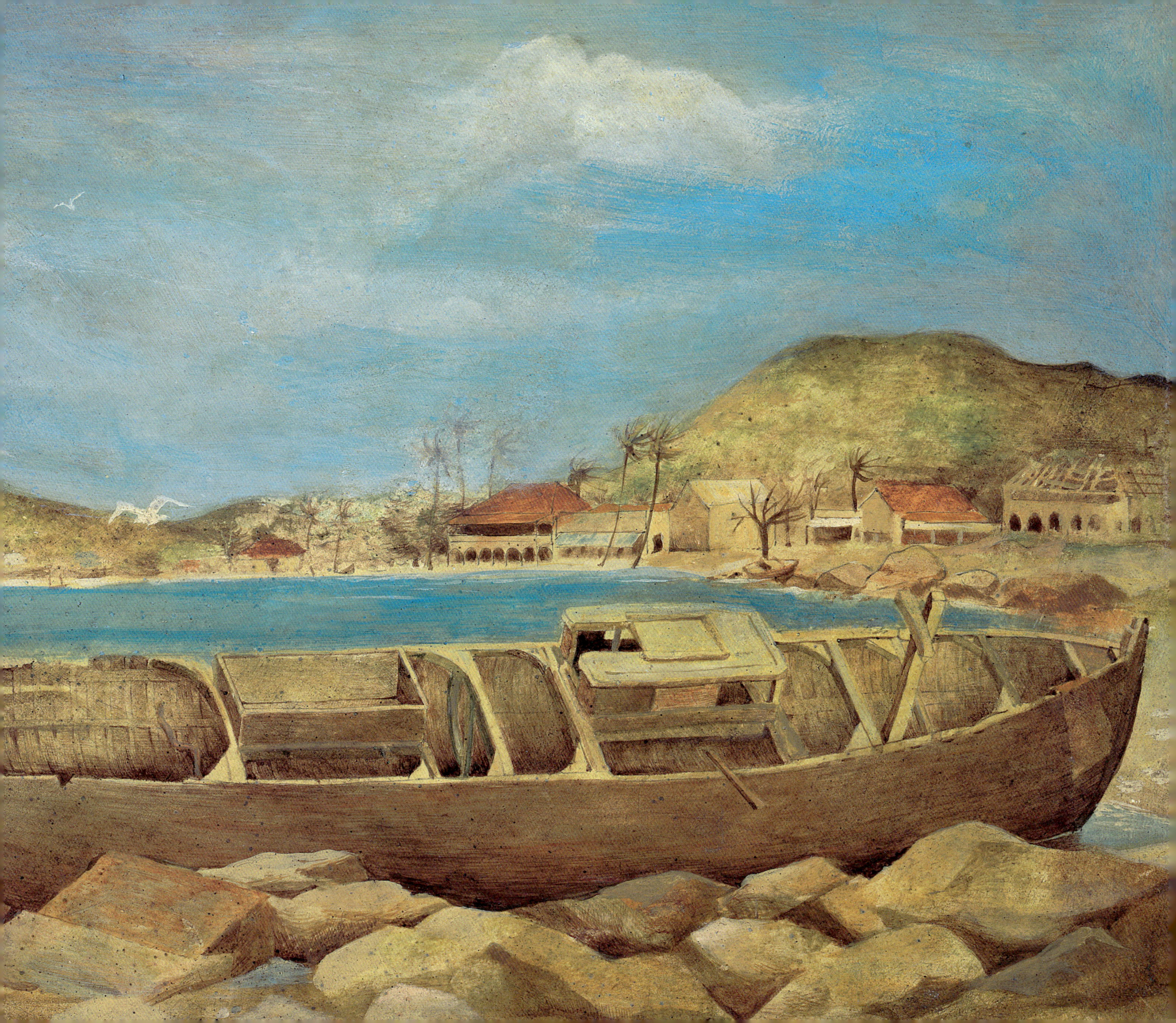

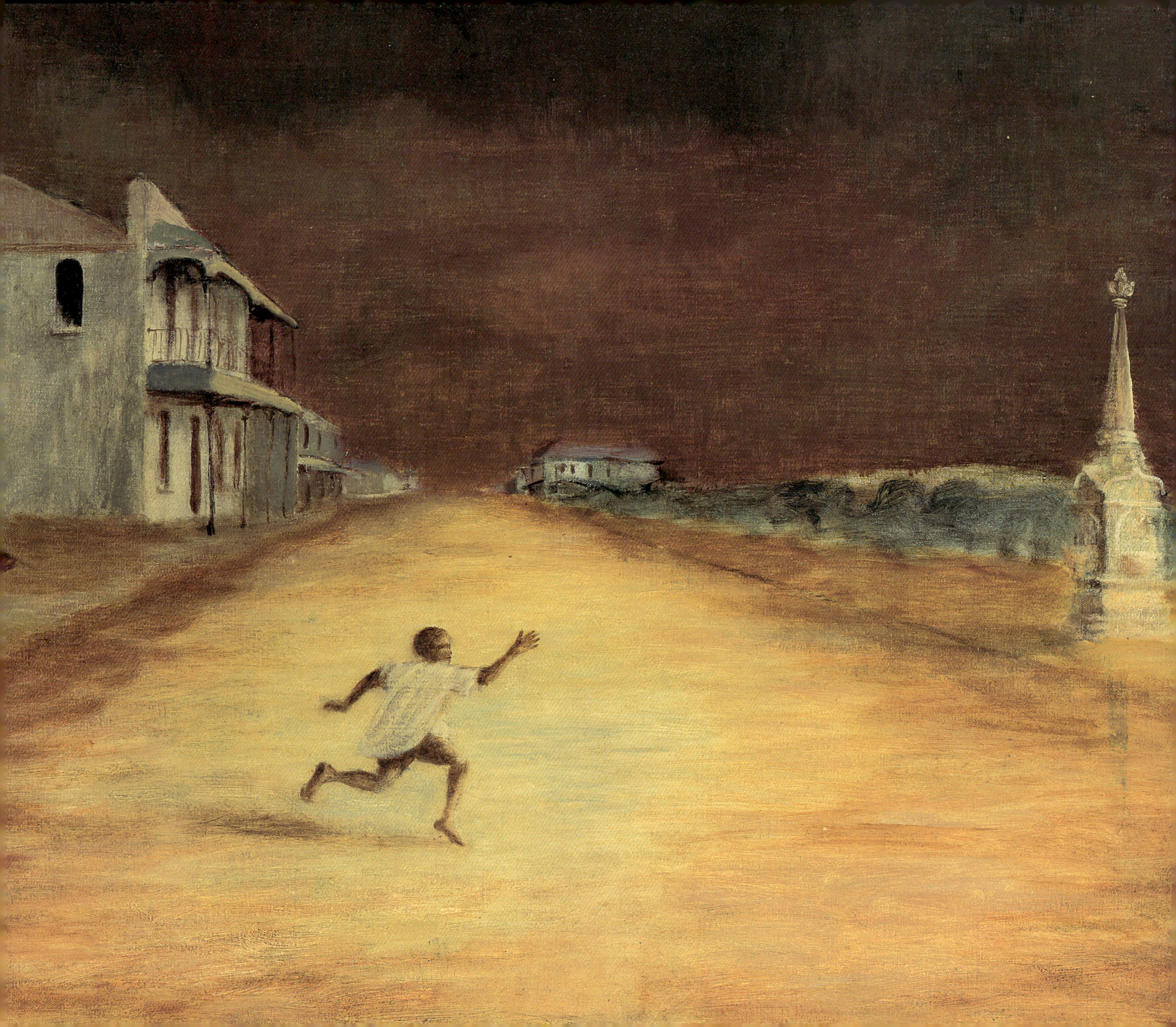

On the contrary, Margaret Preston, Grace Cossington Smith, Russell Drysdale, Arthur Boyd, Sidney Nolan, Albert Tucker, John Perceval and many others continued to paint major landscapes. But figure subjects became even more important to them and to many other Australian artists, particularly in Melbourne. From the 1950s abstract art became increasingly significant in Australia, particularly in Sydney. At Hermannsburg Mission in Central Australia, a host of Indigenous followers developed around Albert Namatjira, painting watercolour landscapes of their own country. And from the late 1960s onwards, much Australian art practice focused on complex conceptual concerns. In the 1980s painterly figure painting returned with a vengeance in Australia as elsewhere.

Yet after the mid-twentieth century great landscape painters still emerged. In Sydney, it was John Olsen's abstracted and animated expressions of the city and country. And most significantly, in the late 1950s Fred Williams, arguably Australia's finest landscape artist of any time, began his distinguished landscape career, expressing very different and new things about local landscape. After Williams's death in the early 1980s, William Robinson in Brisbane was beginning his distinctive sub-tropical Queensland landscapes. Landscape painting is alive and well in Australia. Indeed, Australia is one of the few countries in the world where landscape art is still a significant part of the art scene. Surely this is partly to do with the strong and unavoidable presence of our peculiarly Australian land and light. It is possibly also due to Australia's striving for a sense of national identity on an island continent. Nonetheless, it is true to say that from the early 1950s landscape has not been the dominant singular presence in our painting as it had been in the preceding century.

Created by our finest artists over 100 years, these paintings of diverse places – familiar or strange, welcoming or forbidding – exemplify the extraordinary and compelling resonance of this continent of Australia.

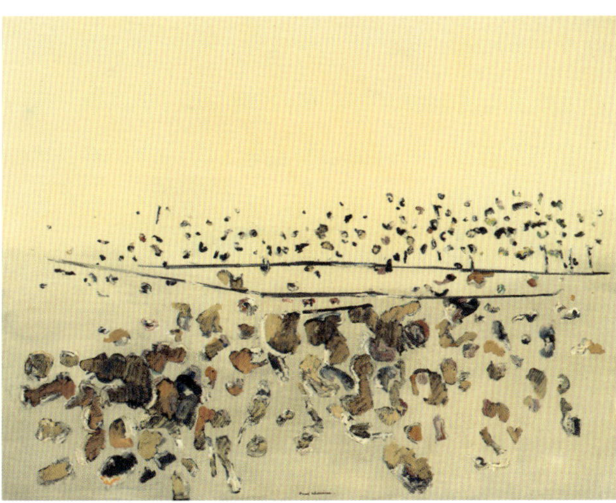

OPPOSITE
Russell Drysdale (1912–1981)
Boy running, Cooktown c. 1952 (detail)
oil on canvas 51.0 x 77.0 cm
Purchased 1959

Fred Williams (1927–1982)
Silver and grey 1969–70
oil on canvas
152.5 x 183.5 cm
National Gallery of Australia, Canberra
Purchased 1976

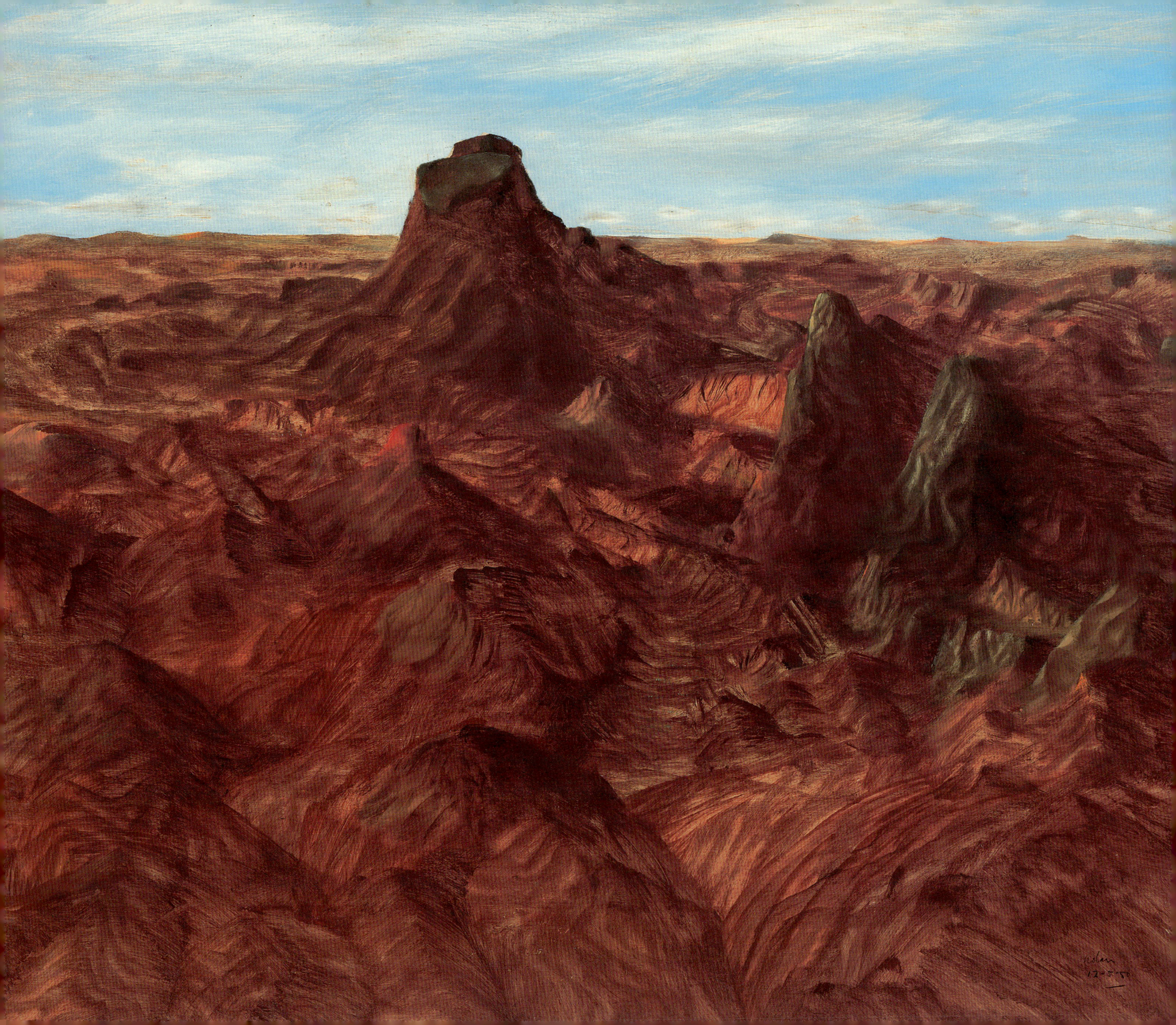

Catalogue

All works in the exhibition are from the collection of the National Galley of Australia.

Measurements are in centimetres (to the nearest millimetre). Height precedes width.

Size indicates image size and does not include frame size.

Birth and death years of artists have been included in parenthesis following the artist's name.

The title originally attributed to the work by the artist or used when it was first exhibited is used, if known. A number of titles have been changed following recent research.

Dates for works have been established based on artists' inscriptions, movements or documentary evidence. A number of dates have been changed following recent research.

Works have been arranged in a roughly chronological order and grouped by city, in accordance with the basic order of the catalogue essay.

Catalogue entries have been written by Beatrice Gralton.

Sidney Nolan (1917–1992)
Inland Australia 1950 (detail)
oil and enamel paint on composition board
91.5 x 121.0 cm
Purchased 1961

Knut Bull (1811–1889)
The wreck of the 'George the Third' 1850
oil on canvas 84.5 x 123.0 cm
Purchased with funds from the Nerissa Johnson Bequest 2001

The wreck of the George the Third depicts the aftermath of the shipwreck in 1835 of the *George the Third* off the coast of Tasmania. Following a four-month voyage from London and bound for Hobart, the 35-metre convict transport ship entered D'Entrecasteaux Channel on the evening of 12 April 1835. Less than 200 kilometres from its destination, the ship struck submerged rock and in the catastrophe that followed 127 of the 220 convicts on board died.[1] Survivors' accounts said the ship's crew fired their weapons at convicts who, in a state of panic, attempted to break from their confines as the vessel went down.

Painted by convict-artist Knut Bull, this image is dominated by a huge sky, with the broken *George the Third* dwarfed by the expanse. Waves continue to crash over the decks of the ship, while a few figures in the foreground attempt to salvage cargo and supplies. This is a seascape that evokes trepidation and anxiety. The small figures contribute to the feeling of human vulnerability when faced with the extremities of nature.

In 1845 Norwegian-born Knut Bull was tried in London Central Criminal Court for the attempted forgery of a 100-dollar Norwegian bill. He was sentenced to fourteen years transportation and arrived in Norfolk Island in 1846. After nine months Bull was transferred to the Saltwater River probation station in Van Diemen's Land. From 1849 he was permitted to work as an artist in the colony under a certificate of general good conduct and by 1853 had received a conditional pardon. He went on to work as a professional painter and teacher and relocated to New South Wales in 1856.

1 Michael Roe, *An Imperial disaster: the wreck of George the Third*, Hobart: Blubber Head Press, 2006, p. 12.

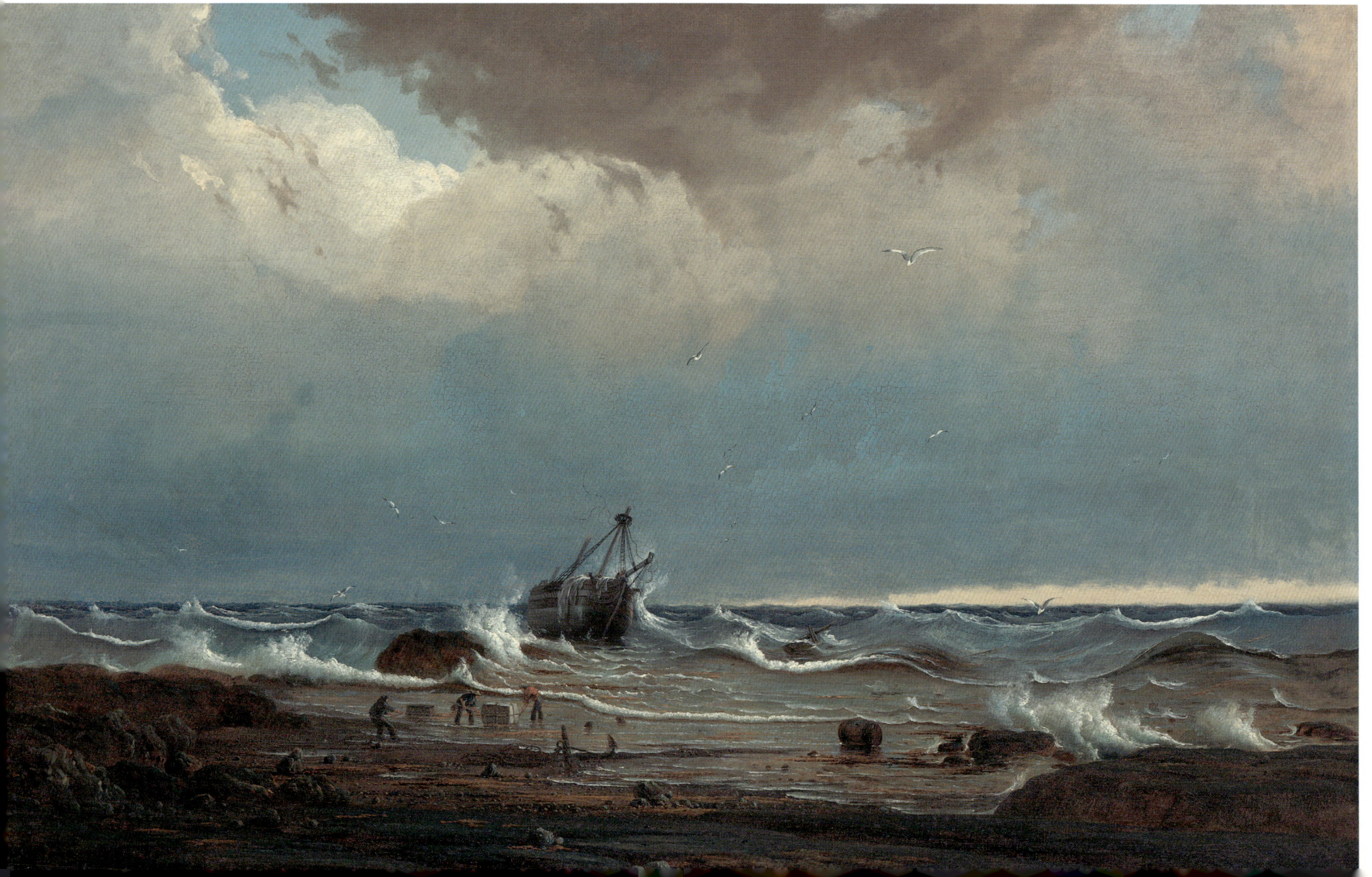

Conrad Martens (1801–1878)
View of Sydney Harbour showing Sydney Cove c. 1850
oil on canvas on composition board 46.5 x 65.0 cm
Rex Nan Kivell Collection: National Library of Australia and the National Gallery of Australia, Canberra

British artist Conrad Martens, who arrived in Sydney in 1835, is best known for his accomplished watercolours of early settlement around Sydney and Brisbane. Martens's mastery of watercolour technique informs this luminous oil painting of Sydney Harbour. He has used oil paint to convey the atmospheric conditions of the sea and sky, and the subtlety of light and tone.

The view is from the north, most likely from Cremorne Point. Martens had settled with his family close by in St Leonards in 1844. Framed by a foreground of native bush, we look over the glistening harbour towards the settlement of Sydney Cove. The distant horizon of the ocean divides the picture, a light-filled sky adding to the beauty of the harbour. Some of the early landmarks of Sydney are visible in this work, including the spire of convict-architect Francis Greenway's Church of St James (constructed in 1824), Government House and Fort Macquarie at Bennelong Point (now the location of Sydney Opera House).

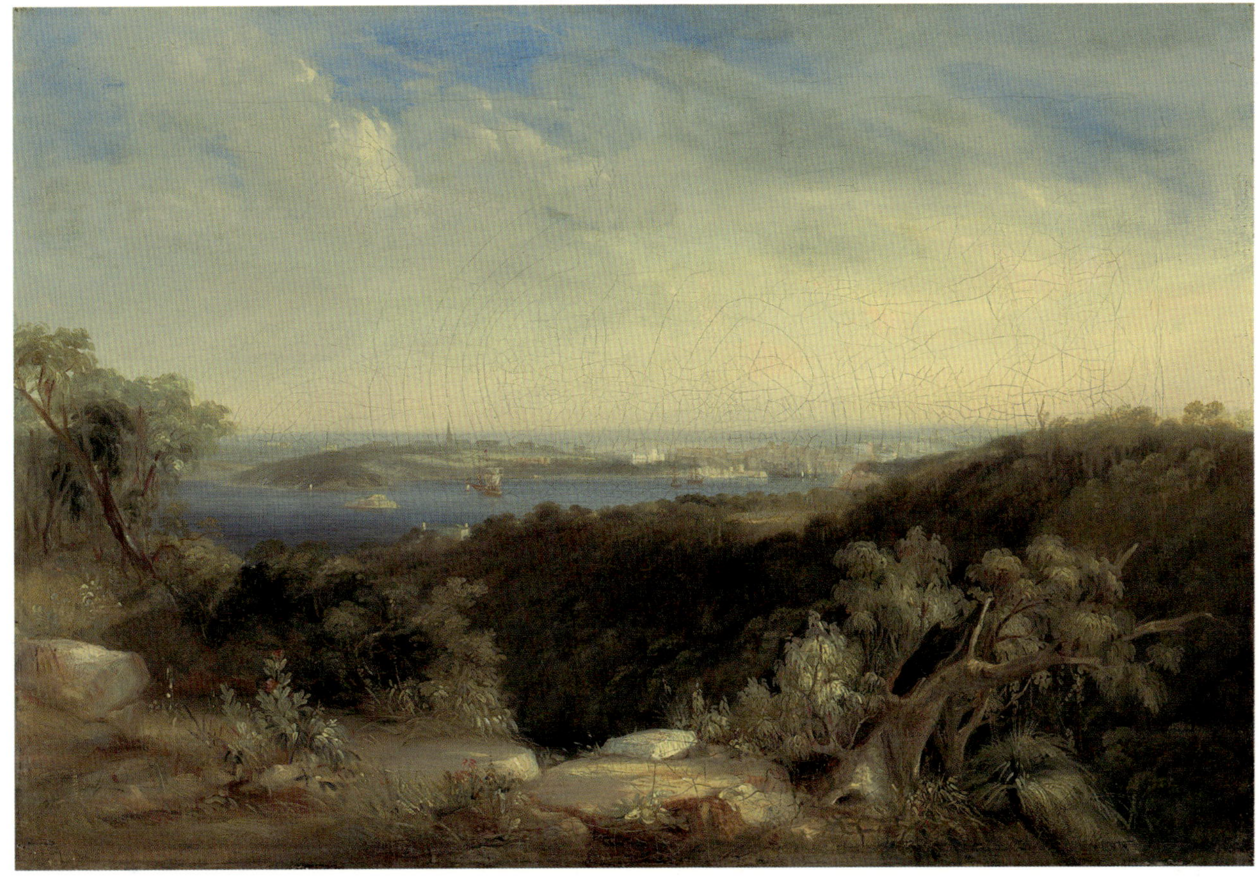

Eugene von Guérard (1811–1901)
Ferntree Gully in the Dandenong Ranges 1857
oil on canvas 92.0 x 138.0 cm
Gift of Dr Joseph Brown AO OBE 1975

For German-born artist Eugene von Guérard the Australian landscape represented a real, lived experience and a vehicle for evoking personal and contemplative ideas. His remarkable image of a fern-tree gully in the Dandenong Ranges, some 40 kilometres east of Melbourne, conveys a sense of the landscape as a spiritual sanctuary. In this painting von Guérard showed the landscape as a rejuvenating life force, untainted by human interference. When he first visited the Dandenong Ranges the area was a dense bushland of temperate rainforests and cool fern gullies. We know from sketchbooks held in the collection of the Dixson Galleries, State Library of New South Wales, Sydney, that von Guérard visited the region twice between 1855 and 1857 and again in 1858.[1] The pages of these books contain a number of drawings which document the lush and largely unexplored forests. This natural resource of high-quality timber was rapidly logged for the growing industries and settlement in Victoria.

Painted on return to the artist's Melbourne studio, *Ferntree Gully in the Dandenong Ranges* is a work that combines von Guérard's meticulous observation of local plant species with his artistic interest in compositional arrangement and the creation of a 'mood' particular to this environment. In this case we are privy to the magical world of a bower – an enclosed gully of natural foliage created by towering tree ferns. A pool of light on the forest floor leads us to two male lyrebirds cast in shadow, one with its characteristic tail feathers raised – a natural mimic of the arch of the fern fronds. The theatrical activities of the lyrebird were one of the early drawcards for tourists to the area, who hoped to witness the singing and dancing of the male bird.

Von Guérard's painting received much positive acclaim in the Melbourne newspapers and a few years after the work was completed, 'fern tree gully', located close to the Fern Tree Gully Hotel, became a popular tourist destination, especially during the summer months. The residents of Melbourne sought the sanctuary of the cool green gullies and active birdlife for their leisure. The work was exhibited at the 1862 *International exhibition* in London where it was noted as an example of the natural beauty and scenery of the colony.

1 Tim Bonyhady, *Australian colonial paintings in the Australian National Gallery*, Canberra: Australian National Gallery, 1986, p. 171.

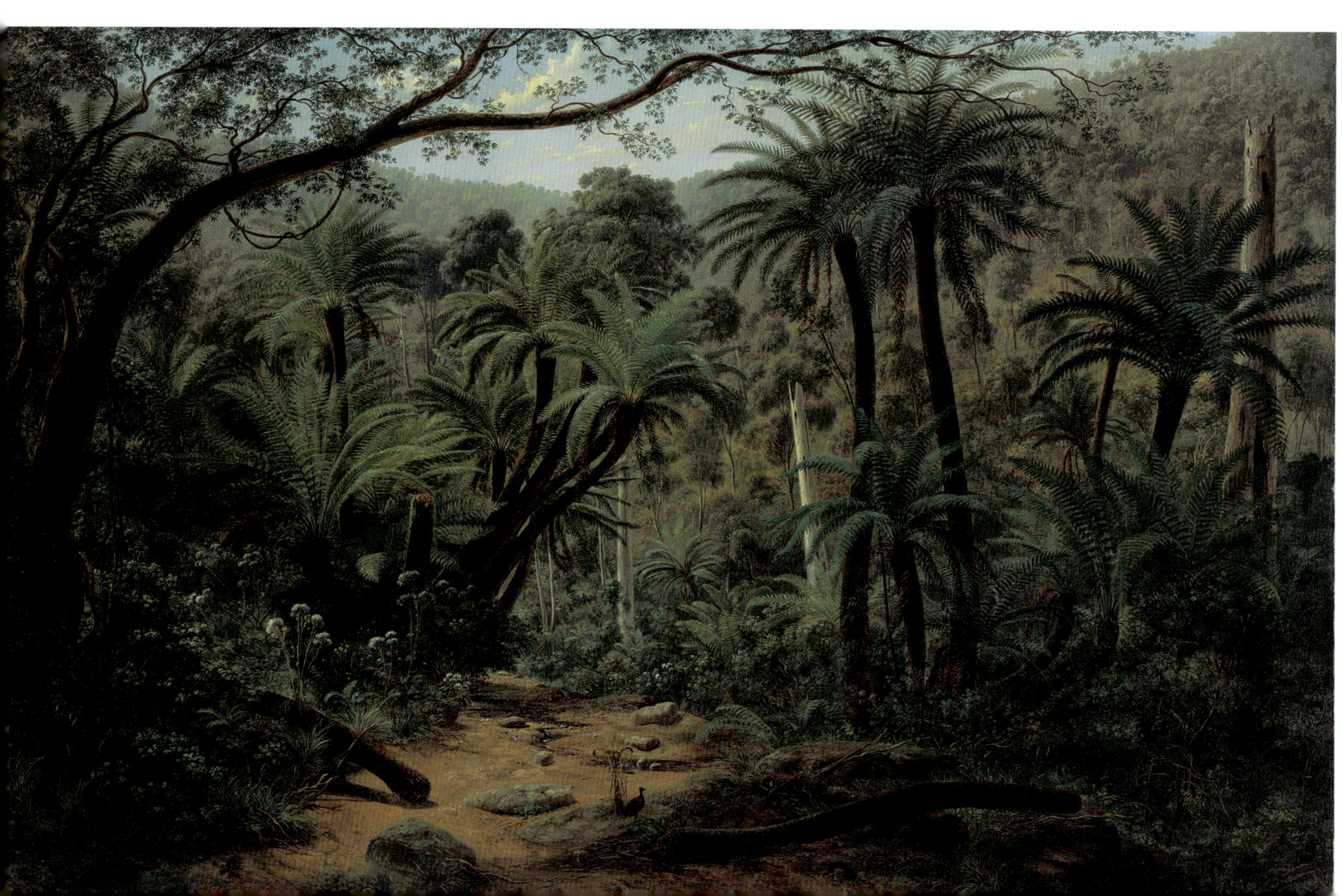

Eugene von Guérard (1811–1901)
Schnapper Point from 'Beleura' 1870
oil on canvas 66.1 x 104.2 cm
From the James Fairfax collection
Gift of Bridgestar Pty Ltd 1995

Eugene von Guérard painted the Australian landscape from the perspective of an observer, an explorer and as a resident. In this view of Schnapper Point, near Mornington Peninsula on Melbourne's Port Phillip Bay (approximately 40 kilometres from the city), von Guérard depicts the beauty of the Australian coast. The work was painted for James Butchart, the owner of the 'Beleura' homestead built in 1863. Von Guérard shows the sweeping views from the property across the bay – an area that had become a popular holiday destination for Melbourne residents.

The scene is alive with activity. A couple gather wood in the foreground while a horseman rides through the bush accompanied by his dogs. In the distance, homesteads are dotted along the peninsula and two sailing vessels can be seen on the glistening blue sea. Von Guérard has created an image of the land undergoing settlement and change as people began to seek alternative places to live beyond the city limits.

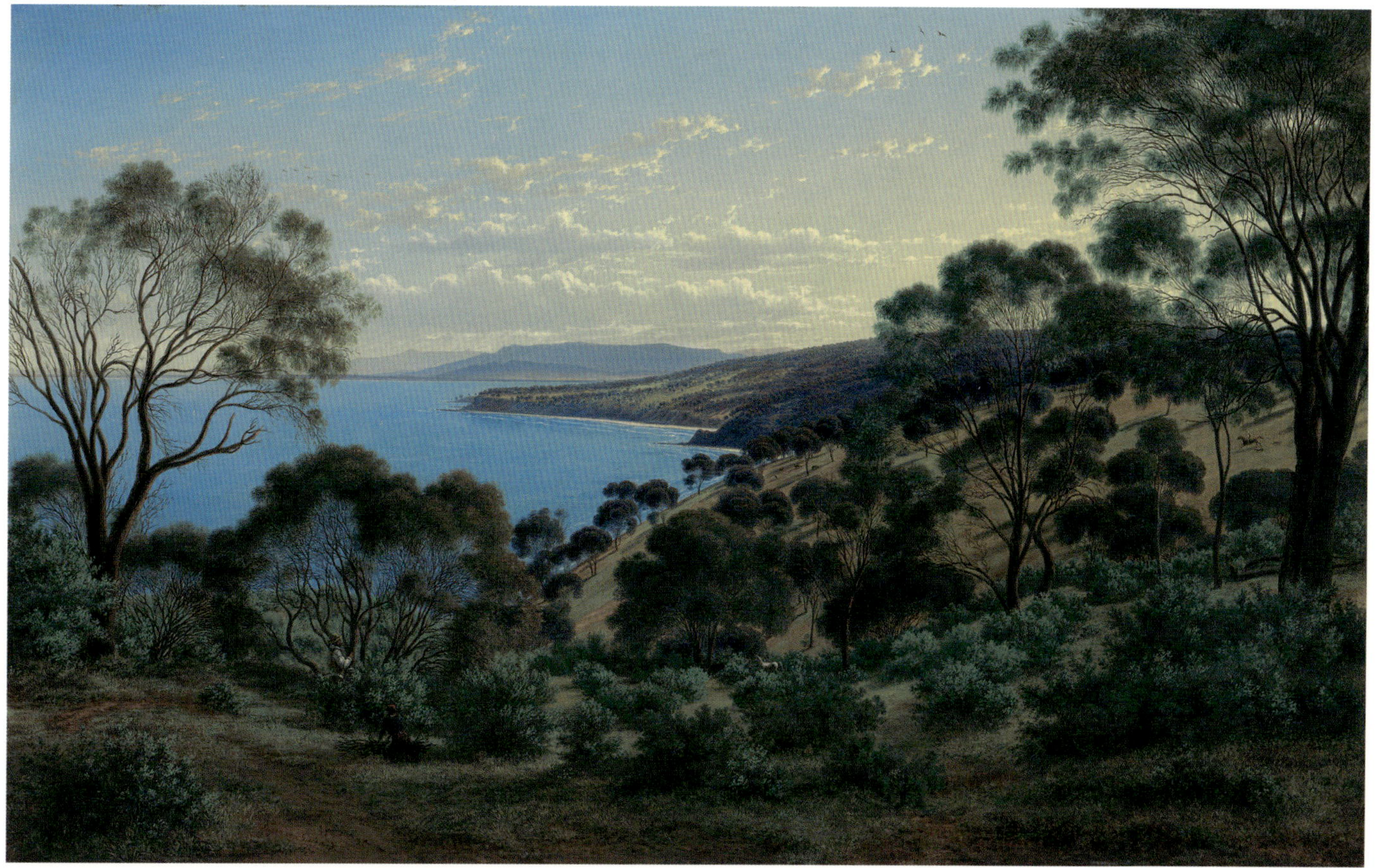

Eugene von Guérard (1811–1901)
Govett's Leap and Grose River Valley, Blue Mountains, New South Wales 1873
oil on canvas 68.5 x 106.4 cm
Purchased 2000

> But to look down on a place which cannot be reached, – into a valley full of trees, through which a stream runs, a green, dark, crowded valley, – and to feel that you are debarred from reaching it by sheer descent of four or five hundred feet of cliff all round, is uncommon … I never saw before so vast a gaping hole on the earth's surface.
> A. Trollope 1873[1]

In the same year that Eugene von Guérard painted *Govett's Leap* and *Grose Rover Valley, Blue Mountains, New South Wales*, the English writer Anthony Trollope published his travelogue Australia and New Zealand, an account intended to describe the Australian colonies to the people of England.

Like the Dandenong Ranges for Melbourne, the Blue Mountains quickly became a tourist destination for Sydney-siders – a sanctuary of cool-climate bushlands, spectacular scenery and native wildlife. In this work von Guérard emphasises the sensation of looking down into a vast valley where human existence feels slight in the company of nature.

Von Guérard visited Govett's Leap in 1859 on his only trip to Sydney, the Blue Mountains and the Illawarra region. He painted *Govett's Leap and Grose River Valley, Blue Mountains, New South Wales* some fourteen years after this visit. Infrared analysis of this picture reveals a considerable amount of underdrawing. This indicates that von Guérard first made an outline drawing of the image on the canvas and then painted over it, working closely to the outline. He would have developed the composition using sketches, drawings and possibly photographs as visual aids.

1 A. Trollope, *Australia and New Zealand*, volume one, Melbourne: G. Robertson, 1873, p. 305.

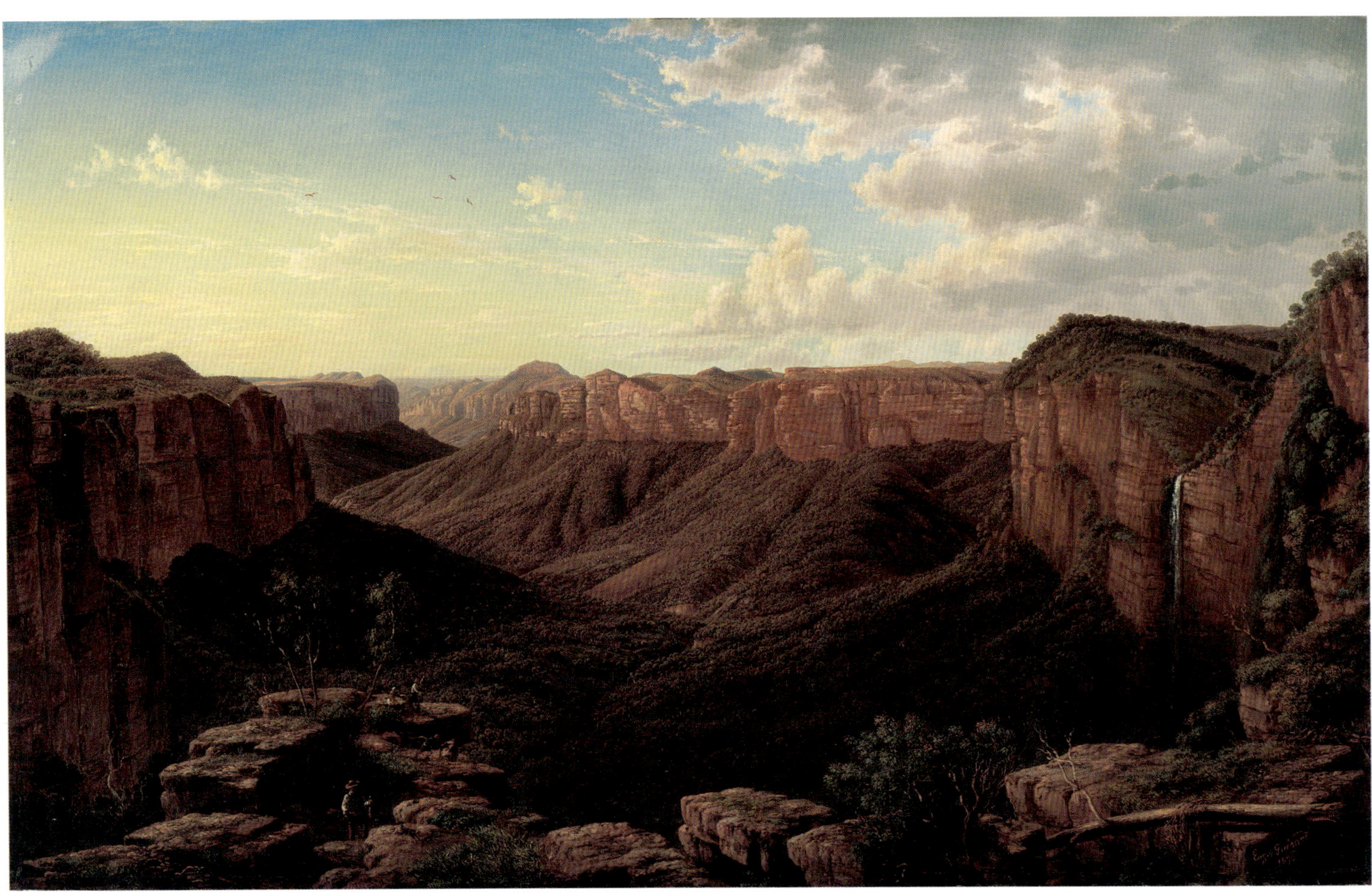

Nicholas Chevalier (1828–1902)
Studley Park at sunrise 1861
oil on canvas 89.1 x 120.0 cm
Gift of Mrs Dorothy Gurner 1959

In the late 1850s and 1860s Studley Park in Kew was a popular picnic spot for the people of Melbourne and a site depicted by numerous artists. *Studley Park at sunrise* is one of Nicholas Chevalier's few paintings from the early 1860s that depicts a local scene. Arriving in Australia at the end of 1854, the Russian-born artist had experience working in commercial lithography and spent his first six years in Australia as a cartoonist for the *Melbourne Punch*. From the early 1860s Chevalier travelled throughout south-east Australia and New Zealand in search of dramatic mountain ranges and seascapes for his subject matter.

In *Studley Park at sunrise* Chevalier shows the Yarra River flanked by tall trees and open bushland stretching through the composition. He was interested in conveying the awe-inspiring beauty of the landscape and the atmospheric effects of nature, such as the morning light and the glistening surface of the water. Choosing to paint the scene at sunrise gave Chevalier an opportunity to explore these artistic concerns and to depict the activity on the river.[1] A group of children are shown gathered on the river bank; a young boy skimming rocks across the glassy water's surface. Hodgson's Punt is also depicted crossing the river. This punt connected the suburbs of Collingwood and Kew. John Hodgson was a Melbourne public servant whose 1860 house gave its name to Studley Park.[2]

1 The work has a 'companion painting' in *The survey paddock at sunset* 1861. This work is held in the National Collection.
2 Tim Bonyhady, *Australian colonial paintings in the Australian National Gallery*, Canberra: Australian National Gallery, 1986, p. 36.

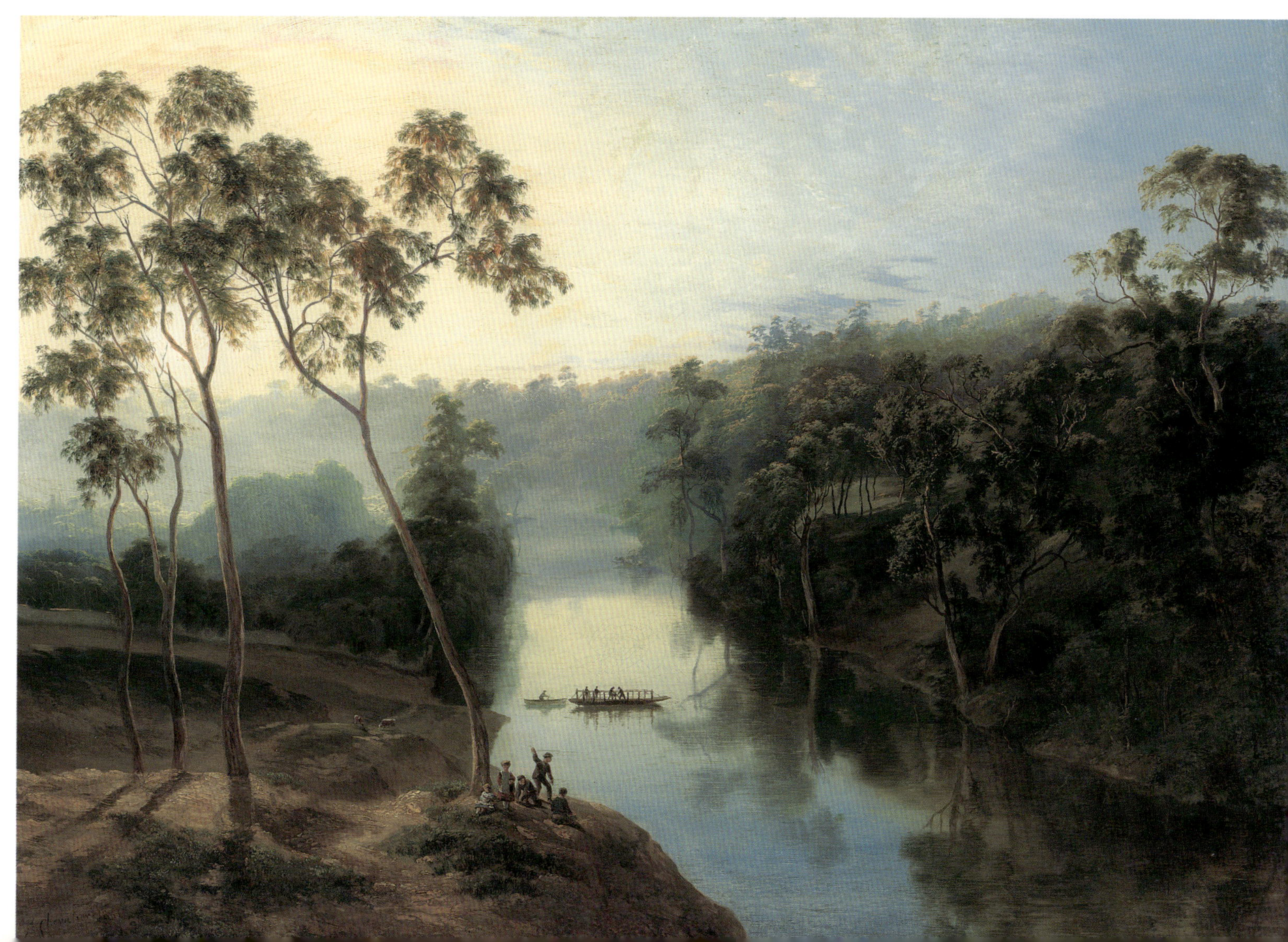

Louis Buvelot (1814–1888)
'Mount Fyans' homestead 1869
oil on canvas 58.6 x 95.3 cm
From the James Fairfax collection
Gift of Bridgestar Pty Ltd 1993

Colonial artists such as Eugene von Guérard, Nicholas Chevalier and Louis Buvelot received many commissions for 'homestead portraits'. These commissions were generally paintings of properties owned by prosperous graziers who were naturally keen to display the results of their hard labours on the land.

Located north of Camperdown in Victoria's Western District, *'Mount Fyans' homestead* was commissioned by brothers William and John Cumming whose father had come to Australia from Scotland. The Cumming family purchased the original property of Mount Fyans in 1856.[1] Buvelot has depicted the homestead at the heart of this picture, flanked by tall trees and surrounded by lush pastures with grazing sheep and cattle.

A companion painting to this work, *'Mount Fyans' woolshed* 1869, was also commissioned by the family and painted by Buvelot. The work is held in the National Collection.

1 W. H. Cumming, *Cumming: from Aberdeen to Hobart, and across to Mount Fyans*, unpublished family history given to Beatrice Gralton in 2006 by Bill Cumming, pp. 32, 65.

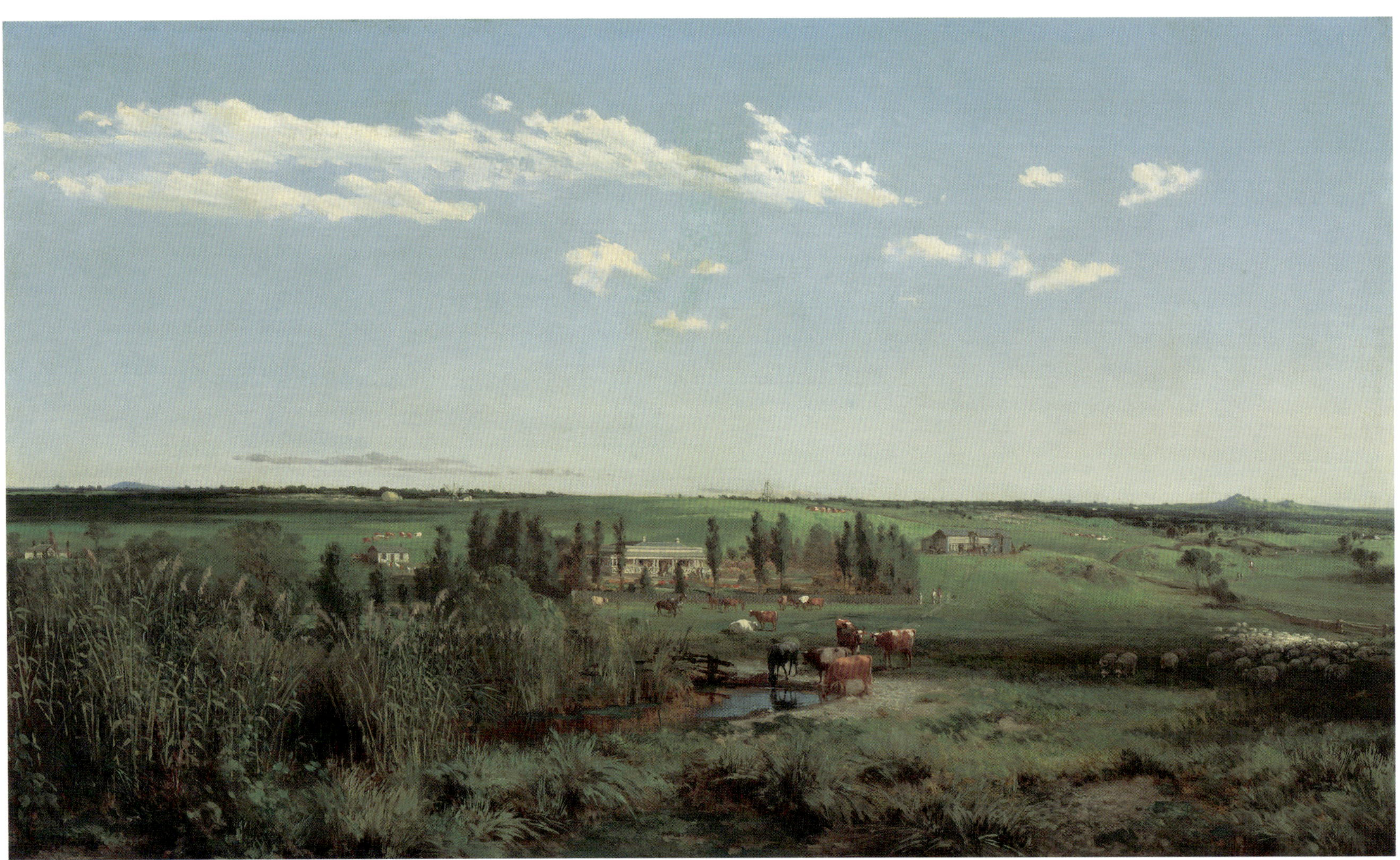

Louis Buvelot (1814–1888)
Near Lilydale 1874
oil on canvas 46.0 x 69.0 cm
Purchased 1977

Swiss-born and trained, Louis Buvelot specialised in painting scenes of the countryside close to Melbourne. Arriving in Victoria in 1865, Buvelot's paintings of settled, domesticated land appealed to city dwellers and pastoralists alike, and he quickly established a successful career as a landscape painter.[1] Admired by his contemporaries, Buvelot differed to earlier colonial artists by attempting to create a more naturalistic image of the Australian bush. Compared to the meticulous observation of Eugene von Guérard, Buvelot's approach was much freer. Moving away from grand scenes and sweeping views, he used softly dabbed brushstrokes and an earthier palette to depict the land as a known and familiar place.

In *Near Lilydale* Buvelot shows the new life and rejuvenation of springtime. A lamb – symbolising the season of spring – follows two women making their way through the landscape. Fresh green grass grows from the damp earth and blue skies are reflected in the surface of the water. Using a basic palette of browns and greens Buvelot skilfully creates the tones observed in the landscape, a subtle gradation between grasses, trees and earth.

1 Tim Bonyhady, *Australian colonial paintings in the Australian National Gallery*, Canberra: Australian National Gallery, 1986, pp. 15–17.

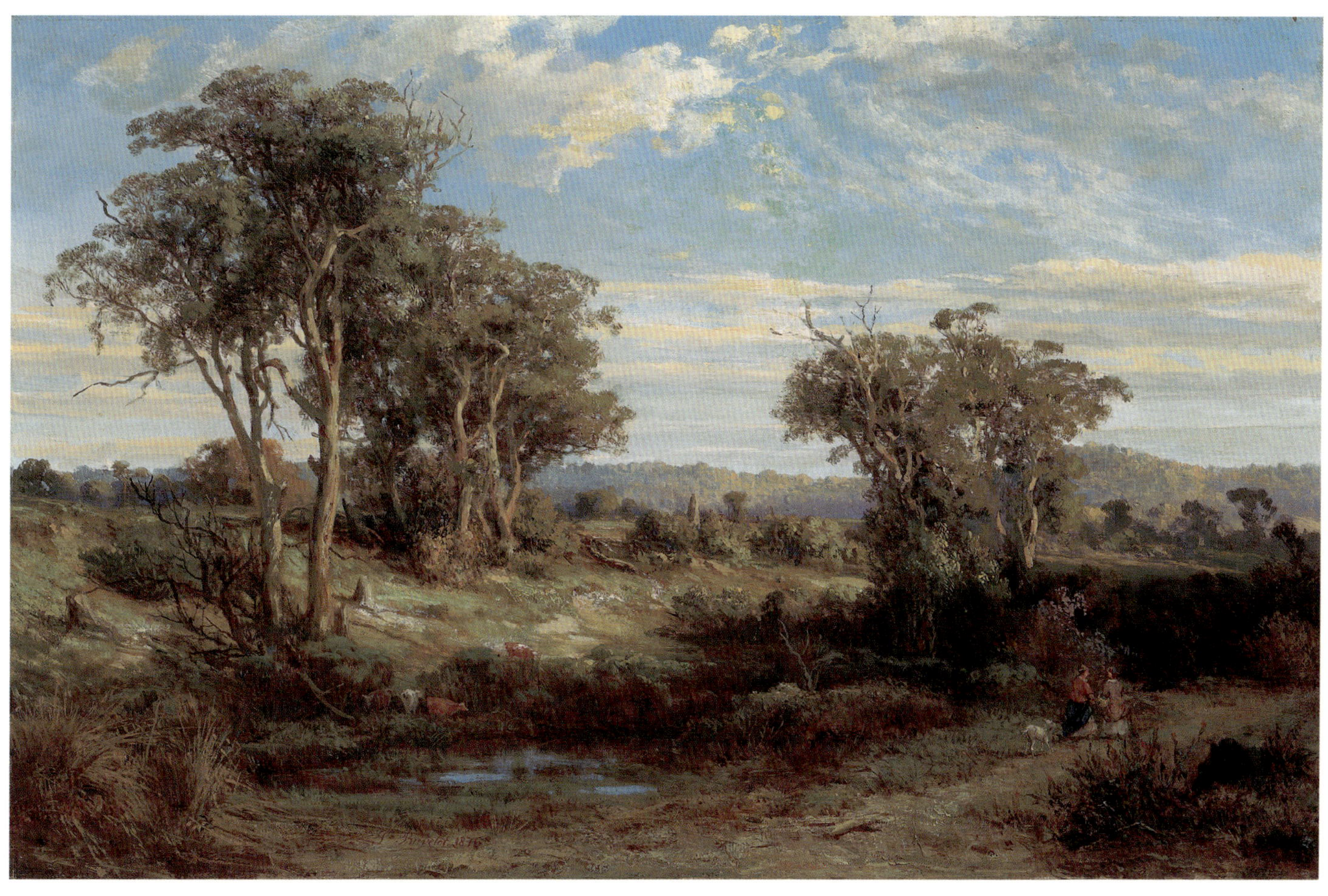

Thomas Baines (1820–1875)
Gouty stem tree, Adansonia Gregorii, 58 feet circumference, near a creek south-east of Stokes Range, Victoria River 1868
oil on canvas 45.2 x 66.5 cm
Purchased 1973

Gouty stem tree, Adansonia Gregorii, 58 feet circumference, near a creek south-east of Stokes Range, Victoria River is an extraordinary image of an enormous water-yielding baobab tree. These trees are native to the north-west of Australia and are easily recognisable by their swollen trunks. The sheer scale of this tree, which dominates the picture, is further emphasised by the two figures at its base. The artist has depicted himself in the lower right-hand side of the painting, sitting underneath a makeshift shelter sketching the scene.

British artist and explorer Thomas Baines was one of a group of eighteen people who formed the 1855 North Australian Expedition party. The purpose of the expedition was to ascertain the existence of natural resources for settlement in the north-west of Australia and to determine if there was an inland river or sea. Under the command of Augustus Charles Gregory the expedition lasted from August 1855 to November 1856, the group reaching the mouth of the Victoria River on the upper north-west coast of the Northern Territory on 15 September 1855.

Baines's official role in the party was as artist and storekeeper – he made hundreds of sketches, recorded weather conditions and kept a detailed journal of daily life. Along with ensuring stocks and stores were managed appropriately, he was expected to 'record' important sites, species, and events encountered on the journey. He did so with the English 'home' audience in mind: the scientific fraternity and the British government who had funded the expedition and were eager to invest in Australia and to encourage the expansion of the Empire.

Gouty stem tree, Adansonia Gregorii, 58 feet circumference, near a creek south-east of Stokes Range, Victoria River was painted in London in June 1868, thirteen years after the expedition. (A sketch for the painting of the baobab tree, held in the collection of the Royal Geographical Society in London, was made on Thursday 10 January 1856.) It is likely that Baines produced these paintings for the purposes of reproduction in the publication *Australia illustrated*.[1]

1 Tim Bonyhady, *Australian colonial paintings in the Australian National Gallery*, Canberra: Australian National Gallery, 1986, pp. 6–9.

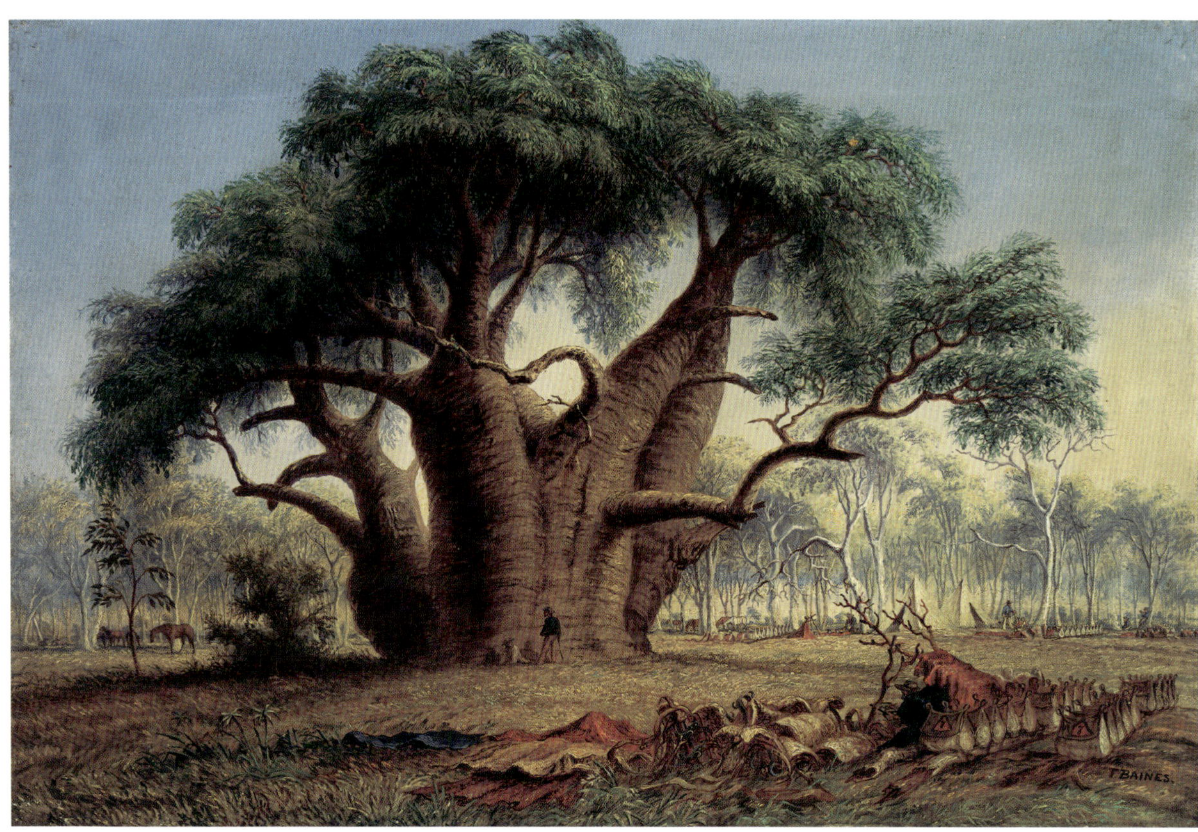

Henry Rielly (1845–1905)
Woodland, vale and hill 1874
oil on canvas 54.0 x 84.5 cm
Purchased 1968

Henry Rielly was a foundation member of the Victorian Academy of Arts, exhibiting annually between 1870 and 1885. *Woodland, vale and hill* was one of eleven works exhibited by Rielly in the 1874 *Academy exhibition*.[1] He painted numerous scenes of the Yarra Valley and the regions surrounding Melbourne and this may be the location of *Woodland, vale and hill*. Rielly was a council member of the Academy and would have known the work of two other council members, Eugene von Guérard and Louis Buvelot, who also exhibited a number of paintings in the 1874 exhibition.

Rielly divided the composition of *Woodland, vale and hill* into five distinct areas: an open foreground of ground-growth, a band of dense woodland, a stretch of valley, a distant mountain range and a large cloud-filled sky. The artist has combined topographic detail with a naturalistic approach in this painting. Unlike Louis Buvelot, Rielly does not attempt to domesticate the landscape; instead, he includes wild horses grazing in the woodland. He has paid most attention to the foreground, portraying a type of gum tree with knarred limbs as well as scraggy foliage and thick ground-growth consistent with a swampy region.

In 2006 the National Gallery of Australia carried out extensive conservation treatment of this painting. It was discovered that two figures and a campfire had been added probably in the mid-twentieth century before the painting entered the National Collection. These elements were removed, revealing a second horse within the composition.

1 *The fourth exhibition of the Victorian Academy of Arts*, exhibition catalogue, 1874. *Woodland, vale and hill* listed as no. 52, p. 8.

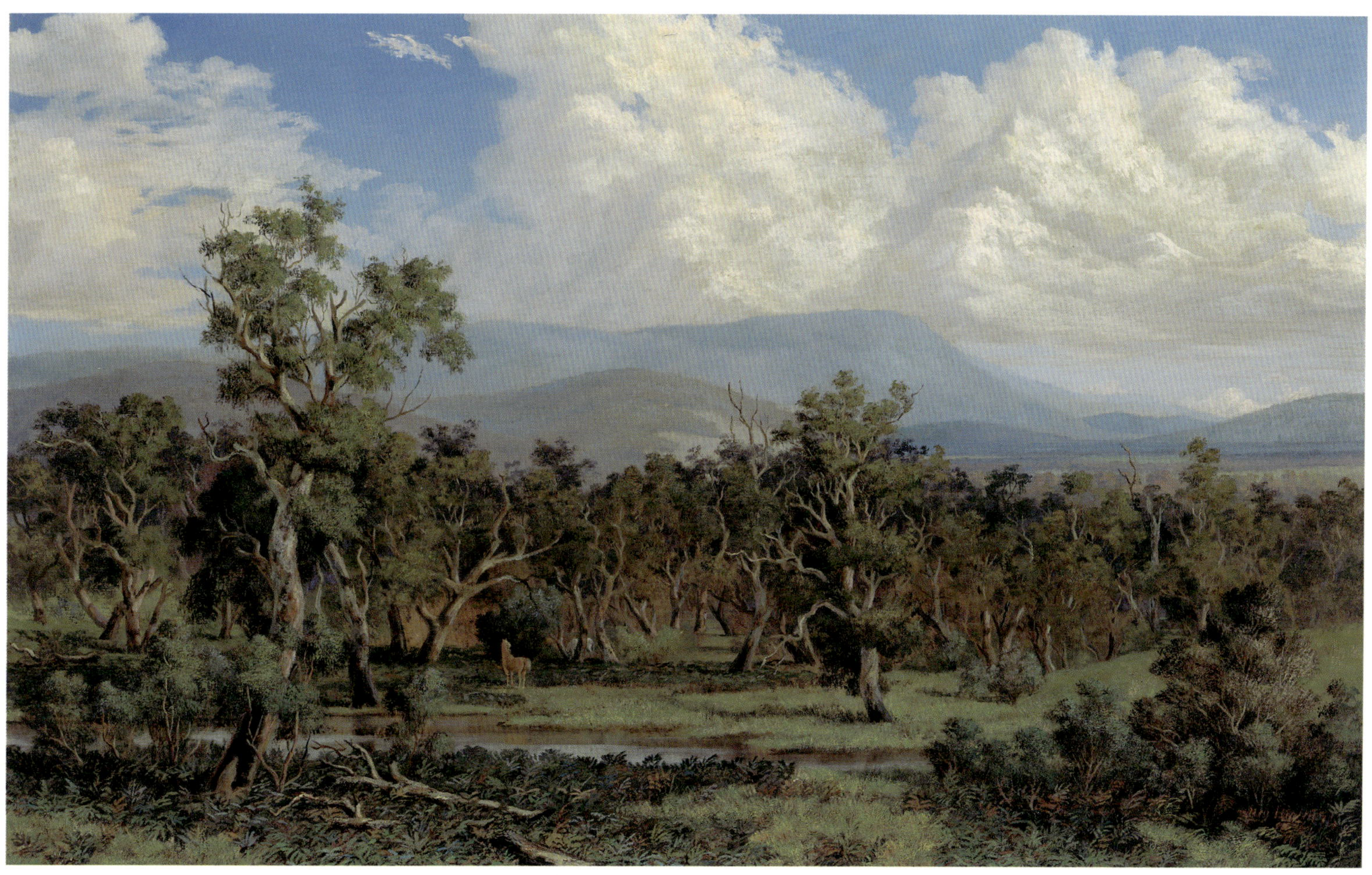

Haughton Forrest (1826–1925)
Mount Wellington from Cascades c. 1885
oil on cardboard 30.6 x 46.4 cm
Purchased 1971

Haughton Forrest painted Mount Wellington, the geographic landmark that defines the city of Hobart, many times. He used colour and scale to convey the inherent drama and atmospheric 'moodiness' of the Tasmanian landscape: luminous pinks and soft cool greys, the glow of the afternoon winter light offsetting the dark damp areas of forest. In *Mount Wellington from Cascades* these colours suggest the air is cold and still, broken only by the movement of birds. The scale of the mountain is also accentuated by the small figures that stroll along the path beside the river.

Primarily a painter of maritime and landscape subjects, French-born Forrest rarely dated his works. He often used photography as a visual aid for his paintings, sometimes referring to the work of James Watt Beattie who trekked into the Tasmanian wilderness to photograph the spectacular natural environment. These photographs assisted Forrest to portray a level of detail in his own work and to create images of Tasmania that were unfamiliar to the general public.

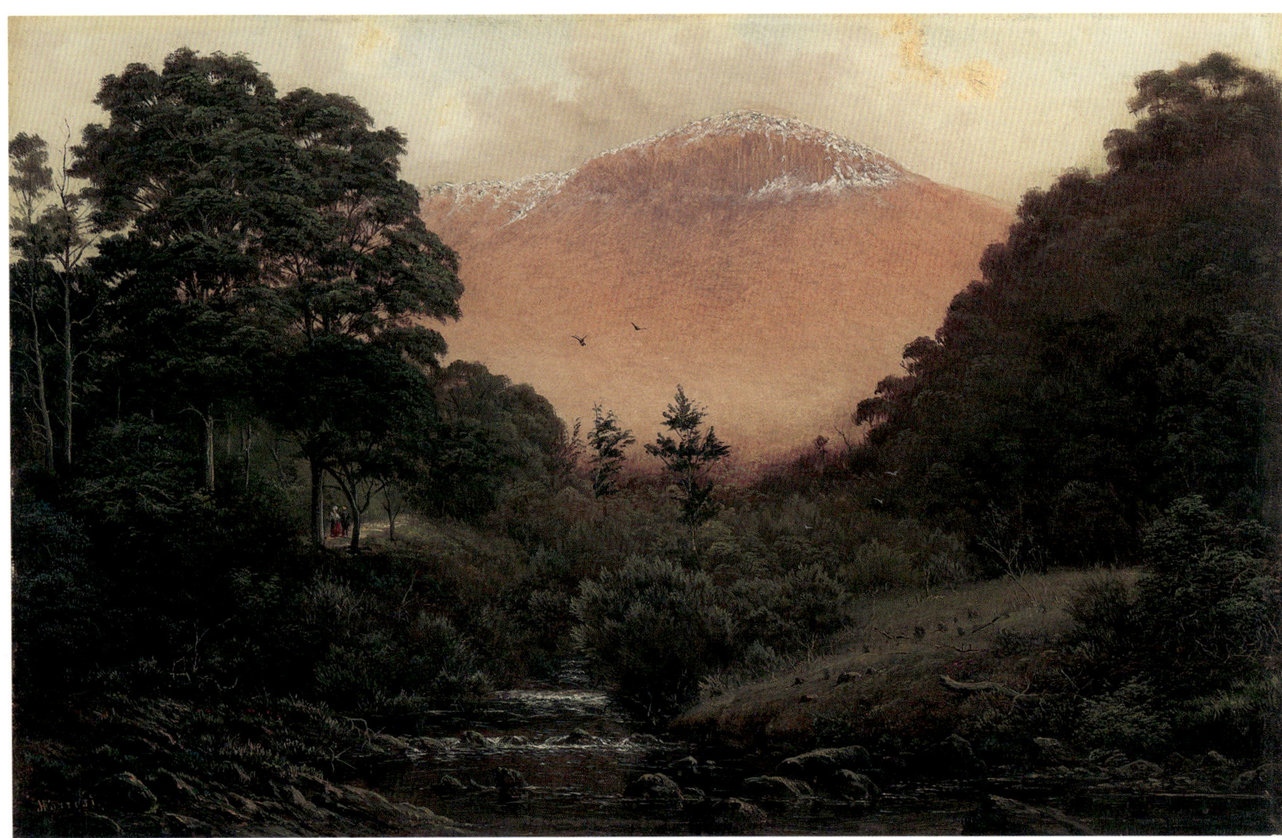

W. C. Piguenit (1836–1914)
On the Nepean, New South Wales 1881
oil on canvas 106.5 x 92.0 cm
Purchased 1976

Tasmanian-born William Charles Piguenit, who moved to Sydney in 1880, was an artist who explored and depicted wilderness landscapes in Tasmania and New South Wales in watercolours, lithographs, photographs and paintings. A versatile draughtsman, Piguenit accompanied a number of journeys into wilderness areas, seeking in his art to convey the inherent beauty in nature. The site of this painting is an area known as 'the Rock' in the Nepean Gorge at Mulgoa, now a suburb near the city of Penrith in the western suburbs of Sydney.[1]

Piguenit painted a number of dramatic vistas and heightened examples of nature. Many of his paintings display a characteristic silver light as well as glassy bodies of water. In *On the Nepean, New South Wales* he explored his interest in the compositional possibilities of reflections in water. The scale of the river valley is emphasised, and it would be easy to overlook the small party of rowers who, in the shadow of the cliff, move quietly up the river towards the bank. In this picture Piguenit reminds us of the idea that the journey is often more important than the destination. Humans take part in this scene, but they are insignificant in relation to nature.

1 Tim Bonyhady, *Australian colonial paintings in the Australian National Gallery*, Canberra: Australian National Gallery, 1986, pp. 151–52.

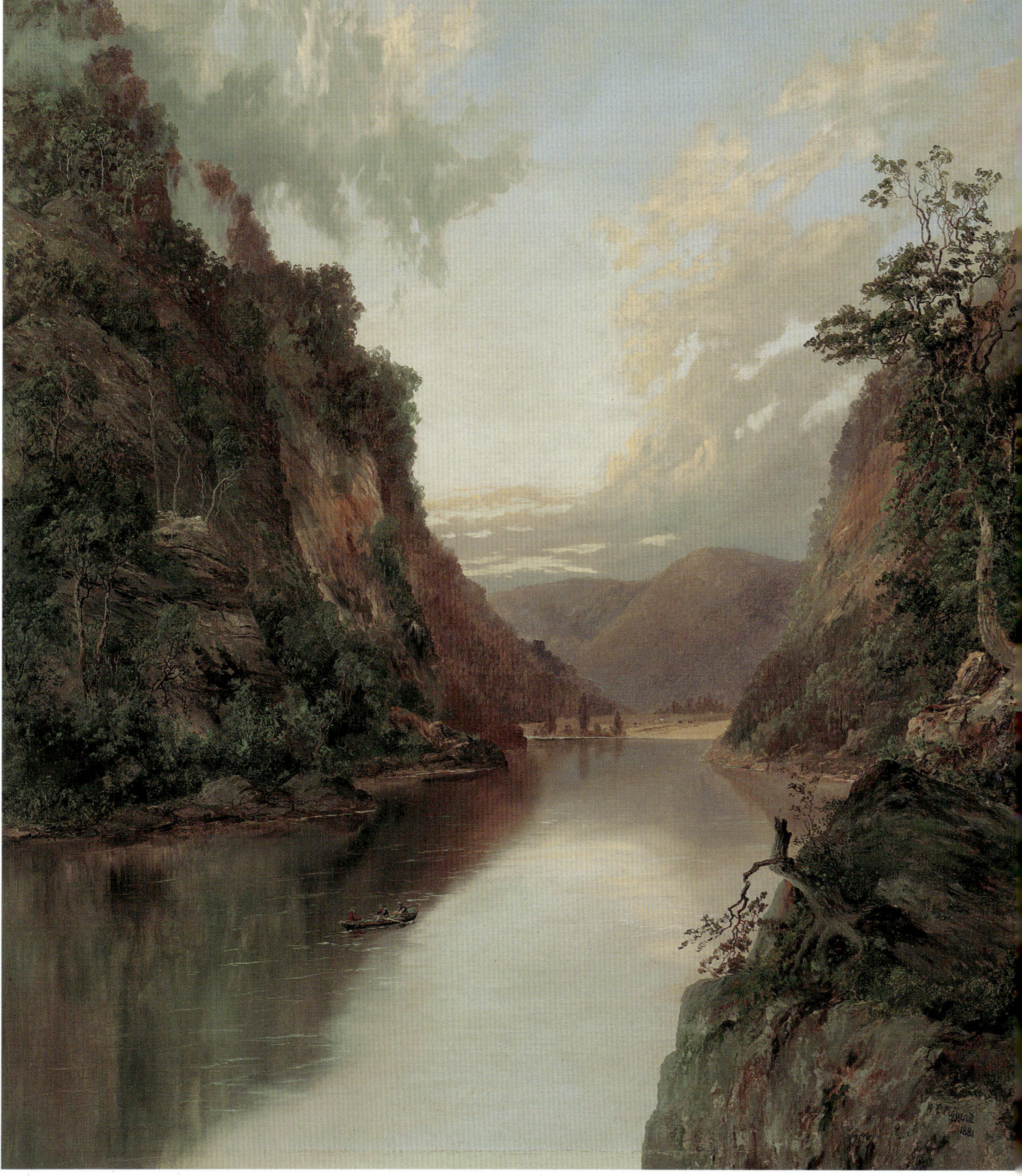

Tom Roberts (1856–1931)
A quiet day on Darebin Creek 1885
oil on wood panel 26.4 x 34.8 cm
Purchased 1969

In the same year that Tom Roberts painted this countryside scene of Darebin Creek on the outskirts of Melbourne, he had returned to Australia from studies and travel in Europe and England. Roberts had absorbed the *plein-air* approach to painting, a technique of sketching in paint directly from nature. He wanted to connect with the natural world, to capture in paint the sensation of momentary light and colour. He considered this sketch to be a finished work, a picture of the moment for the moment. While Roberts continued to work on other paintings in his studio, his *plein-air* approach in this and subsequent paintings was a significant departure from the conventional technique of making drawings and sketches outside and returning to the studio to paint the 'finished' scene.

In the small and exquisitely painted *A quiet day on Darebin Creek* Roberts displayed his skills in working in the open air. His deft and measured application of paint captures the reflection of light in the waters of the creek. Roberts has depicted an artist painting outdoors, placing him low down in the scene which has a high horizon. His use of subtle tonal colours unifies the composition and contributes to a painting that feels complete.

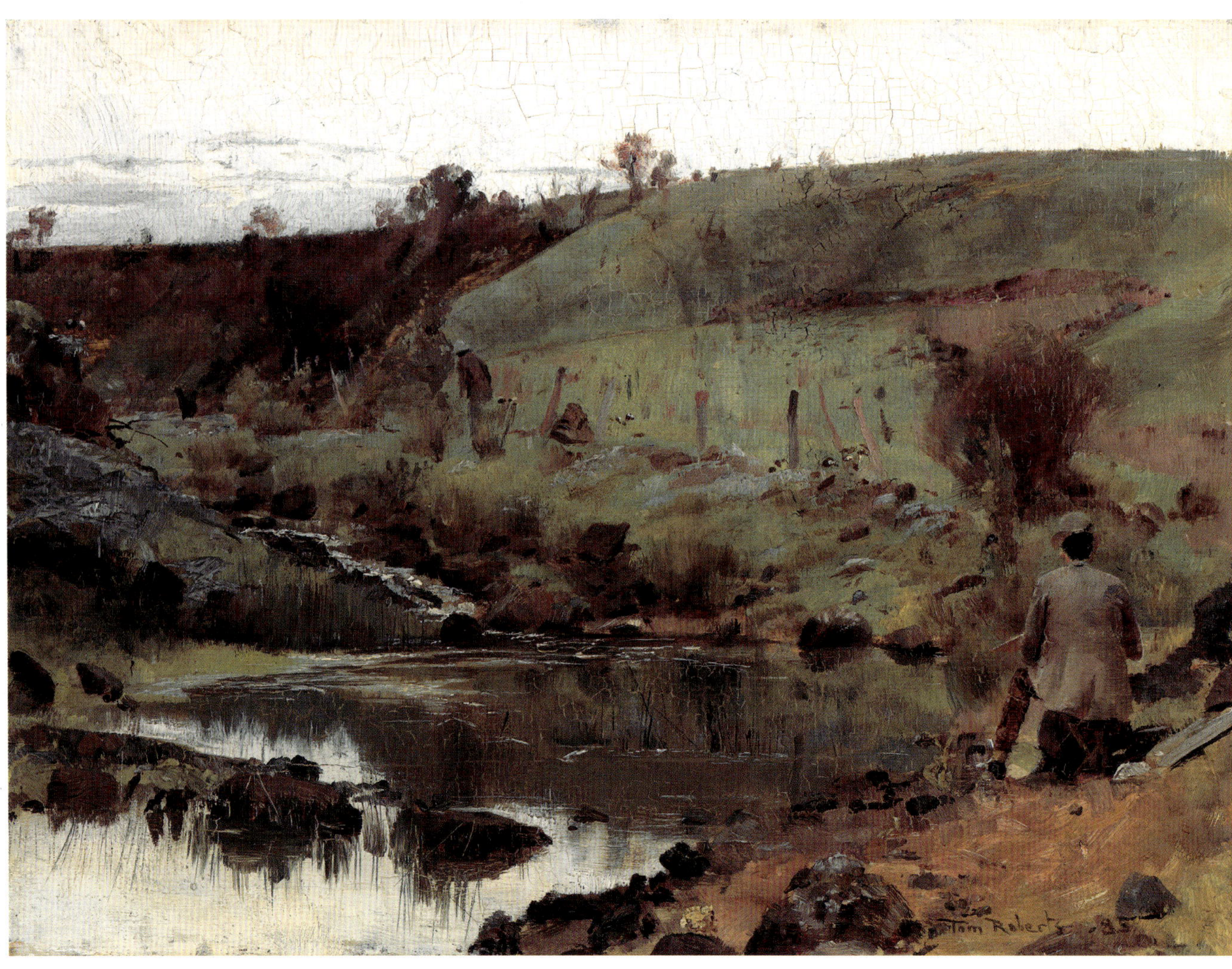

Tom Roberts (1856–1931)
A Sunday afternoon c. 1886
oil on canvas 41.0 x 30.8 cm
Purchased 1984

By 1882 a railway had been constructed between Melbourne and the township of Box Hill, and in 1885 Tom Roberts, Frederick McCubbin and Louis Abrahams first visited the area to paint. The artists set up camp on land owned by a local farmer and friend to the artists, David Houston.[1] Along with other artists, including Arthur Streeton and Jane Sutherland, the group painted the local bushland. Roberts made a number of works in this area, such as his well known *The artist's camp* 1886, while Streeton painted *Evening with bathers* 1888 (both in the collection of the National Gallery of Victoria, Melbourne).

In *A Sunday afternoon* Roberts depicts an intimate picnic. Framed by spindly gums and bathed in dappled light, a young couple relax in the bush, the woman reading to her companion from a newspaper. A belief in the health benefits of the country air was becoming popular with city dwellers who sought recreational activities in the bush or by the ocean. Roberts's observant eye has resulted in such small details in this scene as the trail of smoke from the man's pipe, the dark wine bottle on the crisp white cloth and the light falling softly on the leaves of the eucalypts.

1 Leigh Astbury, 'Memory and desire: Box Hill 1855–88', in Terence Lane (ed.), *Australian impressionism*, Melbourne: National Gallery of Victoria, 2007, p. 51.

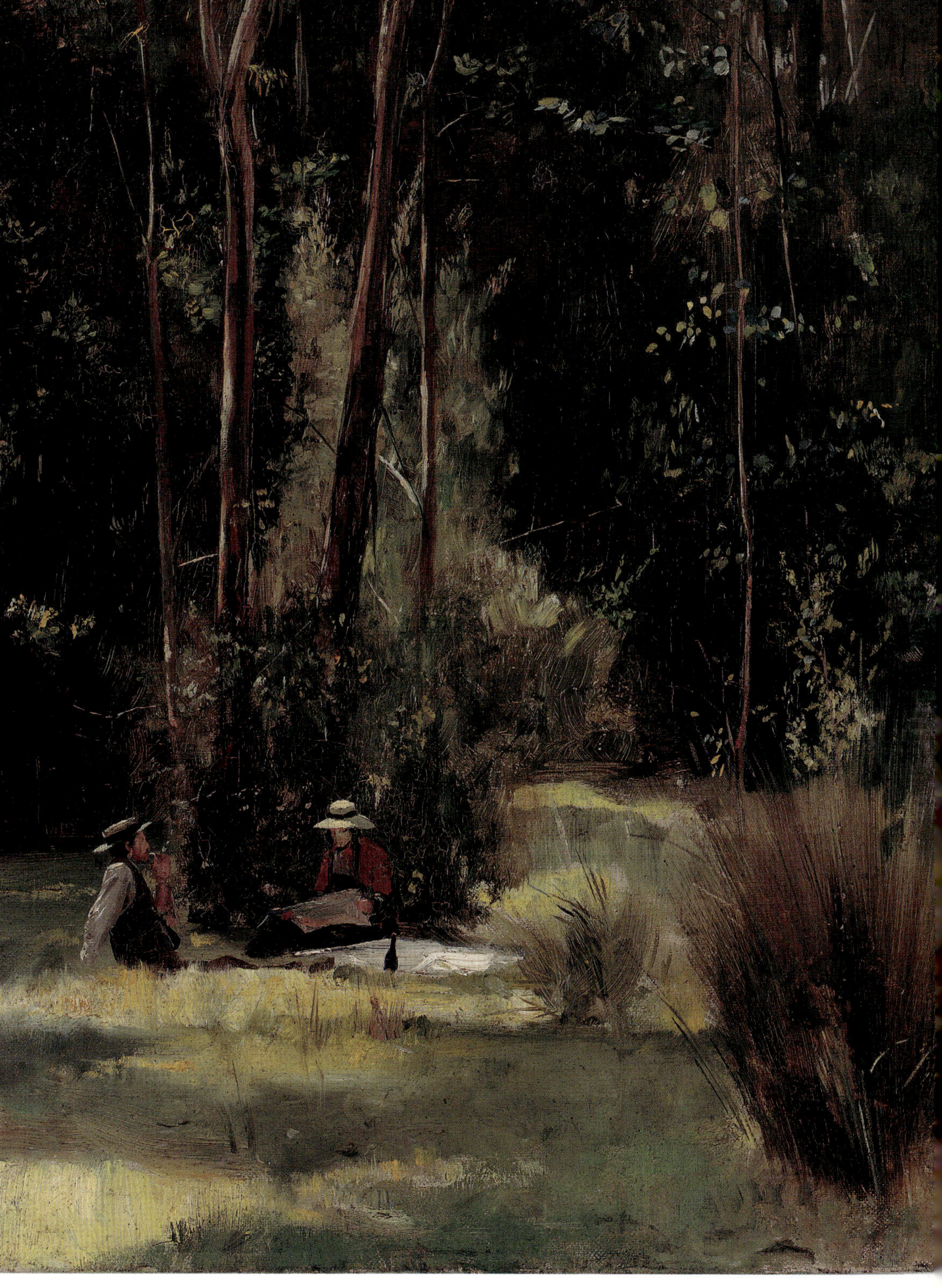

Charles Conder (1868–1909)
Ricketts Point, Beaumaris 1890
oil on wood panel 12.0 x 21.5 cm
Purchased 1973

Charles Conder would have sat right by the water's edge when he painted this joyous impression of Melbourne bay-side activity. Much of the scene is dominated by water – the reflective shallows of the foreground comprising a significant portion of the composition. Behind the strip of sand and rock a band of ocean stretches to the horizon.[1] In this scene Conder explores the elements of light and colour and depicts the activity of visitors to the beach. Women in long dresses search for seashells, a small group watches a sailboat travel across the bay and a child paddles in the foreground.

Working primarily in Sydney and Melbourne between 1884 and 1890, Conder suggested in much of his work the subtle moods and poetic qualities of nature. He painted with the energy and enthusiasm of a young man, delighting in the visual world around him and spurred on by the friendly rivalry of his painting companions, Tom Roberts and Arthur Streeton. In *Ricketts Point, Beaumaris* his bold composition and free application of paint combine to form a picture that still looks fresh almost 120 years after it was completed.

1 Mary Eagle identifies this location as Ricketts Point. See Mary Eagle, *The oil paintings of Charles Conder in the National Gallery of Australia*, Canberra: National Gallery of Australia, 1997, p. 61.

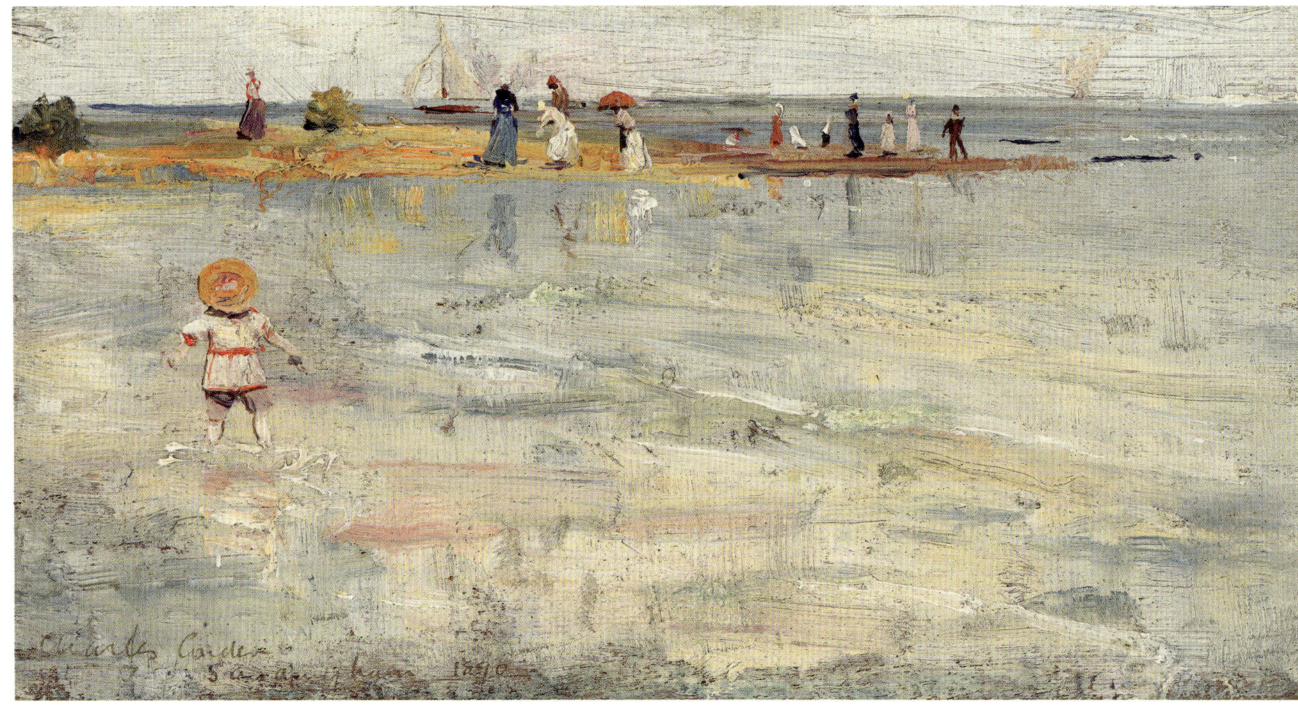

Arthur Streeton (1867–1943)
The selector's hut (Whelan on the log) 1890
oil on canvas 76.7 x 51.2 cm
Purchased 1961

The selector's hut (Whelan on the log) is an iconic image of the 'pioneering spirit' that underpinned Australian nationalist attitudes of the late nineteenth century. Although most Australians lived in coastal cities and towns, it was the bush that was used as a symbol of Australian sentiment. In *The selector's hut (Whelan on the log)* Arthur Streeton depicted these iconic elements of the land. The 'blue and gold' of sky and earth are encapsulated by the great scale of the sky, the golden grass and shimmering light, a slender silhouetted gum tree and a bush pioneer.

By 1888 a railway had been constructed between Melbourne and the suburban fringe at Heidelberg. Towards the end of that year Streeton had set up 'camp' in an old house on Eaglemont estate, which was located close to Heidelberg at Mount Eagle. Mr C. M. Davies, part owner of the estate, had offered the house to the artist.[1] Early in 1889 Streeton was joined by Charles Conder and Tom Roberts. The camp provided the perfect working environment – a reasonably isolated bush location that was still close to the city. Streeton found much inspiration in the area, nicknaming Eaglemont 'our hill of gold'.

Jack Whelan was the caretaker and farmer of the Eaglemont estate and shared the house with the artists over the summer of 1888–89. In *The selector's hut (Whelan on the log)* Streeton has presented Whelan as a bush selector – a type of pioneering 'hero' who farmed the large properties of landowners.

1 Terence Lane, 'Painting on the hill of gold: Heidelberg 1888–90', in Terence Lane (ed.), *Australian impressionism*, Melbourne: National Gallery of Victoria, 2007, p. 123.

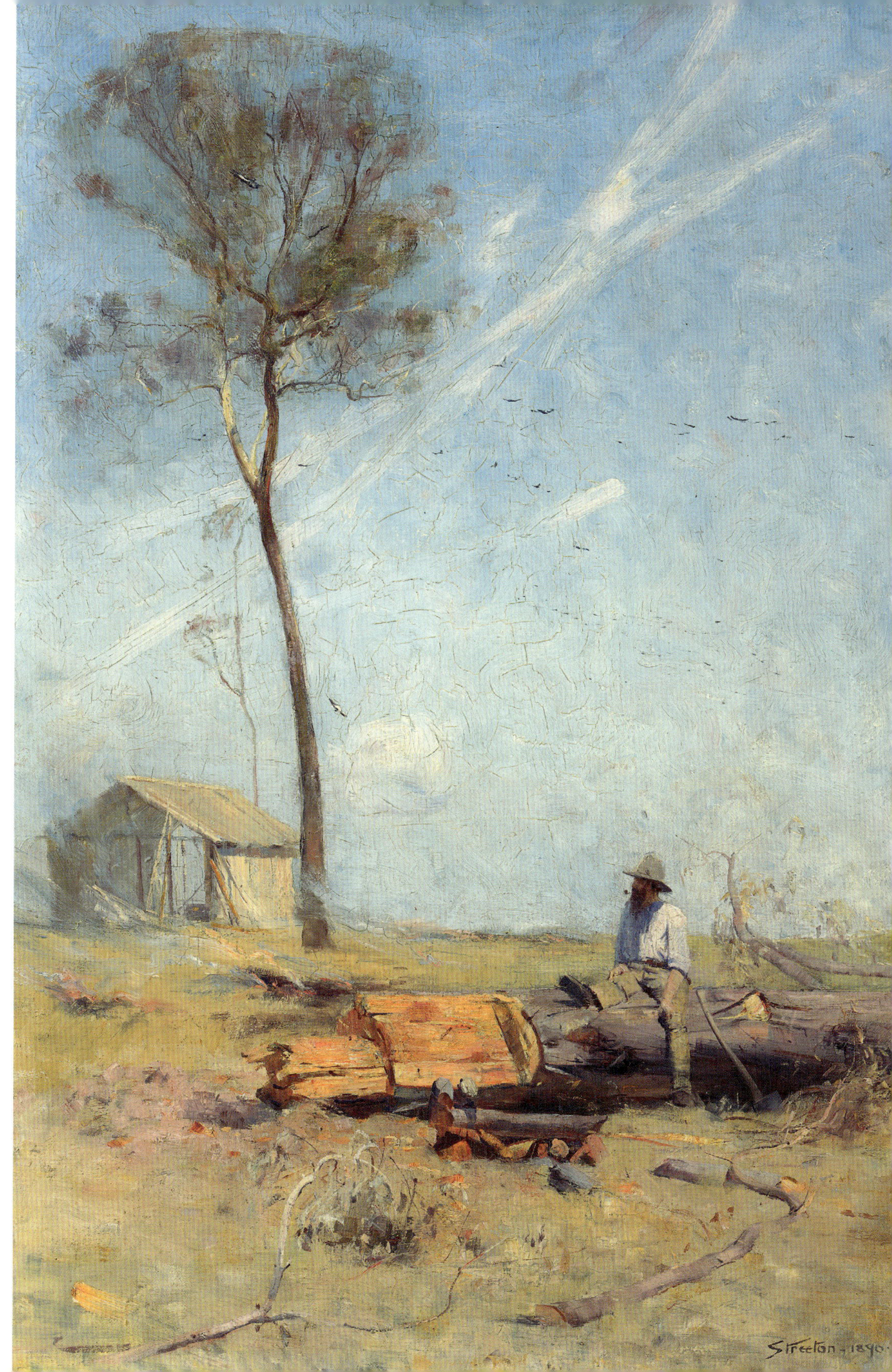

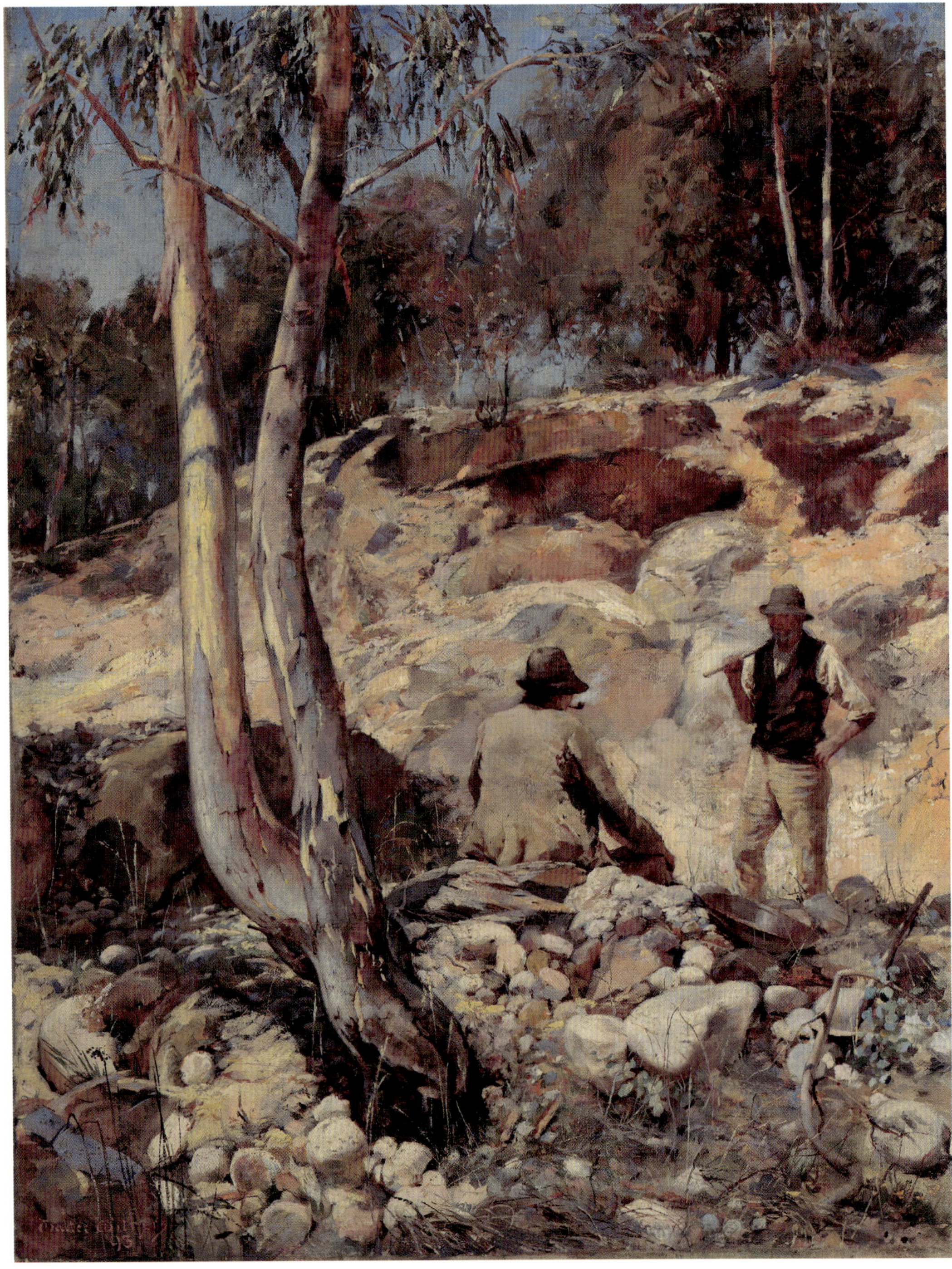

Walter Withers (1854–1914)
The fossickers 1893
oil on canvas 67.7 x 49.0 cm
Gift of Mrs Alec de Bretteville 1969

Gold, gold, gold, gold!
Bright and yellow, hard and cold;
Molten, graven, hammered, rolled,
Heavy to get, and light to hold;
Stolen, borrowed, squandered, doled.[1]

Fossickers were miners who searched through mined earth in the hope of finding undiscovered gold. In Walter Withers's depiction the fossickers are almost camouflaged within the land, blending inconspicuously with the colours of the earth. Under a gum tree the two men take a break in the midday sun. In the foreground of the picture the artist has depicted the texture of the gum tree and rocks in sharp focus, while the large rock-face in the background has been eroded by the impact of heavy mining.

An English artist who arrived in Melbourne in 1883, Withers worked mostly around Heidelberg and Eltham. He visited the town of Creswick 18 kilometres north of Ballarat and 129 kilometres north-west of Melbourne where he painted landscapes and mining subjects. In January 1893 Withers conducted outdoor painting classes in Creswick.[2] Percy Lindsay, who is known for his paintings of Creswick and the surrounding area, attended these classes as a young artist.

1 J. C. F. Johnson, *Getting gold: a gold-mining handbook for practical men*, London: Charles Griffin & Company, 1904, p. 1.
2 Andrew McKenzie, *Walter Withers: the forgotten manuscripts*, Lilydale, Victoria: Mannagum Press, 1987, p. 120.

Percy Lindsay (1870–1952)
Miners and cradle, Creswick c. 1893
oil on canvas 40.5 x 30.5 cm
Purchased 2006

The discovery of gold in the regions north-west of Melbourne in 1851 triggered a huge influx of miners to the district. With many men seeking fortune from mining, the populations of small towns grew rapidly and, during the height of the gold rush, Creswick, some 18 kilometres north of Ballarat, had a population of more than 25 000 people.

In *Miners and cradle, Creswick* Percy Lindsay presents the physical labour of cradle mining: the backbreaking trawling and sifting of the earth in search of gold. The industrious miners wheel their barrows of earth up and over the heavily worked land. Lindsay painted this picture outdoors, seeking to capture the momentary conditions of light and atmosphere.

Unlike many of his contemporaries, as a young artist Lindsay did not settle in Melbourne to study or pursue painting as a profession. In 1895 he attended the National Gallery School in Melbourne for less than a term, returning shortly after to his hometown of Creswick. The works Lindsay produced in Creswick between 1890 and 1900 are his best pictures. These rural scenes are important images by an Australian artist – who was born and trained locally – depicting his region.

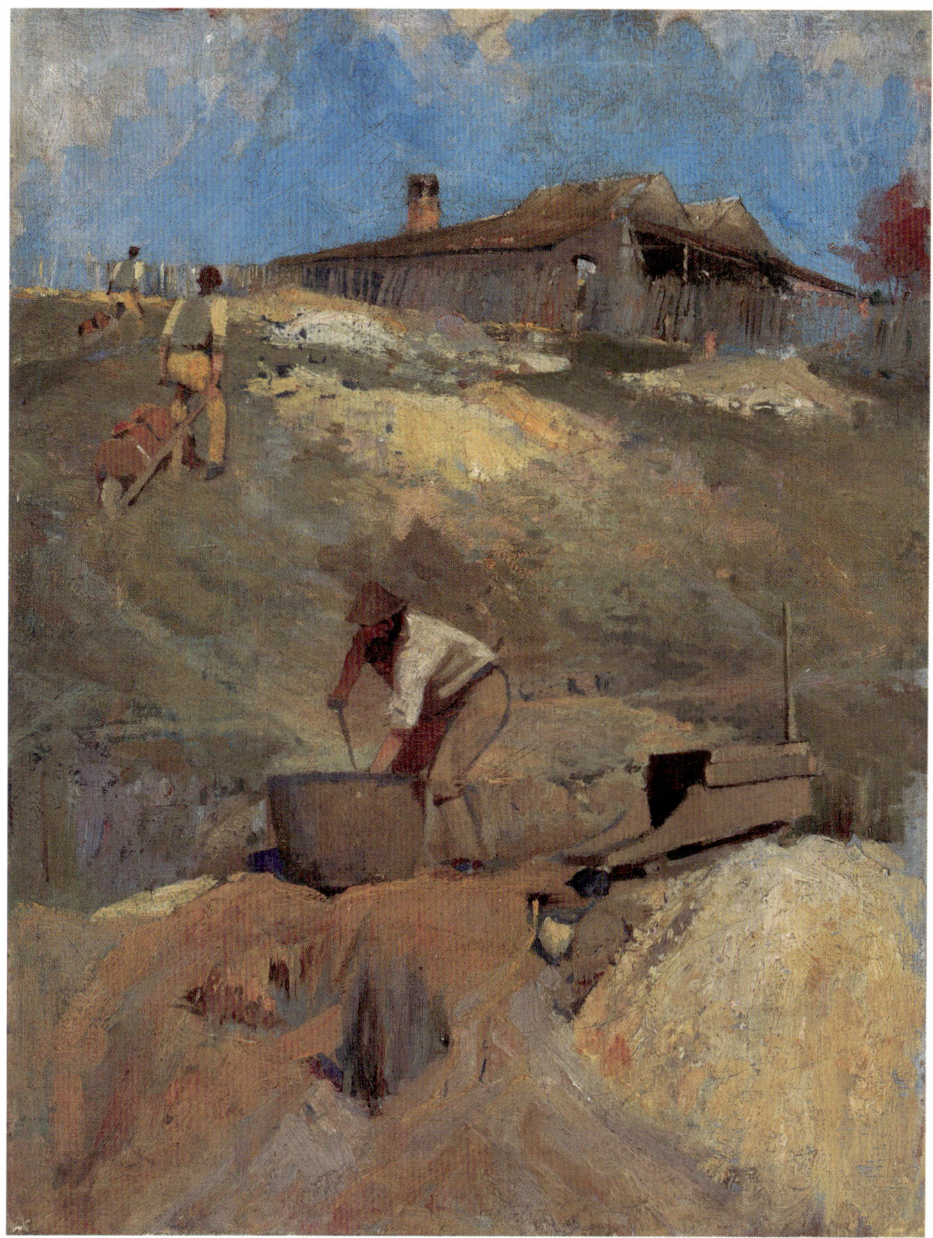

Arthur Streeton (1867–1943)
Sirius Cove c. 1895
oil on wood panel 68.8 x 16.8 cm
Purchased 1973

In December 1892 Arthur Streeton moved from Melbourne to Sydney to join his friend Tom Roberts who was living at Curlew Camp at Sirius Cove near Mosman. Streeton spent the next four years based at this camp. He was captivated by the jewel-like beauty of Sydney Harbour – a public playground and private universe of endless creative possibility.

In *Sirius Cove* Streeton has depicted a glorious slice of the harbour. He used the vertical grain of the wood panel that he painted on, and its natural colour, to produce a study in positive and negative space, of flattened shapes and tonal contrasts that advance and recede. The image unfolds vertically like a Japanese scroll. Streeton used sweeping calligraphic-style brushstrokes – fluid and intuitive yet carefully considered and attentive to detail.

In this image a calm body of water mirrors an overcast sky. The harbour appears still and quiet yet is host to a range of human activities. A small rowing boat is shown on the water, a distant ferry advances and a path leads up the hill indicating the location of the artists' camp.

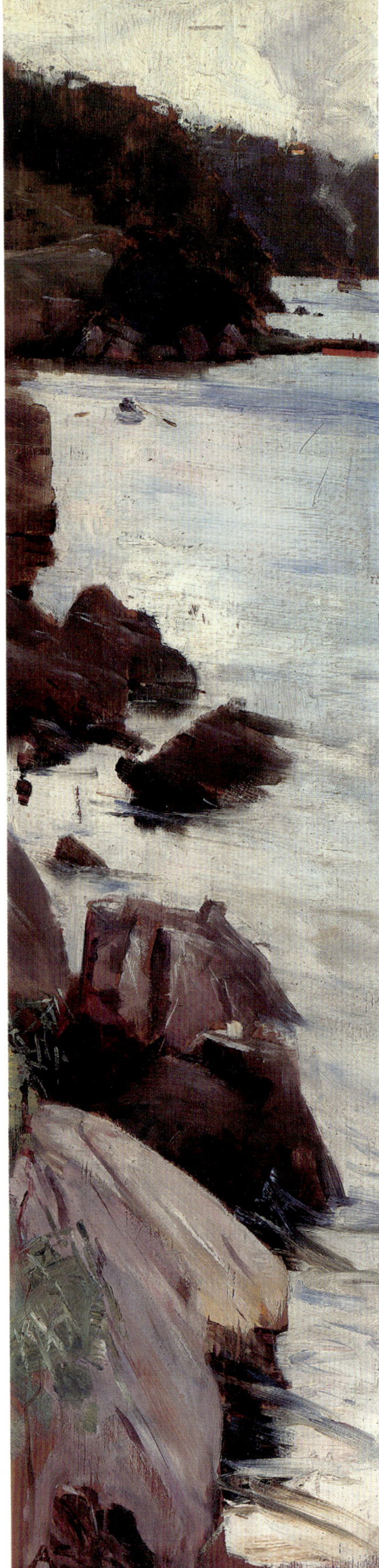

Arthur Streeton (1867–1943)
Sydney Harbour: A souvenir c. 1897
oil on canvas mounted on cardboard 64.9 x 40.3 cm
Gift of S. H. Ervin 1962

Arthur Streeton depicted scenes of city life on Sydney Harbour – such as Sirius Cove, the ferry at McMahon's Point and the bustle of Circular Quay – yet he also created a number of allegorical images. From the late 1880s Streeton had painted symbolist landscapes using the female form to indicate a particular season, mood or state of nature.

Sydney Harbour: A souvenir was possibly painted after Streeton had left Sydney and was based in London.[1] The work is a romantic and personal memento of the four years he spent on the harbour at Curlew Camp near Mosman. Framed by the bush setting a group of spirits dance in the landscape. Against the sandstone rocks their transparent forms seem weightless. At the centre of the composition is the magnetic blue of Sydney Harbour, the water glimpsed through rich vegetation. A passing ship is a reminder of everyday reality and the presence of the city.

1 Mary Eagle, *The oil paintings of Arthur Streeton in the National Gallery of Australia*, Canberra: National Gallery of Australia, 1994, pp. 129–31.

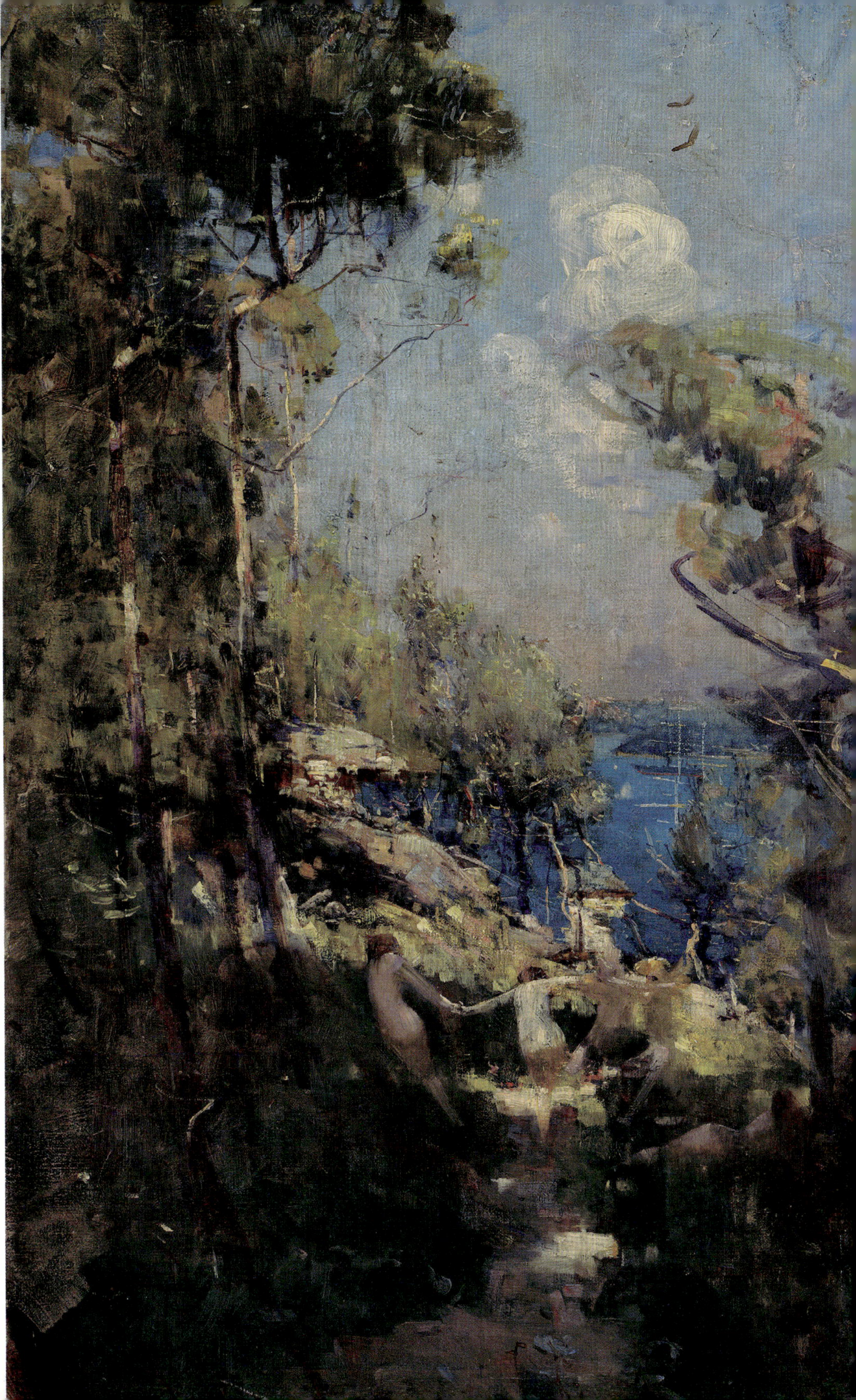

Sydney Long (1871–1955)
Feeding time 1896
oil on canvas 56.0 x 76.5 cm
Purchased 1963

Sydney Long's *Feeding time* is an image of a crisp winter morning with a young woman feeding calves and chickens. This is a quiet scene of rural domesticity, the farmhouse and fence indicating an established property. The location of this work is most likely Griffiths's farm, a property on the Richmond side of the Hawkesbury River west of Sydney.[1] From the late 1880s this region was a popular painting site for a number of Sydney-based artists, including Julian Ashton, Charles Conder and Arthur Streeton, who went there to paint outdoors in a tranquil, rural environment, just beyond the city limits.

Feeding time is an earthy and rustic picture in which Long has positioned the female figure in the land as both the subject of the work and as a metaphor for the notion of woman as worker, carer and nurturer. In later works Long developed his interest in the role of women in bush mythology and allegory, and it was as a symbolist artist that he became best known.

Feeding time was exhibited in September 1896 at the *Society of Artists Spring exhibition* at the Cliff Gallery in Pitt Street, Sydney. A sketch of the work was also reproduced in the exhibition catalogue.

1 Joanna Mendelssohn, *The life and work of Sydney Long*, Cremorne: Copperfield Publishing Co., 1979, p. 53.

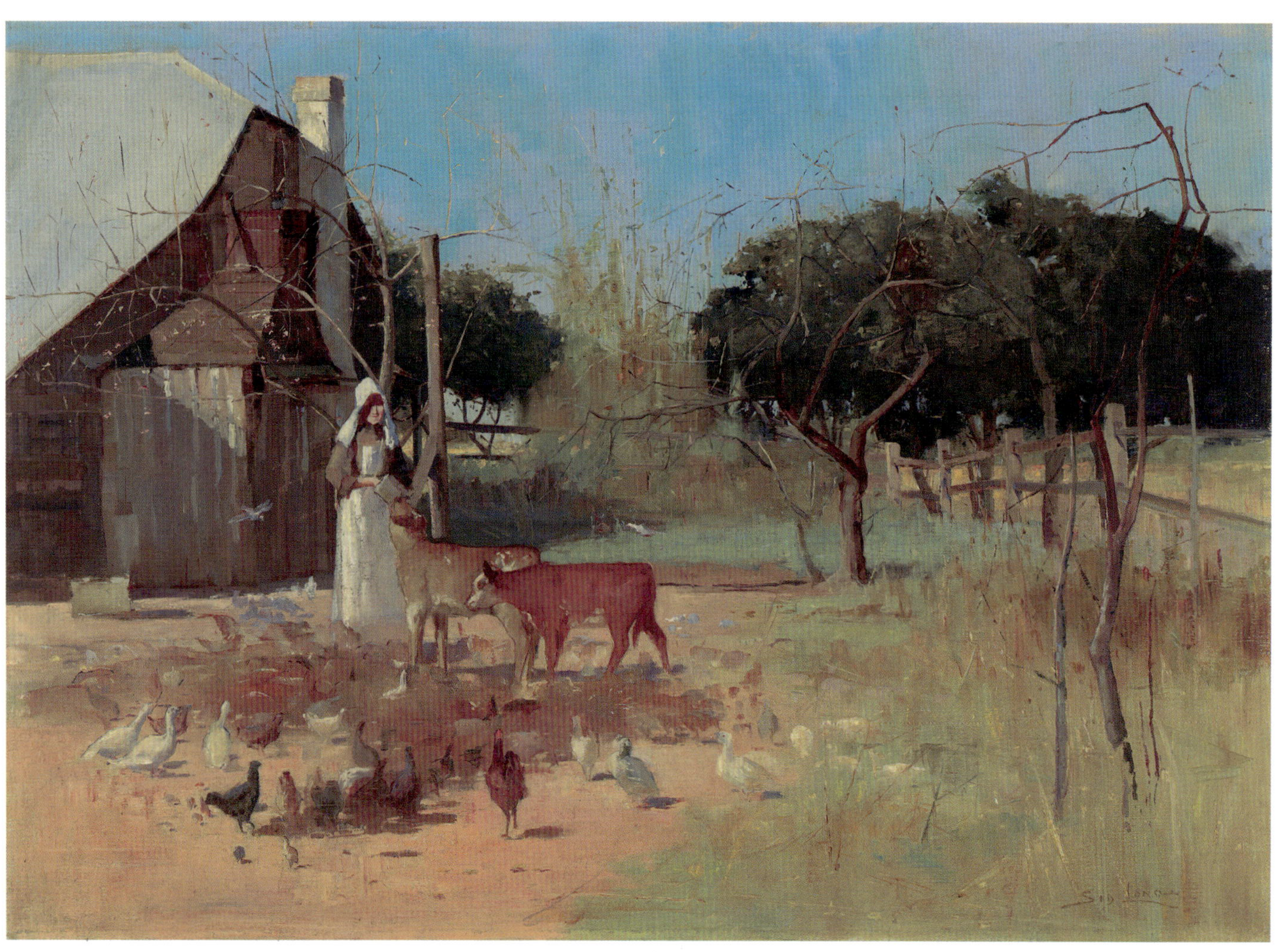

Harry Garlick (1878–1910)
The drover 1906
oil on canvas board 60.8 x 45.4 cm
Purchased 1972

Harry Garlick painted *The drover* in response to the 'Federation drought', which began in 1895 and reached its climax in the summer of 1901–02. Officially lasting until 1903, the drought had a devastating effect on the sheep, cattle and wheat-farming industries throughout much of Australia. Garlick had painted earlier responses to the drought, such as *Drought stricken* 1902 (present whereabouts unknown). It is possible that *The drover* was painted in the Orange or Bathurst regions of western New South Wales where Garlick was born and lived until 1896. In the heat of the midday sun a drover leads his flock along an arid stock route, the artist's use of perspective emphasising the distance between the drover and his flock and the hills on the horizon.

The drover is indicative of Garlick's interest in pastoral scenes. As a young man he travelled each week from Orange to Bathurst to attend painting classes with Sydney painter Arthur Collingridge. After relocating to Sydney from Orange in 1896 he attended night classes with Julian Ashton, worked as a clerk and occasionally published drawings and cartoons in the *Bulletin*. Garlick was one of a number of artists, including Julian Ashton, Sydney Long, Charles Conder and Arthur Streeton, who visited Griffiths's farm on the Richmond side of the Hawkesbury River on outdoor painting trips.

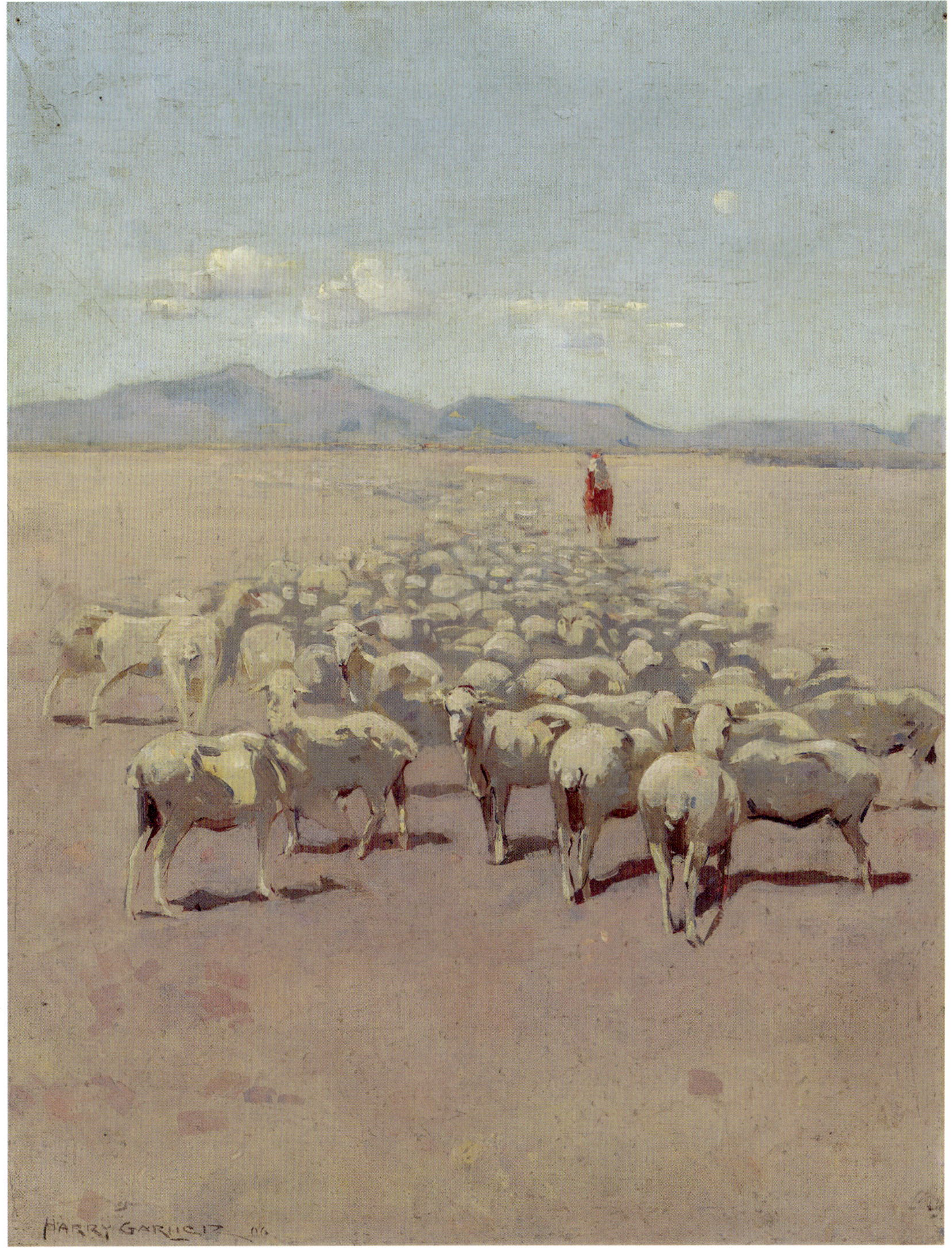

Frederick McCubbin (1855–1917)
The coming of spring 1912
oil on canvas 68.8 x 102.0 cm
Purchased 1972

In *The coming of spring* Frederick McCubbin demonstrated his longstanding interest in evoking qualities of light and the atmospheric conditions particular to each season. He skilfully manipulated the surfaces of his paintings to create a sense of dappled light and used luminescent colours and layers of paint to develop a rich and textured finish.

The view in this work is from the artist's garden on Kensington Road in Melbourne's South Yarra, looking over the river to the industrial suburb of Richmond. McCubbin completed a number of paintings from this garden, delighting in the seasonal variation and the subtleties of the environment. In *The coming of spring* the banks of the Yarra River are covered with the new growth of the season; a cow in the foreground grazes on the soft, damp grasses. Looking into the distance we see Richmond and the city of Melbourne beyond.

McCubbin's paintings of his home environment are important statements by the artist, who claimed that:

> It is precisely the pictures of things familiar to us of homely subjects … which most appeal to us and more often therefore rise to true greatness … the farm with its neighbouring clump of gum trees, the fields that merge into wayward forests, the winding road with its bullock wagons, men and women toiling, horses and cattle and all things that savour of man.[1]

1 Bridget Whitelaw, *The art of Frederick McCubbin*, Melbourne: National Gallery of Victoria, 1991, p. 104.

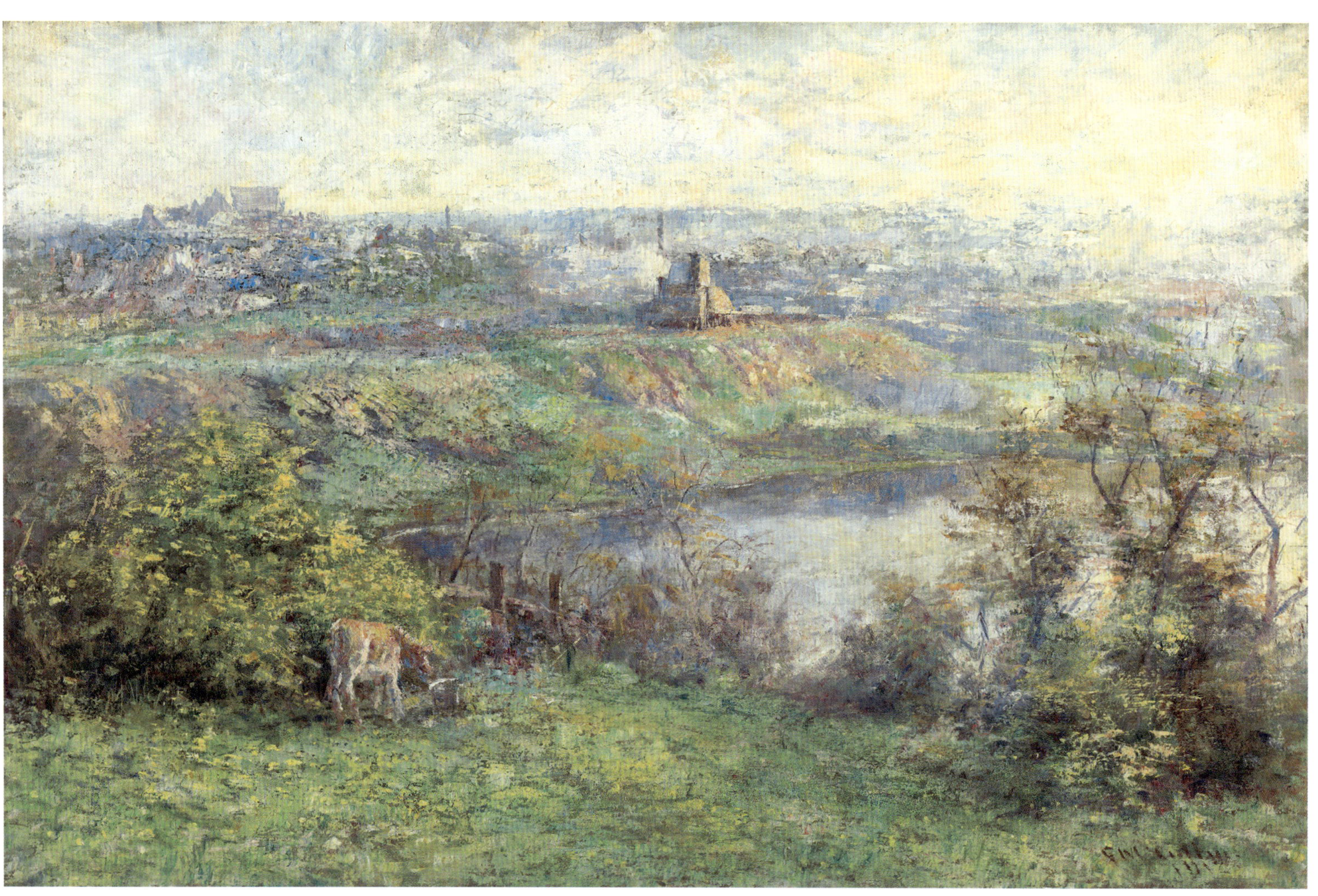

Frederick McCubbin (1855–1917)
Girl in forest, Mount Macedon 1913
oil on canvas 50.8 x 76.2 cm
Purchased 1962

In *Girl in forest, Mount Macedon* Frederick McCubbin revisits a central theme in his oeuvre: the activities of children in the Australian bush. He had previously painted scenes of children lost in the bush – narratives of innocence and vulnerability within the landscape. McCubbin also explored the magical worlds invented by children through storytelling and imagination. In works such as *What the little girl saw in the bush* 1904 (private collection, reproduced p. 28) he sought to capture ideas of creative freedom and expression that children unselfconsciously bring to their surrounds.

In *Girl in forest, Mount Macedon* a young girl wanders through the bush carrying a basket, possibly collecting wildflowers or berries. She is small beside the large trees and thick growth, her white dress setting her apart from her environment. McCubbin has paid close attention to the study of dappled light through trees and foliage. Areas of the canvas appear abstracted and flecks of colour are layered over each other using a palette knife. Moving back from the work the scene comes into focus – a glorious image of gold, pink and violet; bracken, bark and gum.

Girl in forest, Mount Macedon depicts the bush close to 'Fontainebleau', the McCubbin's residence at Mount Macedon about 60 kilometres north-west of Melbourne. The child in the image is the artist's youngest daughter, Kathleen, who posed for her father numerous times.

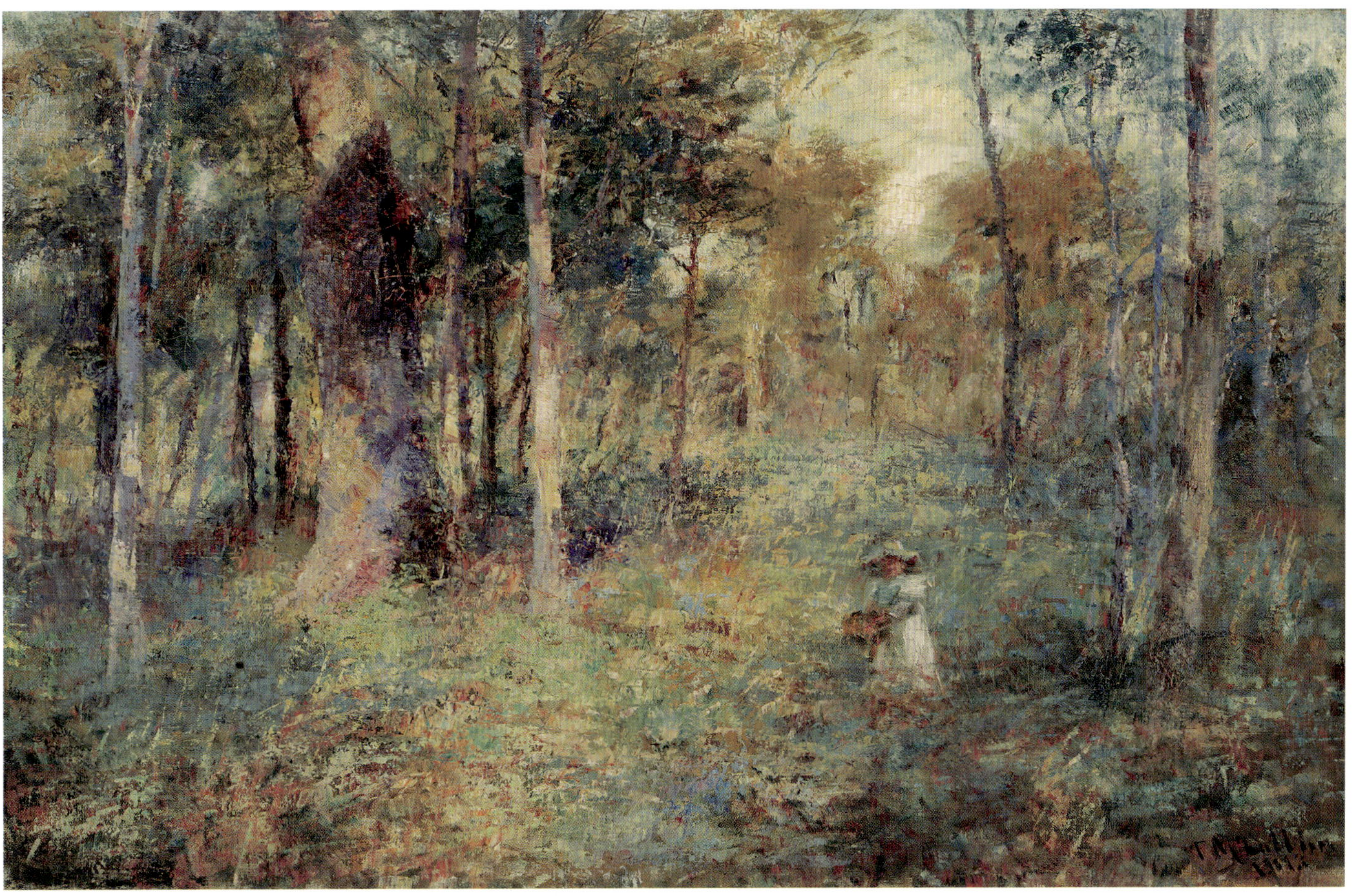

Elioth Gruner (1882–1939)
Autumn morning c. 1916
oil on canvas mounted on cardboard 34.5 x 44.4 cm
The Oscar Paul Collection, Gift of Henriette von Dallwitz and of Richard Paul in honour of his father 1965

> It must have been with queer exultation of inspired emotion that Gruner, wrapped up in chaff-bags to keep the chill out of his blood, watched for those clear, colourless dawns to arrive, with a palette set to a key that would paint the unpaintable, light itself.
> Norman Lindsay 1918[1]

Autumn morning belongs to a group of pastoral landscapes by Elioth Gruner that were painted in the Emu Plains district near the Blue Mountains west of Sydney. Based in Sydney, Gruner made many painting excursions throughout much of New South Wales. The subtle, tonal qualities of *Autumn morning* exemplify Gruner's primary interest in the effects of light on the landscape.

In *Autumn morning* Gruner depicts cattle gathered under the expanse of a tree in the first light of day. The dark silhouette of the tree contrasts with the cool whites, greys and lilacs of the foliage and sky. These colours convey the crisp conditions of an autumn morning, the sense of frost dissipating with the warmth of the rising sun. The composition is dominated by the tree, which stretches out across the sky, its limbs casting shadows across the grass. The low horizon accentuates the scale of the tree and its solid trunk and sinuous branches resemble the shape of inverted human lungs, a complex arrangement of connective tissue and blood vessels. In *Autumn morning* the tree is transformed into a metaphor for breath and the vitality of nature.

1 Norman Lindsay, *Elioth Gruner: twenty-four reproductions in colour from original oil paintings*, Sydney: Shepherd Press, 1947, n.p.

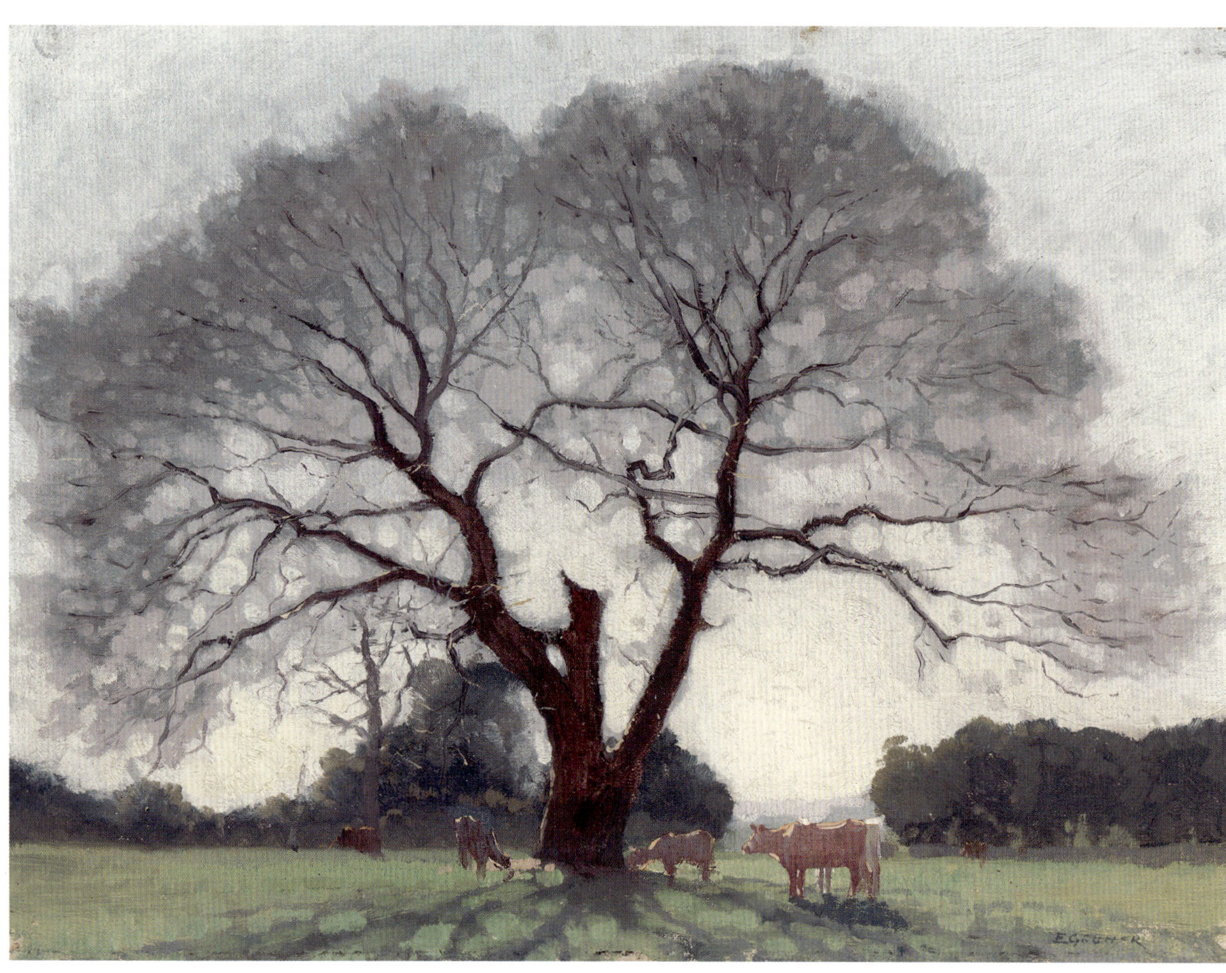

Elioth Gruner (1882–1939)
Murrumbidgee Ranges, Canberra 1934
oil on canvas 51.6 x 89.0 cm
Bequest of Stuart A. Johnston 1964

In 1934 Elioth Gruner made one of several visits to the Canberra region where he painted *Murrumbidgee Ranges, Canberra.* In 1928 Gruner had purchased a car, which gave him the means to travel throughout the countryside on painting trips. He first visited Yass and Canberra in 1929 and was impressed by the crisp, clear light of the area. Over the next ten years he returned several times and completed some of his major late works in the district.

Murrumbidgee Ranges, Canberra is an arrangement of several views looking south-west from Canberra towards the Tidbinbilla and Brindabella ranges. While there are no Murrumbidgee Ranges as such, the Murrumbidgee River runs between Canberra and the Tidbinbilla Range. Gruner would have painted this work outdoors, and possibly in one sitting. Through his use of colour he has captured the sharp light of the Canberra region and the cool velvety softness of the surrounding mountains. He has also depicted signs of settlement, including sheep grazing quietly near the 'bush capital', distant trails of smoke and a car heading west towards the Murrumbidgee River.

Murrumbidgee Ranges, Canberra was awarded the 1934 Wynne Prize for landscape painting at the Art Gallery of New South Wales, Sydney. Indeed, Gruner won the prize seven times between 1916 and 1937. In 1937 *Murrumbidgee Ranges, Canberra* was exhibited in London in the *Artists of the British Empire overseas exhibition* at the Royal British Colonial Society of Artists.

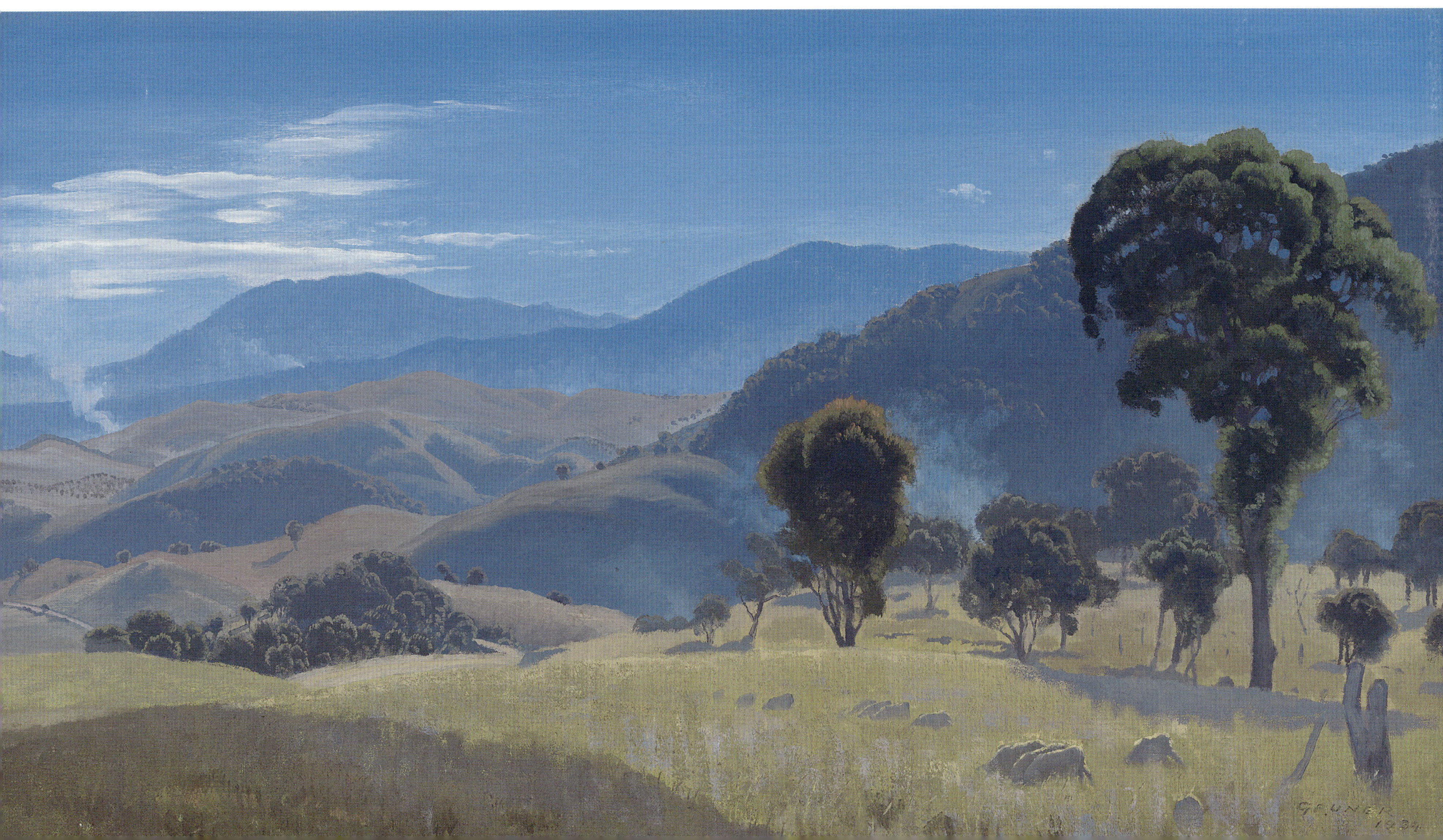

Tom Roberts (1856–1931)
The quarry, Maria Island 1926
oil on canvas 61.0 x 50.5 cm
The Oscar Paul Collection, Gift of Henriette von Dallwitz and of Richard Paul in honour of his father 1965

In February and March of 1926 Tom Roberts spent six weeks painting in Tasmania. During this period he visited Maria Island, a former penal station and mining township located across the Mercury Passage off the east coast of the main island.

The quarry, Maria Island is a late example of Roberts's depiction of human labour on the land. This is a narrative landscape filled with anticipation. Roberts presents an active mine in the heat of the midday sun – a flash of earth beneath clear blue sky. Careful geometric balance of the composition accentuates the dramatic vertical drop and sheer size of the quarry. The sweeping precipice is counterbalanced by opposing triangular masses of rock and sky. Dwarfed within this scene and disguised by the colours and tones of their environment, eight miners work the quarry. Their dangerous activity of blasting the stone is heightened by the scale of the limestone cliffs.

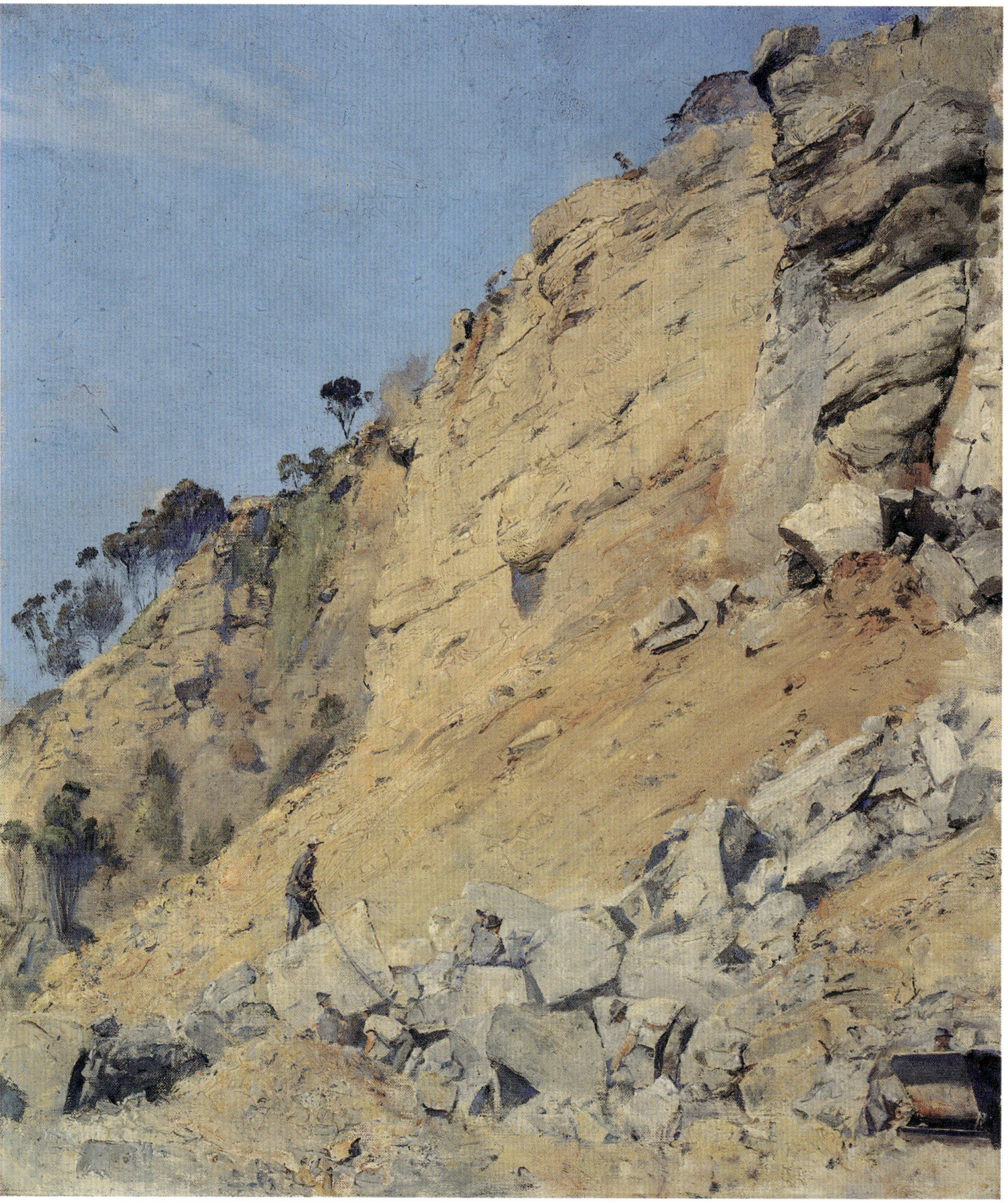

Arthur Streeton (1867–1943)
Land of the Golden Fleece (1926)
oil on canvas 50.7 x 75.5 cm
The Oscar Paul Collection, Gift of Henriette von Dallwitz and of Richard Paul in honour of his father 1965

In *Land of the Golden Fleece* Arthur Streeton presents a view towards Mount William from the southern end of the Grampians mountain range in Victoria. Looking down and across a property at Willaura (owned by Streeton's friend Walter Cain),[1] Streeton depicts a flock of sheep grazing, a dam and a windmill. Shadows move across the land and Streeton has used colour to give the image a sense of space, painting the distant Grampians with blues and greys to make them recede, and using warm yellows in the foreground to make the golden fields appear closer to the viewer.

Land of the Golden Fleece displays an open and opulent pastoral Australia: full of potential, grand in scale and scenic in beauty. In this work Streeton presented a country rich in 'blue and gold', earth and water, sky and land. Australia was a land of youth and possibility. Following the death of many thousands of Australians during the First World War, and the devastation of the landscapes of France and Belgium, artists such as Streeton looked to the land as a symbol of national pride and prosperity – a reaffirmation of place and identity.

1 Mary Eagle, *The oil paintings of Arthur Streeton in the National Gallery of Australia*, Canberra: National Gallery of Australia, 1994, p. 184.

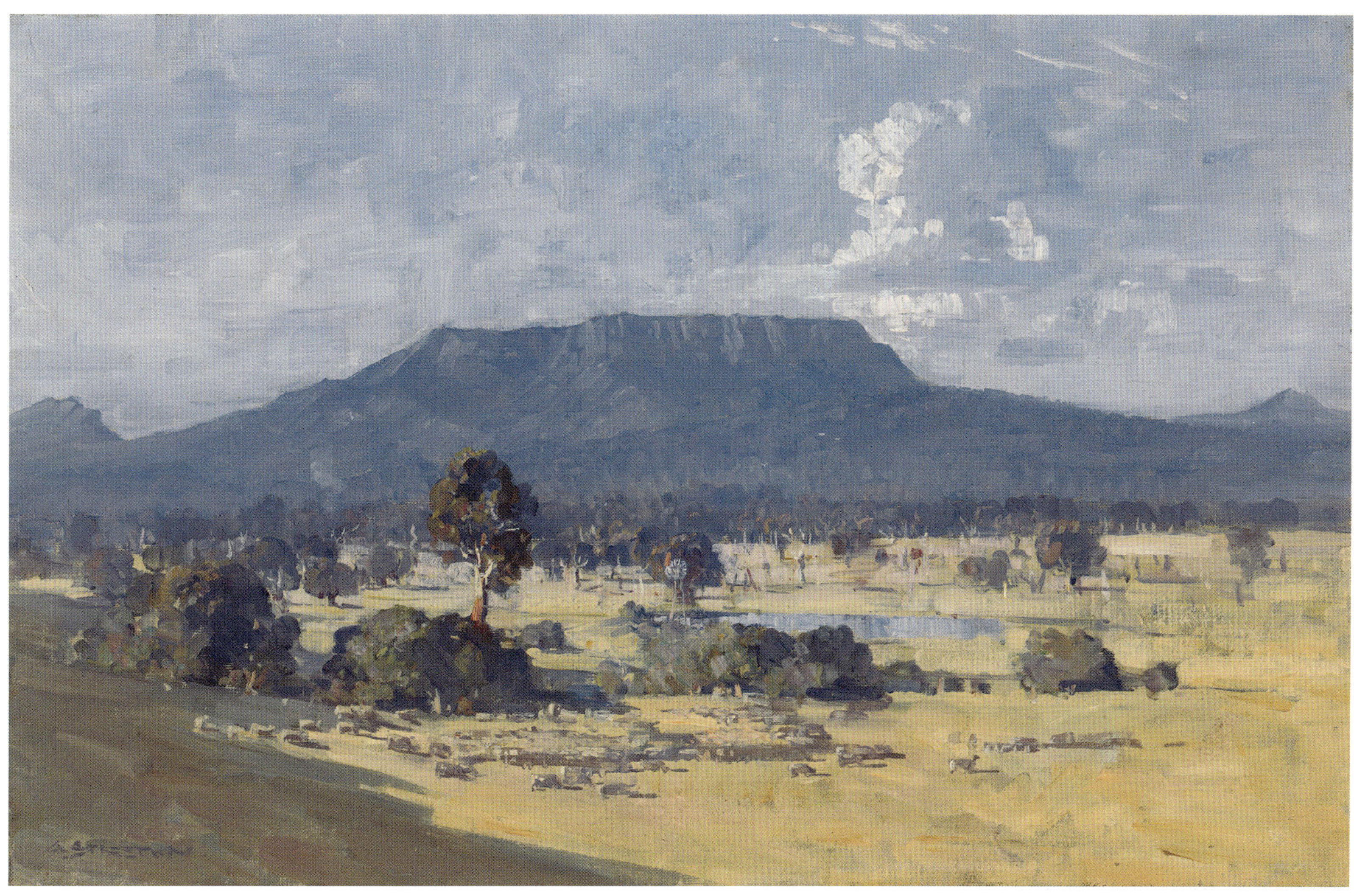

Max Meldrum (1875–1955)
Shadows, landscape with trees c. 1925
oil on canvas on wooden panel 37.0 x 34.0 cm
Bequest of Mary Meyer in memory of her husband
Dr Felix Meyer 1975

Shadows, landscape with trees is an atmospheric and intimate study of nature belonging to a series of 'tree paintings' completed by Max Meldrum between 1917 and 1925. In this work Meldrum has captured a slice of a larger scene, and has used the tree-trunks to frame and balance his composition. Omitting branches and foliage, he has paid close attention to the patches of dark shadow and dappled light on the grassy hill.

Meldrum was a Melbourne artist and teacher who championed a theory of painting based on the importance of tonal values. He believed it was the artist's task to observe nature accurately and that painting was an application of the science of optical truth and tonal relations. He believed that there were no lines in nature and that they should therefore be abolished from art. As a student Meldrum was awarded the 1899 National Gallery School Travelling Scholarship which enabled him to go to Paris and see works by artists including Rembrandt, Van Dyck, Velázquez, Corot and Whistler. Meldrum's interest in these artists and in the realist tradition of art had a deep impact on his theories of 'depictive' art – of understanding and creating an image of what we see.[1]

Meldrum returned to Melbourne in 1911 and by 1916 had established his own art school where he taught artists including A. E. Newbury and Clarice Beckett. He had an argumentative personality and the opinions he expressed in his many public talks polarised the Melbourne art community. In 1919 he published his theories (based on a 1917 lecture titled 'The invariable truths of depictive art') in a book, *Max Meldrum: his art and views*.

1 Peter Perry & John Perry, *Max Meldrum and associates: their art, lives and influences*, Victoria: Castlemaine Art Gallery and Historical Museum, 1996, pp. 20–21.

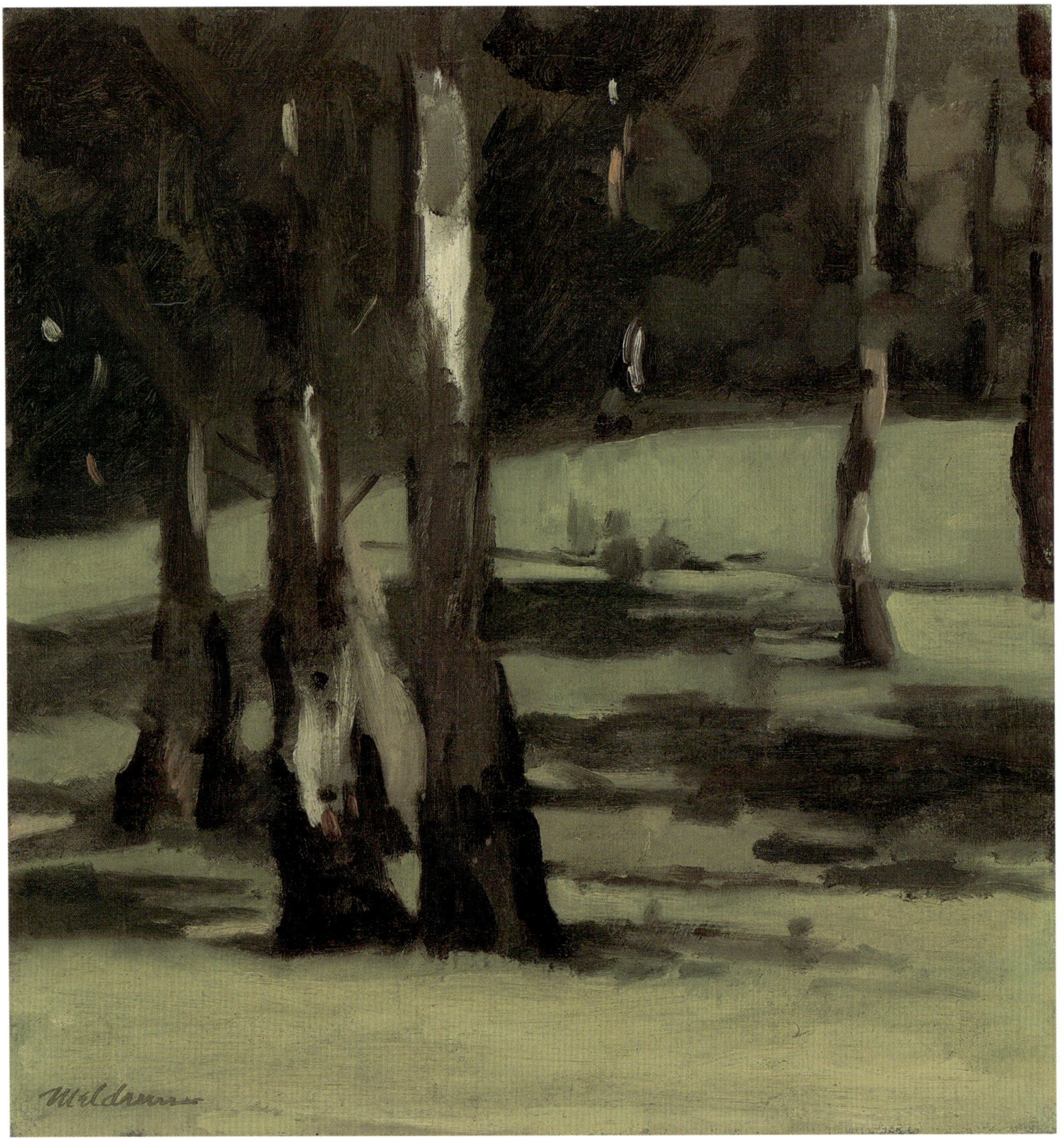

A. E. Newbury (1891–1941)
Eltham 1919
oil on academy board 30.8 x 23.2 cm
Purchased 1979

In *Eltham* A. E. Newbury used soft brushstrokes and carefully blended colour to suggest the stillness and light of a misty Melbourne day. He approached the composition with an economy of colour and form, and sought a similar balance and symmetry to that of Japanese prints. By truncating the gum trees he created an illusion of depth in the overall image. Newbury emphasises contrasts in texture, such as the rough bark base and smooth stretch of the larger gum. This attention highlights the tree against the more muted, almost abstracted planes of colour that form the background.

Newbury sought to portray the simple, strong beauty of the Australian bush. He concentrated his efforts on depicting his local surrounds, and spent much of his life painting around Eltham, the Melbourne suburb where he lived. He also occasionally painted at the South Yarra home of Frederick McCubbin. Between 1916 and 1920 Newbury painted a number of works in the tonal manner championed by Max Meldrum. He initially studied at Melbourne's National Gallery School under Frederick McCubbin and Bernard Hall before attending classes with Meldrum from 1916. Newbury went on to develop works that were primarily concerned with the effect of light on the landscape.[1]

1 Peter Perry & John Perry, *Max Meldrum and associates: their art, lives and influences*, Victoria: Castlemaine Art Gallery and Historical Museum, 1996, p. 113.

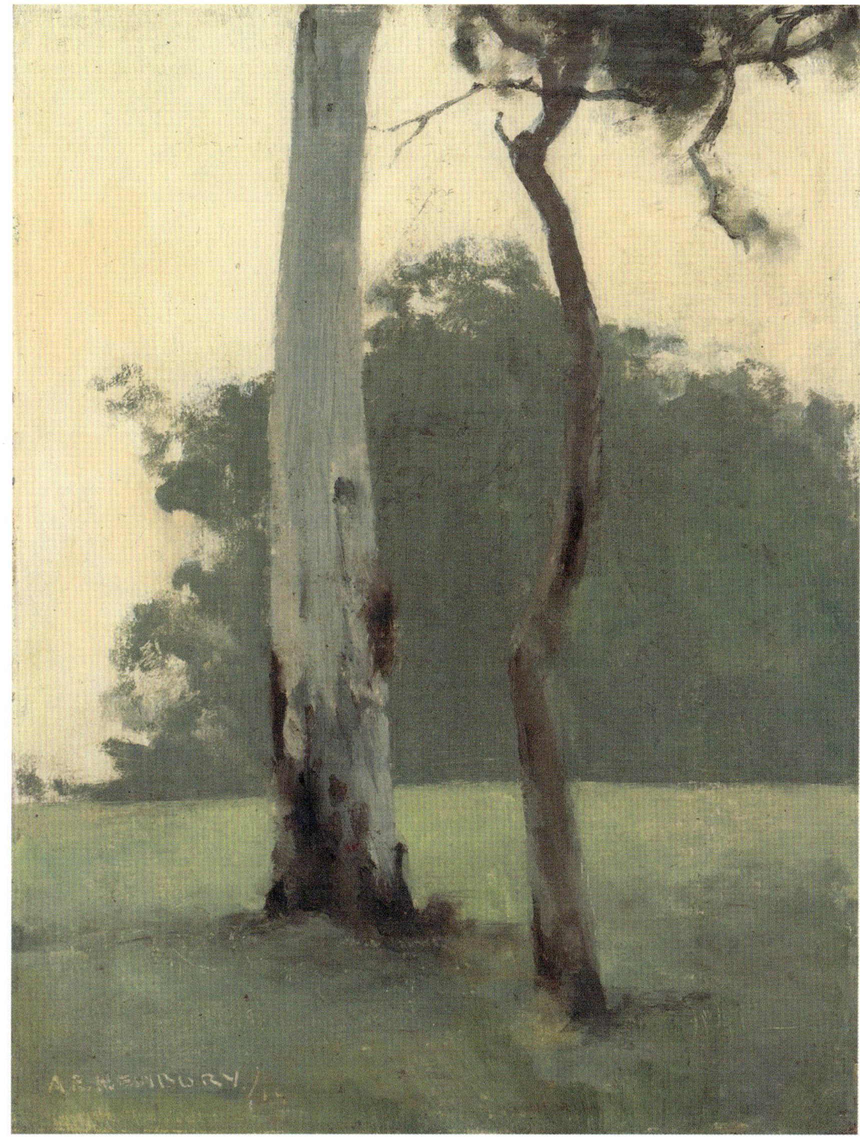

Clarice Beckett (1887–1935)
Beaumaris seascape c. 1925
oil on cardboard 50.0 x 49.0 cm
Purchased 1971

> [My aim is] to give a sincere and truthful representation of a portion of the beauty of Nature, and to show the charm of light and shade, which I try and set forth in correct tones so as to give nearly as possible an exact illusion of reality.
> CLARICE BECKETT 1924[1]

Clarice Beckett's lyrical and evocative landscapes of Melbourne remained largely unknown to Australian audiences during her lifetime. Beckett was a dedicated artist who, despite dismissive reviews and few sales, continued to paint and exhibit regularly. She first studied in Ballarat, and then from 1914 to 1916 studied with Frederick McCubbin at the National Gallery School. In 1917 she attended Max Meldrum's public lecture on tonal painting at Melbourne's Athenaeum Theatre and, impressed by his theories, enrolled in his classes. While Beckett was considered a 'Meldrumite' – a devotee of her teacher's theories of tonal values as the best means of depicting nature – she adapted his ideas to create her own unique vision of the Australian landscape.

Beckett always painted outdoors, usually in the early morning or evening, around the bays and streets of her family home in Beaumaris, a beachside suburb of Melbourne. She sought to convey in her paintings the beauty of her local environment; be it through the afterglow of a bright sunset, the shimmering heat of a tarred road or headlights shining through misty Melbourne rain. She excelled in depicting particular effects of nature, such as haze, rain, mist and smoke. *Beaumaris seascape* is a meditative image of a still sea, a tree-lined cliff and distant coastline. Beckett has paid close attention to the subtle effects of light and shade reflected in the body of water. The soft lilac and pink hues of the sea, coastline and sky dissolve into bands of colour. The subject is so tonally reduced it appears to be almost abstracted.

1 Clarice Beckett, *Twenty Melbourne painters*, 6th annual exhibition catalogue, 1924.

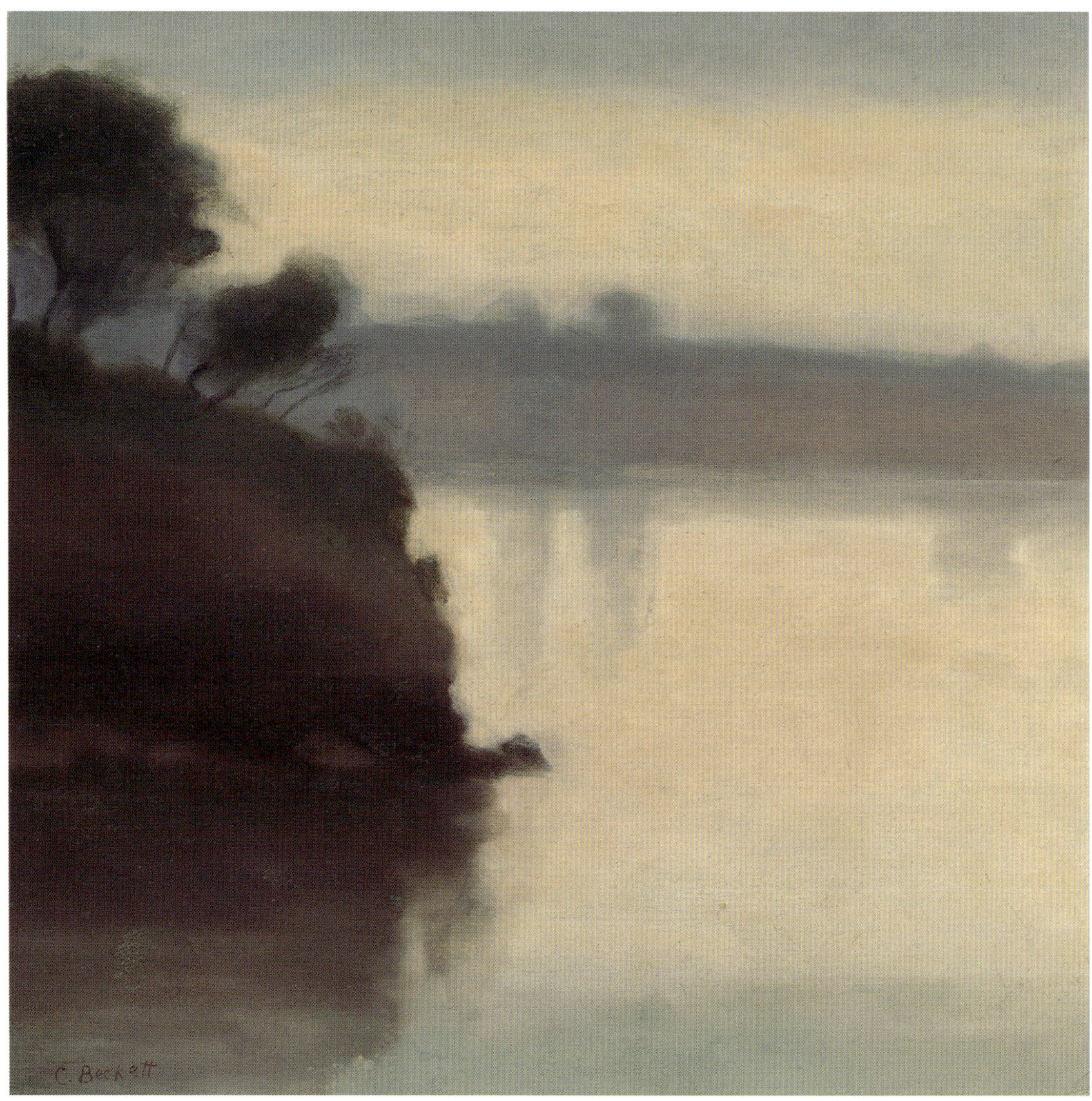

Clarice Beckett (1887–1935)
Sandringham Beach c. 1933
oil on canvas 55.8 x 50.9 cm
Purchased 1971

Clarice Beckett's *Sandringham Beach* is a dynamic and modern composition of sand, bathing boxes and beach walkers. Beckett depicted the scene from an unusual perspective – from a cliff looking down onto the beach. Captured in the glare of a summer day, the smooth body of sand appears to shimmer with 'white heat'. Backing onto scruffy vegetation, the bright stripes of the bathing boxes are the most solid aspects of the composition. While these beach shacks were a key motif in the artist's oeuvre, it is the perspective Beckett explored and the use of colour that transform this image. She recorded her unusual view by even including a craggy ti-tree branch that sprawls across the centre of the picture.

Sandringham Beach is one of Beckett's largest paintings; she generally chose to work on smaller panels. In contrast to Charles Conder's *Ricketts Point, Beaumaris* 1890, the ocean only occupies a small portion of Beckett's view. Painted around forty years after Conder, the beachgoers in Beckett's composition are shown strolling along the water's edge and a game of beach cricket is captured taking place between two young boys. The bright modern swimsuits and exposed skin of the walkers has been brushed onto the canvas with soft dabs of colour. The playful atmosphere of *Sandringham Beach* encapsulates Australia's love affair with the beach as a key site of recreation and relaxation.

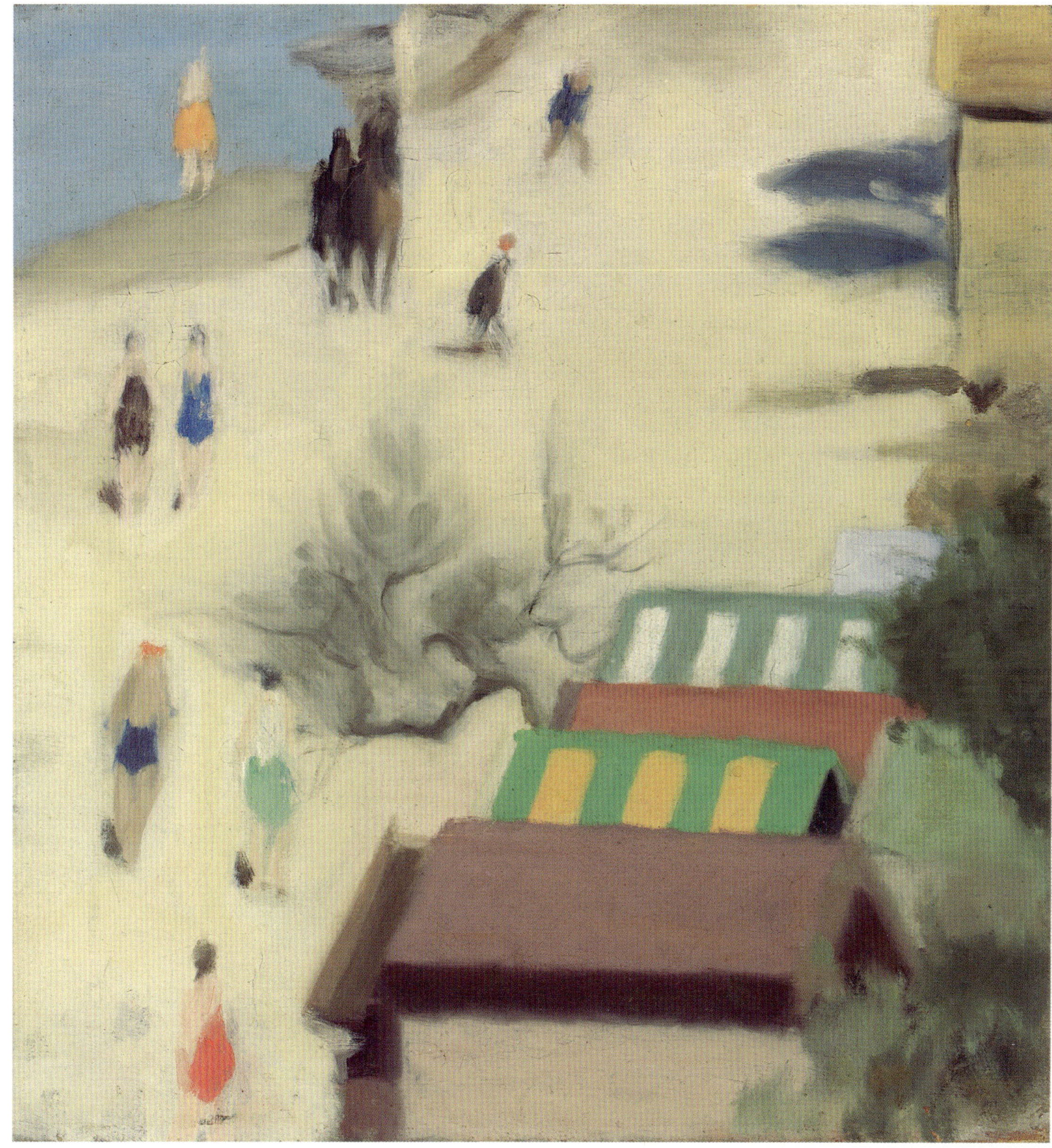

Eric Thake (1904–1982)
Kosciusko and the Murray Flats at Towong 1932
oil on canvas 29.6 x 73.0 cm
Purchased 1979

Kosciusko and the Murray Flats at Towong is a panoramic image of the Great Dividing Range, Murray River and surrounding region. Painted during the Great Depression, the work was intended by Eric Thake for the owner of one of the local properties, although this did not eventuate. Thake wrote: 'Mr Drummond was the man that I painted this picture for, or at least with a view to his buying it. He was very interested, but not financially. During the Depression the price of a steer was probably nowhere near the modest price I asked for this picture.'[1]

The graphic line and simplified forms of this painting derive in part from Thake's training in commercial art, design and printmaking. His studies with the Melbourne teacher George Bell from 1925 to 1928 would have informed his modernist approach to form, space and colour. This painting developed from a number of sketches – a process that involved 'a lot of sifting out and refining and rearrangement, until I come right down to as simplified form as possible'.[2]

Thake depicts the varied topography of the region. The Murray River is shown curling through the foreground, flanked by clumps of trees and pastures – some soft and green, others eroded with only dead trees remaining. The undulating hills are dotted with details and landmarks including grazing cattle, fence posts and the Bringenbrong Bridge and Station. Further into the distance Thake has depicted the mountains and snow-capped peaks of the Great Dividing Range and Australia's highest mountain, Kosciuszko. At the bottom of the work a motorcar is shown driving along a dirt road, an indication of modernity within the land.

1 Eric Thake, inscription on the backing board of *Kosciusko and the Murray Flats at Towong*.
2 Eric Thake, interview by Hazel de Berg, 19 October 1961, Canberra: National Gallery of Australia, transcript, p. 102.

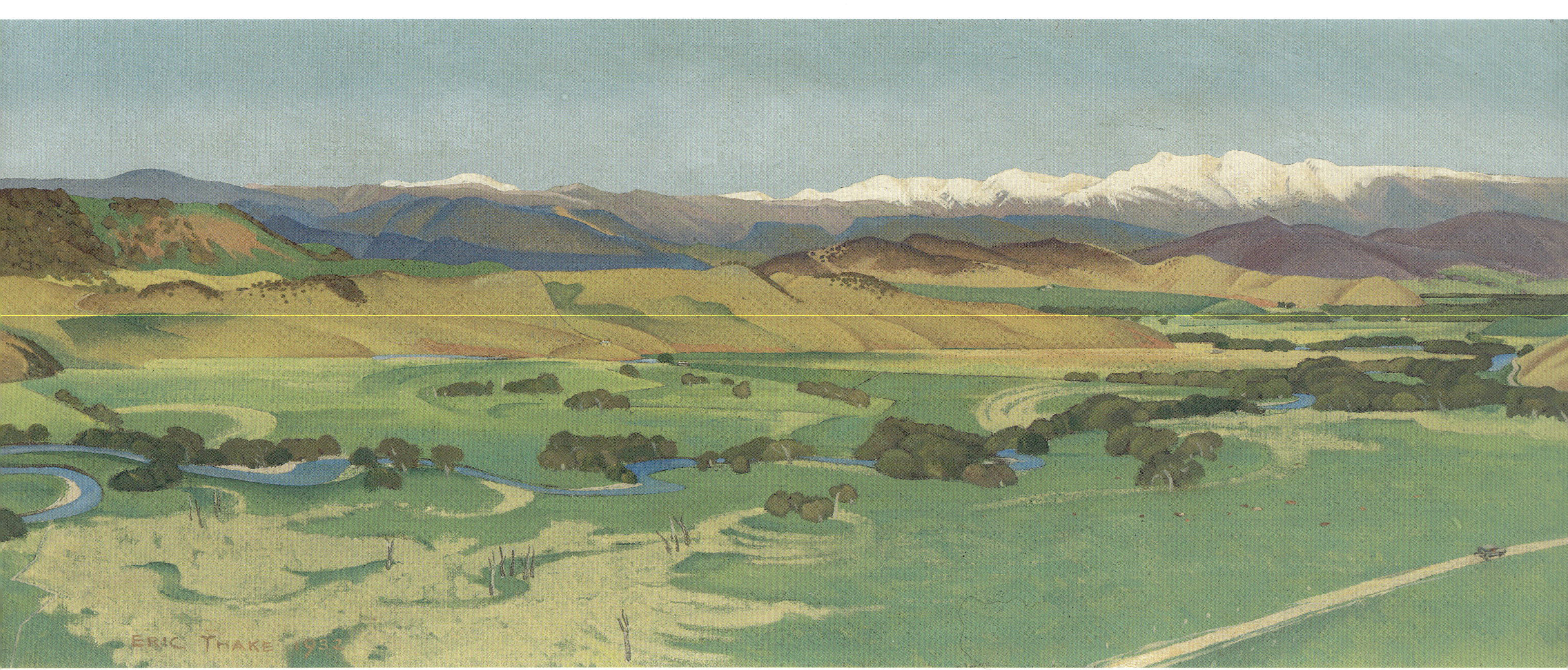

Sam Atyeo (1910–1990)
Norfolk Island pine, Metung 1933
oil on canvas 67.7 x 47.7 cm
Purchased 1973

Sam Atyeo championed the role of modern art in Melbourne. He studied architecture at the Melbourne Technical College and between 1927 and 1932 attended the National Gallery School. Atyeo worked across a variety of media, including furniture and building design, but he believed that painting was the first place to explore new ways of interpreting visual culture.[1]

Norfolk Island pine, Metung depicts a couple having a picnic at the beach under a large native pine tree. Behind the figures the beach stretches out and a headland can be seen on the horizon. The man and woman are John and Sunday Reed – friends of the artist and supporters of modern art in Australia. Atyeo wrote to Sunday in 1933 from Metung (a small coastal town in East Gippsland, about 300 kilometres east of Melbourne) describing the painting and including a small pencil sketch. He noted: 'This is a picture I painted on Saturday of a big pine tree, on a cliff, against the sea, with you and John in the foreground. You are reading and John is looking out to sea.'[2]

This painting reveals Atyeo's interest in the structure and composition of Cézanne's painting and the colour and rhythm of van Gogh's work. The tall Norfolk pine dominates the work. The trunk cuts vertically through the image and the craggy limbs of the tree stretch out at all angles. Atyeo has simplified the forms and re-created the bristly foliage of the tree through dabbing and dynamic brushwork. He placed light and dark tones of colour next to each other, and in some areas left the canvas unmarked. He has angled the brushstrokes to lead the eye through the composition, arching around the beach to the horizon and sky. The overall effect is one of light and volume.

1 Sam Atyeo, excerpt from talks given in 1932, NGA Artist's File.
2 Sam Atyeo, letter to Sunday and John Reed, undated. Reed Papers, LaTrobe Collection, State Library of Victoria, Melbourne.

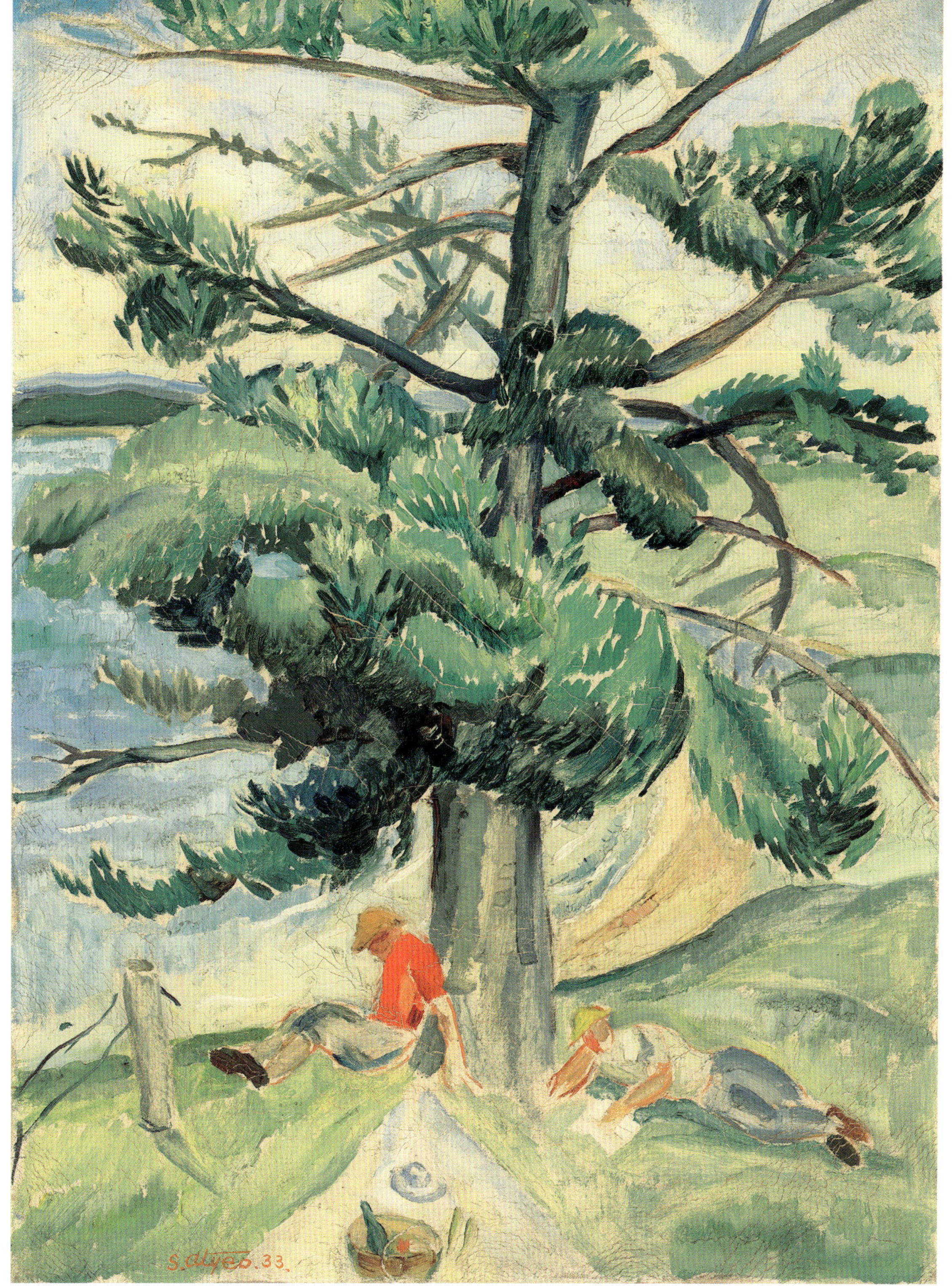

Roland Wakelin (1887–1971)
Barn near Tuggerah 1919
oil on composition board 17.7 x 22.0 cm
Gift of Daniel Thomas 1981

> All will agree that a work of art should possess balance in its design, should be a cosmos, the total of whose parts make a unity. Everyone knows that 5+2+3 equals 10. To the colourists Yellow + Violet + Blue in the right proportions similarly constitute a unity.
> Roland Wakelin 1919[1]

In 1919 Roland Wakelin and Roy de Maistre held a controversial and experimental exhibition *Colour in art* at Gayfield Shaw's Art Salon in Sydney. *Barn near Tuggerah* is possibly one of eleven works included in that exhibition. Wakelin and de Maistre were influenced by the colours of Cézanne, Gauguin and van Gogh. They were also interested in Synchromism, an art theory developed by American artists Morgan Russell and Stanton Macdonald-Wright who believed that colour and tone could be arranged in the same way that a composer arranges notes and chords. De Maistre had developed his own colour-music scale where the spectrum of colours related to the notes of the major and minor musical scales. The colour-music paintings attempted to create a unique visual language based on these principles.

Wakelin visited Tuggerah (a town on the Central Coast north of Sydney) on painting trips where he worked directly from nature. *Barn near Tuggerah* is a carefully composed image of simplified shapes and lyrical colour. Elements within the landscape have been reduced to basic forms and planes and Wakelin has carefully worked the painted surface, applying paint in short thick strokes. Radiating bands of vibrant greens shape the hillside while the trees and sky are carefully defined by soft dabs of turquoise-blue and green. The overall effect suggests a contemplative encounter with the environment.

1 Roland Wakelin, *Colour in art*, Canberra: National Gallery of Australia Research Library, documentary files on Roland Wakelin, 1919, p. 2.

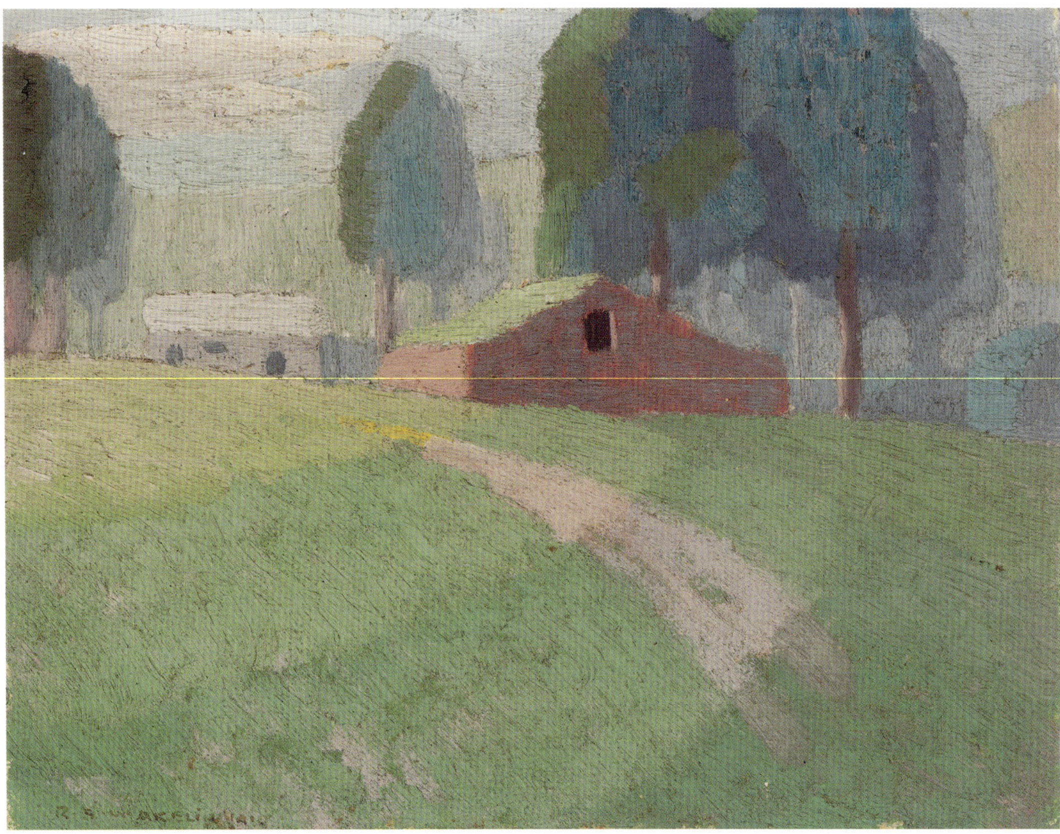

Roy de Maistre (1894–1968)
Forest landscape c. 1920
oil on cardboard 35.4 x 40.6 cm
Purchased 1971

> [Colour] brings the conscious realisation of the deepest underlying principles of nature … it constitutes the very song of life and is, as it were, the spiritual speech of every living thing.
> ROY DE MAISTRE 1919[1]

In *Forest landscape* Roy de Maistre adapted the subject of a felled tree to create a painting concerned with modernist principles of form, rhythm, symmetry and colour. Tree trunks have been reduced to angular planes of colour and the composition is united by vivid greens that portray the forest floor and foliage. De Maistre has explored a range of colour tones, using subtle shifts in greens, reds and browns throughout the painting.

Forest landscape belongs to a period when de Maistre was interested in the broken-colour approach of Cézanne and the relationship between colour and music. De Maistre had studied violin and viola at the Sydney Conservatorium, and art at the Royal Art Society of New South Wales and Julian Ashton Art School. Working with musician Adrian Verbrugghen he developed a colour-music scale where the spectrum of colours related to notes of the major and minor musical scales. The colour-music theory was further underscored by de Maistre's interest in the psychological effects of colour and its relationship to the expression of emotional states.

Historically, the subject of the felled tree in the Australian bush has reflected artistic interests in rural industry, the natural grandeur of Australian forests and, in some instances, an awareness of conservation issues related to loss and destruction. The felled tree and rock formation dominate the foreground of *Forest landscape*. The vitality of colour suggests the cycles of nature and regeneration, and the striking flesh-colours of the wood imply sympathy towards the complex natural environment.

1 Roy de Maistre, in *Colour in art*, exhibition catalogue, The Art Salon, Penzance Chambers, 29 Elizabeth Street, Sydney, 1919.

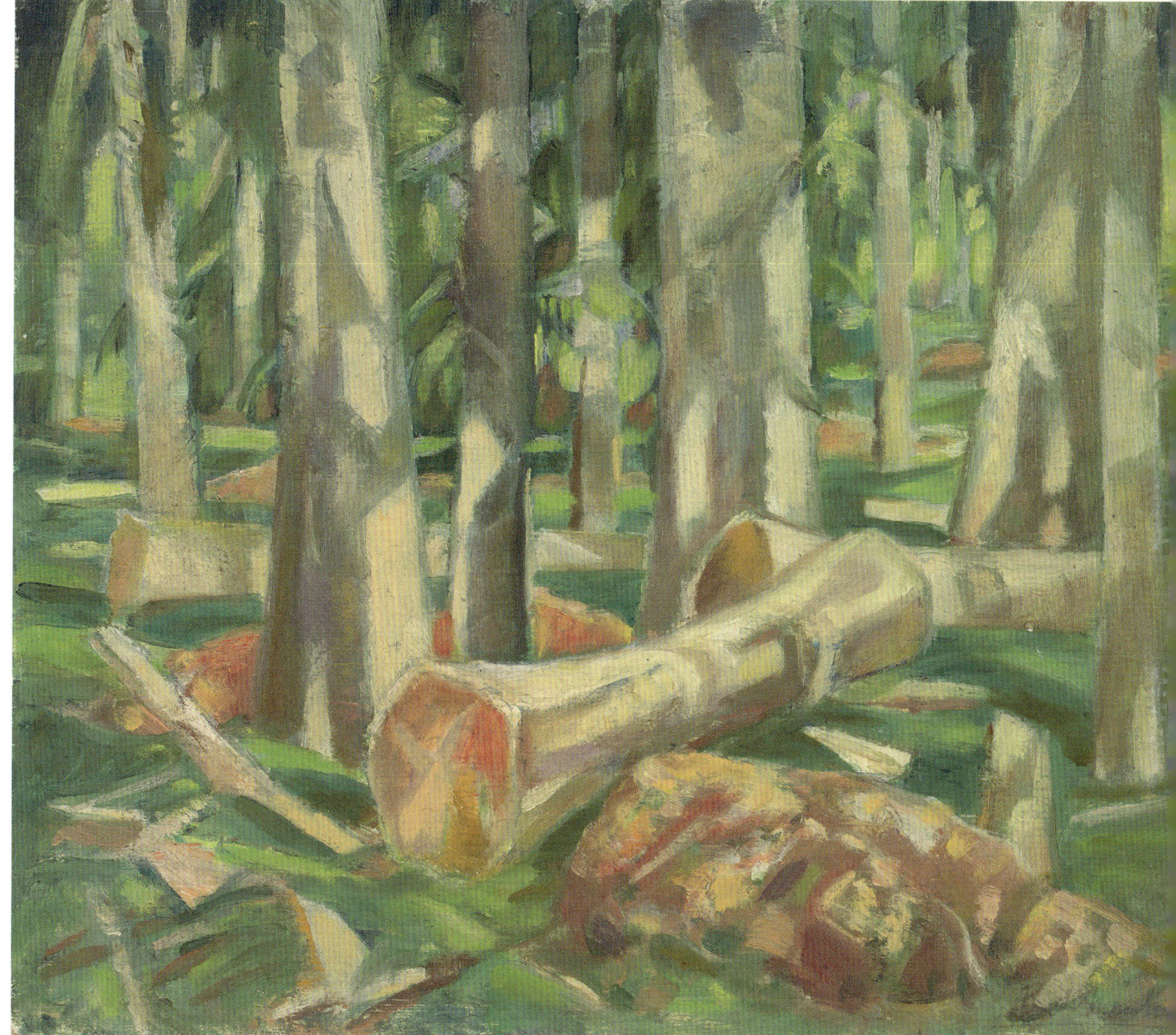

Grace Cossington Smith (1892–1984)
The Bridge in building 1929–30
oil on pulpboard 75.0 x 53.0 cm
Gift of Ellen Waugh 2005

> My chief interest, I think, has always been colour, but not flat crude colour, it must be colour within colour, it has to shine; light must be in it.
> GRACE COSSINGTON SMITH 1965[1]

Grace Cossington Smith's *The Bridge in building* is a dynamic image of one of Australia's most iconic landmarks under construction. One of a number of artists who recorded the development of the Sydney Harbour Bridge, Cossington Smith transformed the scene into a synthesis of industry and nature – of modern construction observed through radiating colour and bands of light. In *The Bridge in building* Cossington Smith has used contrasting colours of purple and orange to depict the angular structures of the bridge and crane. The sky is formed by concentric bands of luminous yellows and blues, with each brushstroke carefully placed on the canvas.

Between 1928 and 1930 Cossington Smith made a number of sketches of the bridge from Milson's Point on the northern side of Sydney Harbour. She created 'map-like' drawings, carefully annotated with notes on colour and form. These studies were used to develop paintings of the bridge, such as *The Bridge in-curve* c. 1930 (National Gallery of Victoria, Melbourne). Cossington Smith delighted in depicting the structure of the bridge, its formal architecture, and the counterbalance of steel and sandstone. In *The Bridge in building* she adopted a low viewpoint, accentuating the dramatic scale of the sandstone pylon and the arch of the bridge. She further emphasised the scale of the structure by including a group of workers on the top of the arch, the small figures appearing almost ant-like in contrast to the bridge's large form.

A truly modern artist, Cossington Smith celebrated the Sydney Harbour Bridge as a work-in-progress, documenting what was for many Sydney residents a symbol of energy and hope during the years of the Great Depression. Indeed, *The Bridge in building* is a celebration of modernity – a modern subject approached in a modern style.

1 Grace Cossington Smith, interview by Hazel de Berg, 16 August 1965, Canberra: National Gallery of Australia, transcript, p. 1484.

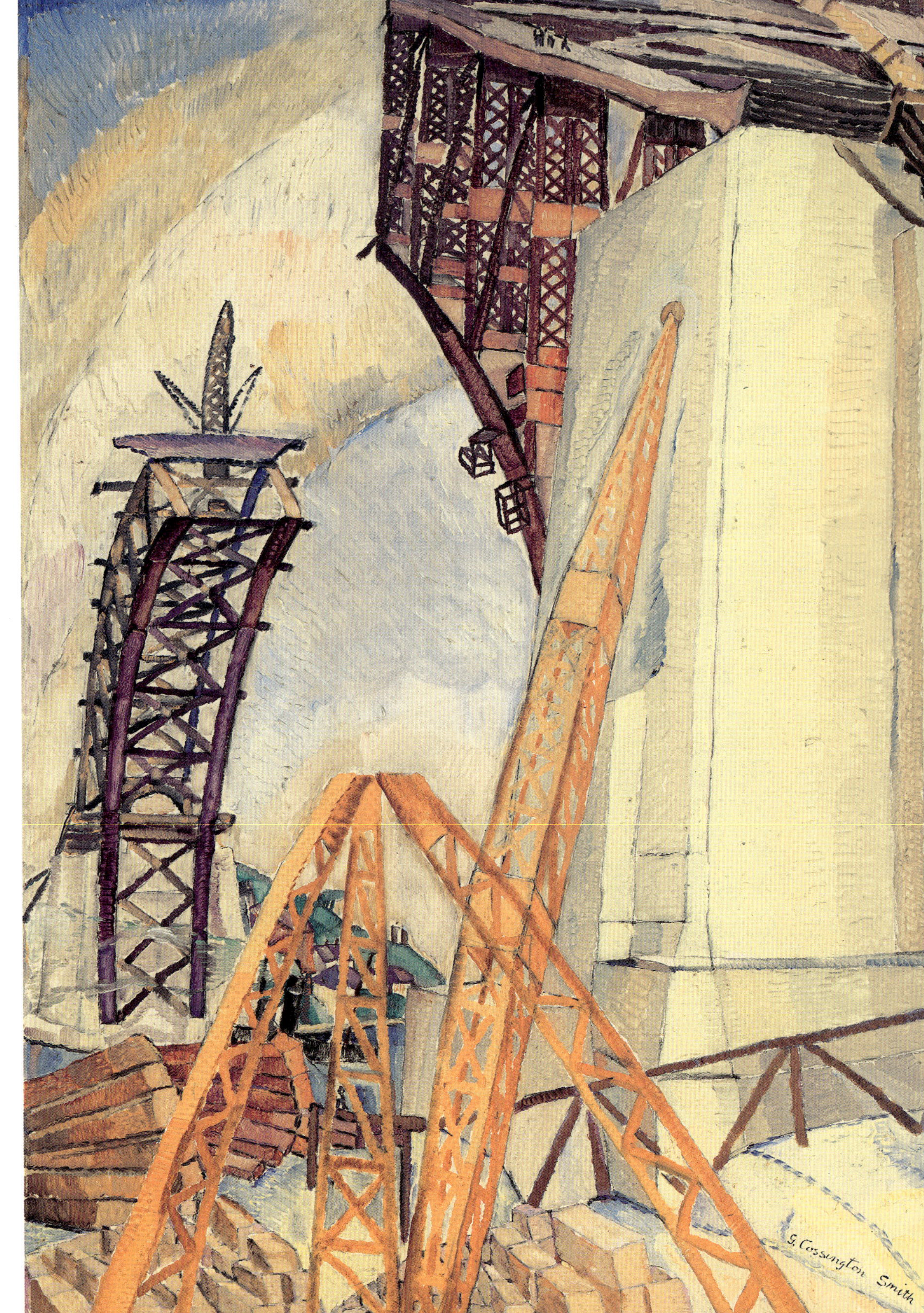

Rah Fizelle (1891–1964)
Elizabeth Bay 1931 or 1932
oil on canvas mounted on composition board 45.0 x 38.0 cm
Purchased 1971

After a period of study and travel in Europe between 1927 and 1931 Rah Fizelle returned to Sydney where he became a teacher and advocate of modernism in Australia. From late 1932 to late 1937, alongside Grace Crowley, he ran the Crowley-Fizelle School at 215a George Street, Sydney. Through their promotion of modern art and, in particular, the principles of Cubism at this school, they influenced a number of artists in Sydney. Their evening sketch club was a meeting place for a small group of artists interested in modernism and abstraction.

Elizabeth Bay is an example of Fizelle's ongoing interest in depicting urban life. The inner-eastern suburbs of Sydney, including Potts Point and Elizabeth Bay, were developed after the First World War and a number of tall apartment buildings were built there. These buildings, many of which are still standing today, helped to shape the urban identity of the area.

Fizelle painted this view looking out from an apartment window, or perhaps from a rooftop. He combined a number of aspects of the scene to create a meticulously balanced composition, emphasising the angular planes of rooftops, awnings and balconies. These angles are counterbalanced by the rounded forms of trees and the distant sweep of Rushcutters Bay. Fizelle simplified nature to basic geometric forms, creating relationships between cubes, spheres and prisms. While the apartments suggest dense urban living, there is an absence of people and activity in the scene which compounds a sense of stillness and silence.

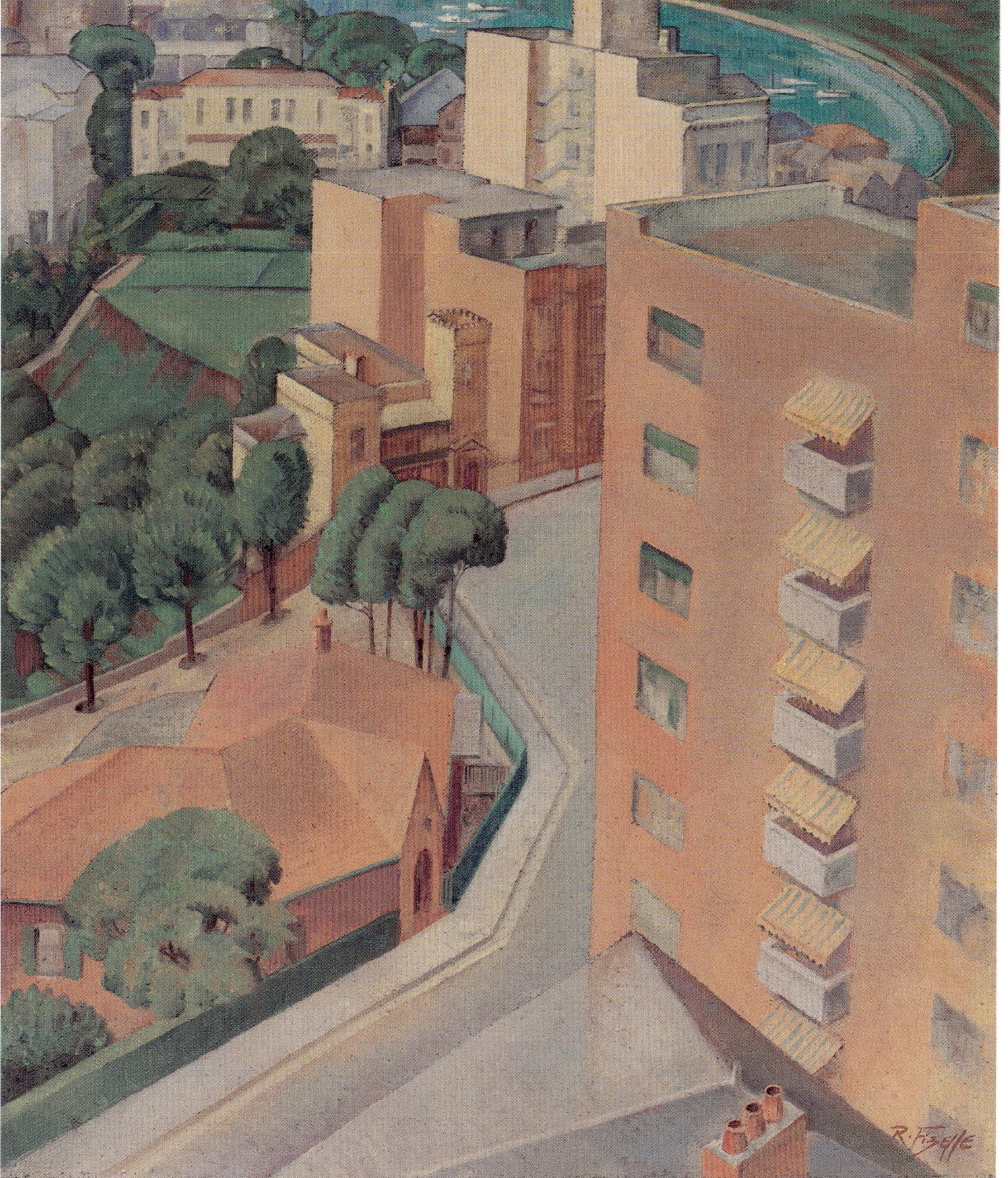

Rah Fizelle (1891–1964)
Pyrmont Power Station from Darling Harbour c. 1935
oil on canvas mounted on composition board 34.7 x 45.8 cm
Purchased 1977

In *Pyrmont Power Station from Darling Harbour* Rah Fizelle has combined his knowledge of French Cubism and dynamic symmetry with his interest in the industrial landscape around Sydney Harbour. After a period of study in Europe, and through his artistic association with Grace Crowley, Fizelle adapted a method of working that emphasised pictorial composition, the simplification of forms into basic geometry and the use of colour to integrate form.

Fizelle has carefully structured the composition in this painting, establishing an ordered relationship between every aspect. Forms have been reduced to basic geometrical elements. The building facades are flattened and the spherical shapes of chimneys and wharf pillars carefully rendered. Dabbing brushstrokes used to depict smoke and sky are repeated in the representation of the luminous body of water. The colours of concrete and faded wood are reflected in the smoggy sky. Colour subtly shifts between background and foreground, creating a sense of compositional harmony and order. Unlike his contemporaries, including Crowley, Fizelle never moved completely into abstraction. He wrote: 'I have always painted more or less in the visual aspect of nature. Landscape and figures have been stylised, and the composition organised with a subjective attitude towards nature.'[1]

1 Rah Fizelle, quoted in *Rah Fizelle*, exhibition catalogue, Sydney: Rex Irwin Art Dealer, 1979, n.p.

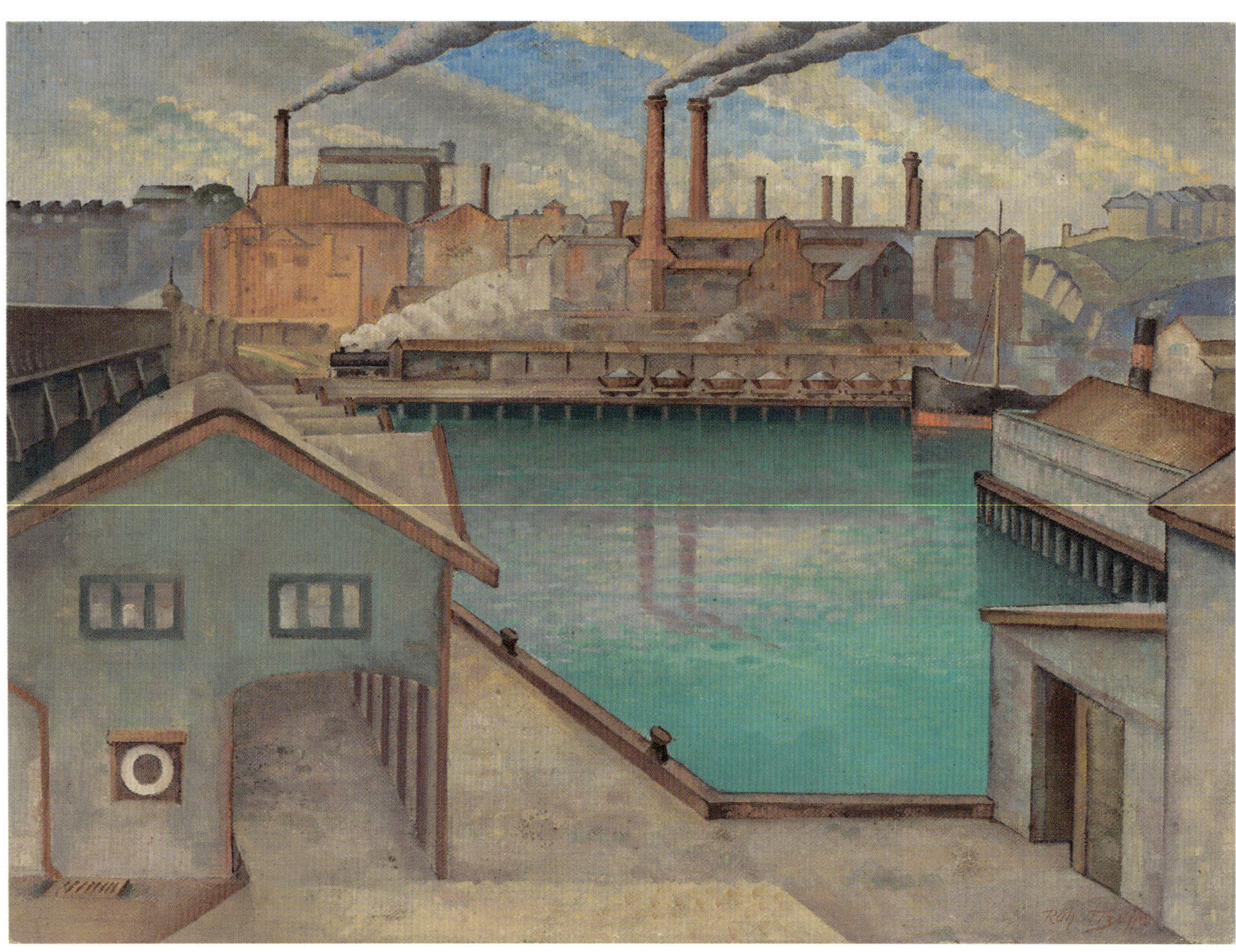

Arthur Boyd (1920–1999)
Landscape with grazing sheep 1937
oil on canvas mounted on composition board 87.1 x 58.9 cm
The Arthur Boyd gift 1975

Throughout his oeuvre Arthur Boyd drew great inspiration from the Australian landscape, developing much of his art in response to particular places. As well as depicting the topographical elements of his environment, Boyd created metaphorical landscapes to locate works that addressed the human condition. Painted when he was seventeen, *Landscape with grazing sheep* displays Boyd's awareness of the 'blue and gold' pastoral paintings of Arthur Streeton and the painterly approach of van Gogh. Paint has been applied thickly – strokes of blue, grey and white forming the sky and dabs of white and light brown conveying a sense of afternoon light across the paddock. At this early stage Boyd was experimenting with a number of styles and techniques, including the thick application of paint with a palette knife.

Landscape with grazing sheep was painted at Rosebud on Victoria's Mornington Peninsula. Boyd had moved to the family cottage at Rosebud in 1936 to live with his grandfather, the painter Arthur Boyd Senior. He stayed at Rosebud for around three years, painting views of the region as well as a number of portraits. The vertical orientation of *Landscape with grazing sheep* is more typical of a portrait painting, while the division of the composition emphasises the great presence of the Australian sky within the landscape. In this quiet and contemplative scene sheep graze on a stretch of dry, grassy land. A grey sky dominates the image and only the rounded forms of sheep and a bail of hay – signs of pastoral settlement – interrupt the horizon.

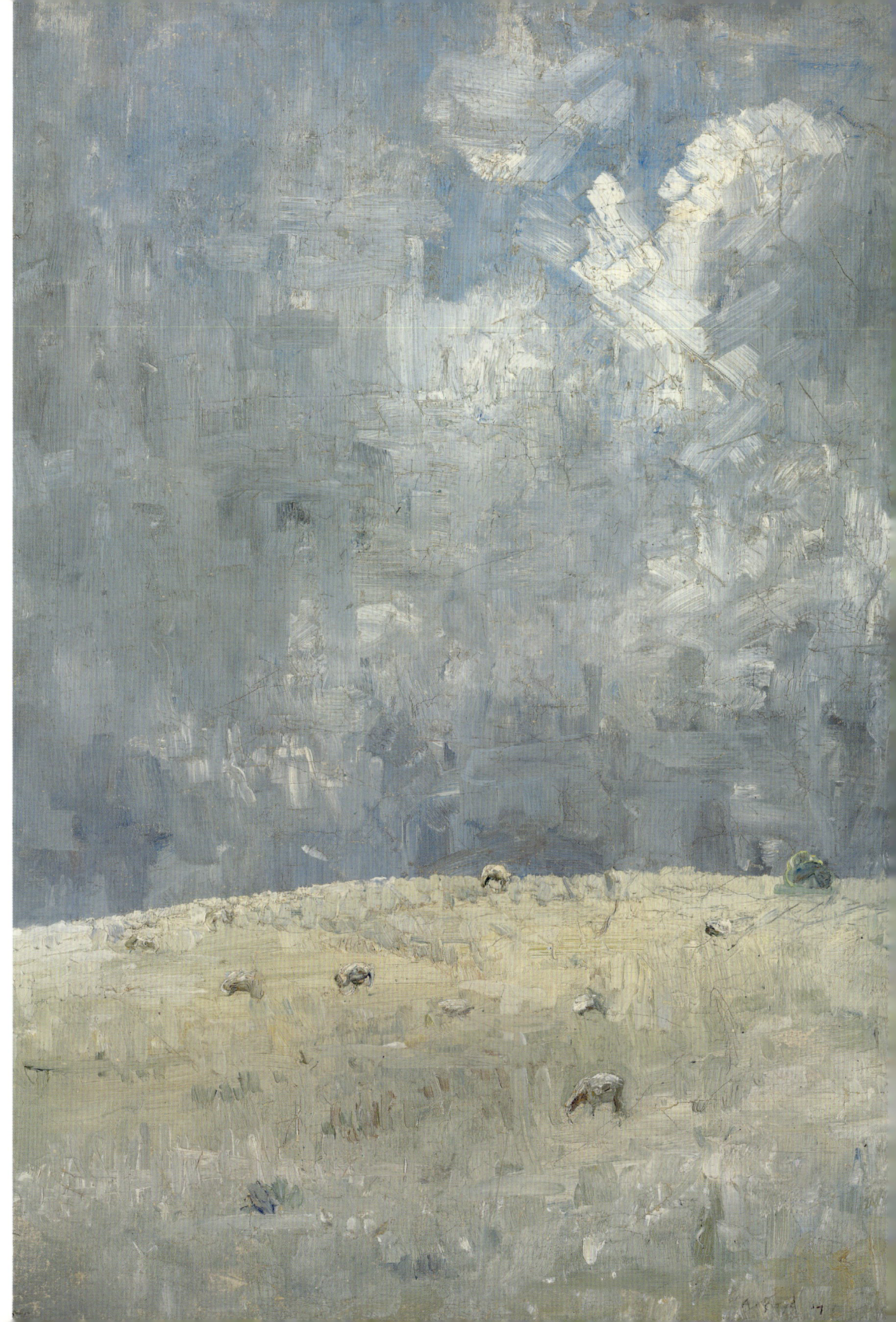

Arthur Boyd (1920–1999)
The hunter I 1944
oil on cotton gauze on cardboard 63.6 x 75.8 cm
The Arthur Boyd gift 1975

Arthur Boyd's paintings during the Second World War reflect the personal turmoil he experienced at the time and his deep opposition to violence. Boyd was conscripted into the army in May 1941 and discharged in March 1944. His paintings from the war years include expressionistic images of human dislocation and suffering; images of crippled, grotesque figures in the streets of St Kilda and South Melbourne. In 1944 he completed a series of dark, dramatic paintings of figures in the Australian bush. The landscapes in these paintings, including *The hunter I,* were inspired by places in Victoria that Boyd had visited while on leave from the army, including the upper reaches of the Yarra, Launching Place, Warburton and Woods Point.[1]

In *The hunter I* Boyd has used private symbols to create an image of personal despair and anxiety. He portrayed the hunter as an exposed and vulnerable figure, naked with closed eyes. As if trapped or lost in the dense, straggly bush the hunter appears to be both part of the landscape and alien within it. Approached by the horned ram (a symbol of lust and corruption in Boyd's work) the hunter attempts to flee, his extended arm a seemingly futile gesture.

1 Barry Pearce, *Arthur Boyd retrospective*, Sydney: Art Gallery of New South Wales, 1993, p. 16.

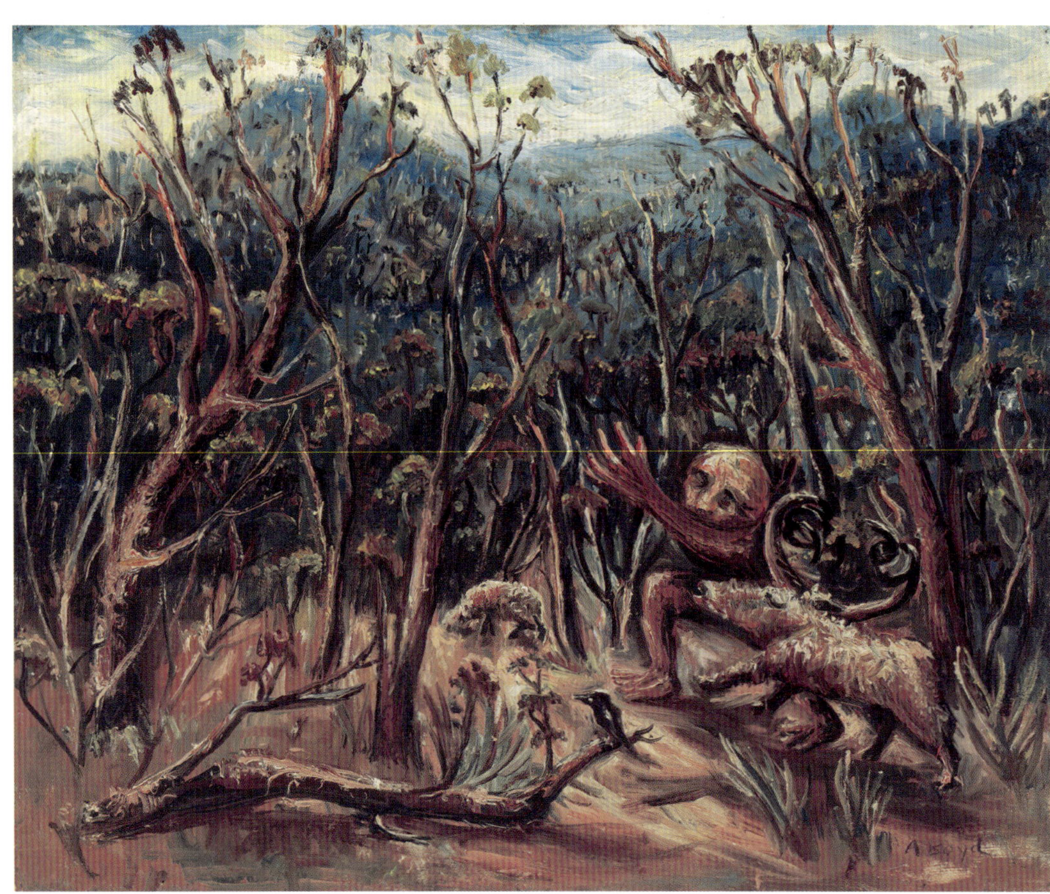

Arthur Boyd (1920–1999)
Boat builders, Eden 1948
oil and egg tempera on composition board 85.6 x 101.7 cm
Purchased 1977

In *Boat builders, Eden* Arthur Boyd depicts activities within the landscape of Eden, a coastal New South Wales town, close to the Victorian border. Eden is known for its forestry and fishing industries, as well as for its beautiful natural landscape. Framed by a bush setting, the boat builders in this image construct their vessel. Boyd has included a number of boathouses and workshops in the painting, as well as the fishing wharf of Eden's Twofold Bay. In the distance are Lookout Point Lighthouse and the distinctive profile of Mount Imlay.

Boat builders, Eden is one of a number of postwar paintings by Boyd likely to have been made at Open Country, the Boyd's family home at Murrumbeena on the eastern outskirts of Melbourne. Elements in the work are inspired by the sixteenth-century Flemish painter Pieter Bruegel. Boyd had seen reproductions of Bruegel's biblical paintings, such as *The gloomy day* 1565 and *Tower of Babel* 1563, in the State Library of Victoria in Melbourne and was interested in Bruegel's depiction of historical subjects and stories within a contemporary landscape. The subject of *Boat builders, Eden* is a reminder of the Old Testament story of Noah's Ark, where Noah's virtuous behaviour saved himself and his family from a great flood. Boyd's image is also a response to the rebuilding of lives and lands that took place following the devastation of the Second World War.

In contrast to the painterly approach of *Landscape with grazing sheep* 1937 or the thick and expressive application of paint in *The hunter I* 1944, Boyd used the more refined paint medium of egg tempera in this work. The semi-transparent pigments have been carefully layered over each other to create a fine, shimmering surface.

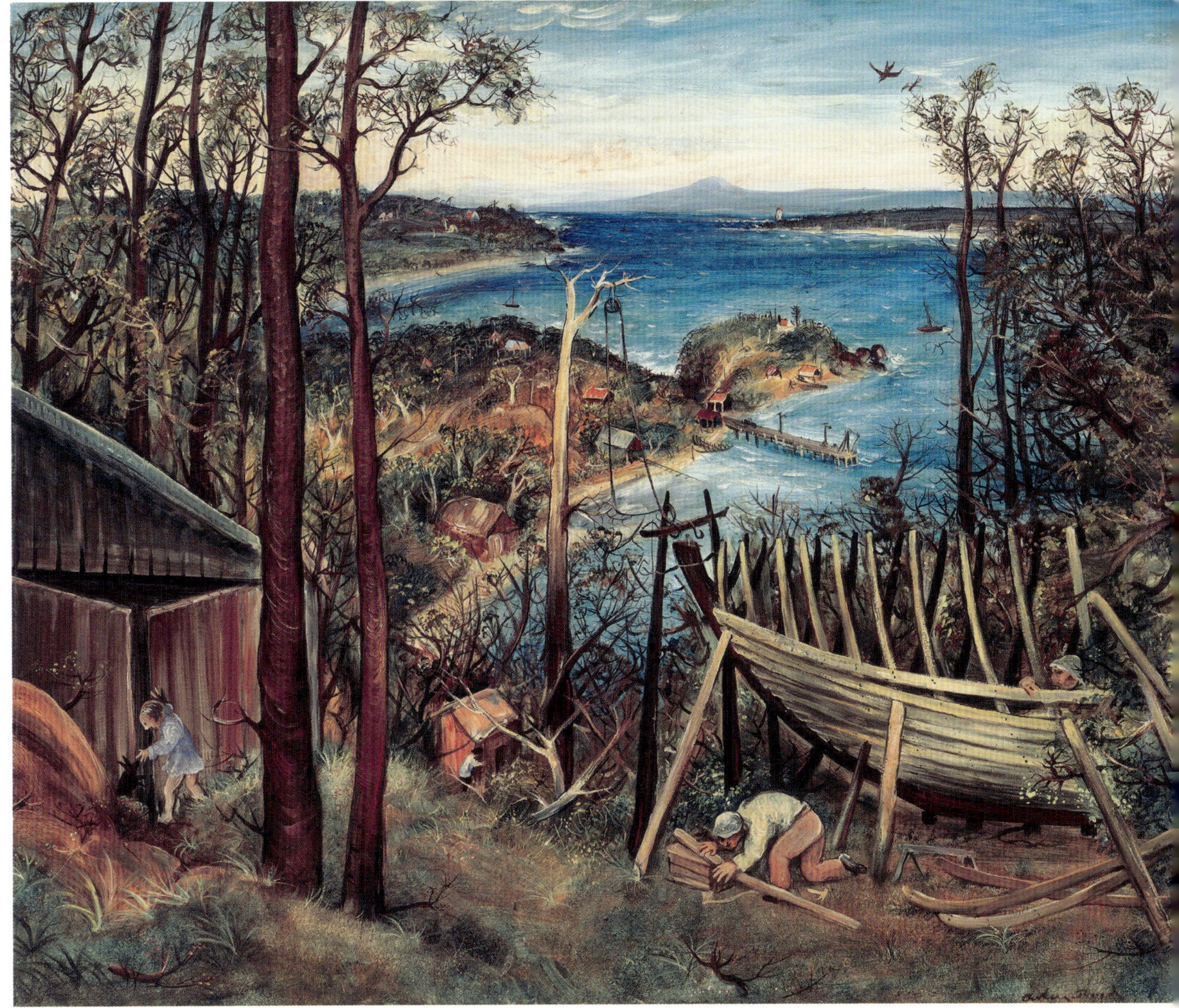

Margaret Preston (1875–1963)
Flying over the Shoalhaven River 1942
oil on canvas 50.6 x 50.6 cm
Purchased 1973

Margaret Preston was used to seeing the earth from the air. By 1942 the artist had visited Europe and North America, and had travelled extensively throughout much of Asia, the Pacific Islands, Central and South America and Australia. During her travels she visited many places and sought out the Indigenous art of other cultures, yet it was the Indigenous art of Australia that inspired her most. Preston travelled extensively throughout remote areas of Australia to see Indigenous paintings and carvings. She studied the collections at the Australian Museum in Sydney and published articles and lectured on Indigenous art.

From 1932 to 1939 Preston lived in the bush at Berowra, close to Ku-ring-gai Chase National Park north of Sydney, where her great passion for the natural environment of Australia was reinforced. During the Second World War, Preston, like many others, developed a strong nationalist sentiment and in 1942 published an article titled 'The orientation of art in the post-war Pacific'. In this article she argued for the development of a 'National Australian Culture' through an exchange of ideas between Indigenous and non-Indigenous artists. She also suggested that Australians should actively exchange ideas with their Asian neighbours.

In *Flying over the Shoalhaven River* Preston combined her knowledge of Indigenous Australian, Asian and western art with a modernist aesthetic. The linear quality of the composition and the flattened areas of colour reflect her skills in woodblock printmaking. Using an earthy palette of browns, greys and ochres, Preston suggested the bush with dabs and dots of paint. She mirrored the overcast sky in the silvery stretch of river and depicted a number of low-lying clouds casting shadows on the earth. While the aerial perspective displays Preston's knowledge of Indigenous Australian and Chinese methods of representing the land from above, the experience of flying over the Shoalhaven River was her own.

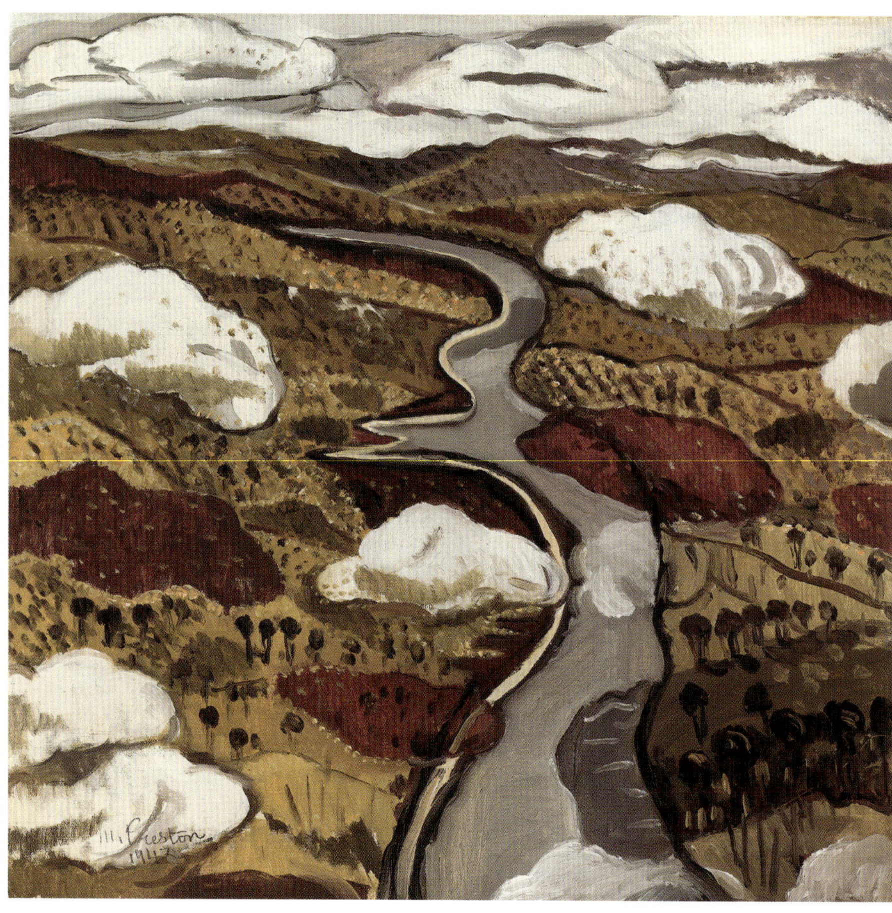

Lloyd Rees (1895–1988)
A South Coast road 1951
oil on canvas 65.7 x 101.5 cm
Purchased 1977

> [*A South Coast road*] is a very important picture in relation to that period. And because I was always fascinated by this road winding around the forms of the hill. And one day I suddenly saw my subject, you know. And I was able to get a space off the motor track and paint that on the spot.
> Lloyd Rees 1978[1]

A South Coast road was painted close to Gerringong on the South Coast of New South Wales. The view is looking north towards Kiama Head. Lloyd Rees painted the work while on a summer holiday with his family at nearby Werri Beach.[2] He first visited the region in 1940 and over the years spent a considerable amount of time in the area, making a number of paintings of the lush landscape around Berry and Kiama. In *A South Coast road* Rees has created a visual journey from the crossroad in the foreground, up and over the hills and towards the town of Kiama. The turns in the road are cut out of the picture plane, emphasising the curves and dips of the scene. The rhythmical lines accentuate the undulating hills and natural contours of the region.

Throughout his long career Rees sought to depict the beauty and light of the Australian landscape. He referred to this as 'chasing nature' – the attempt to capture through painting, drawing or printmaking the elements of colour, form and atmosphere that make a scene inspiring. The lush green colours of the South Coast have been altered by Rees, who said that 'realistically you looked out and in a colour sense it was often too green for me. So sometimes I'd absolutely bring the warmth into it … But then finally I found that colour in my later works becomes a very personal thing. I use the colour that comes happily, you know.'[3]

1 Lloyd Rees, interview by James Gleeson, 18 August 1978, Canberra: National Gallery of Australia Research Library, transcript, p. 26.
2 Anne Gray, 'Lloyd Rees: *A South Coast road*', in Anne Gray (ed.), *Australian art in the National Gallery of Australia*, Canberra: National Gallery of Australia, 2002, p. 216.
3 Lloyd Rees, interview by James Gleeson, transcript, p. 26.

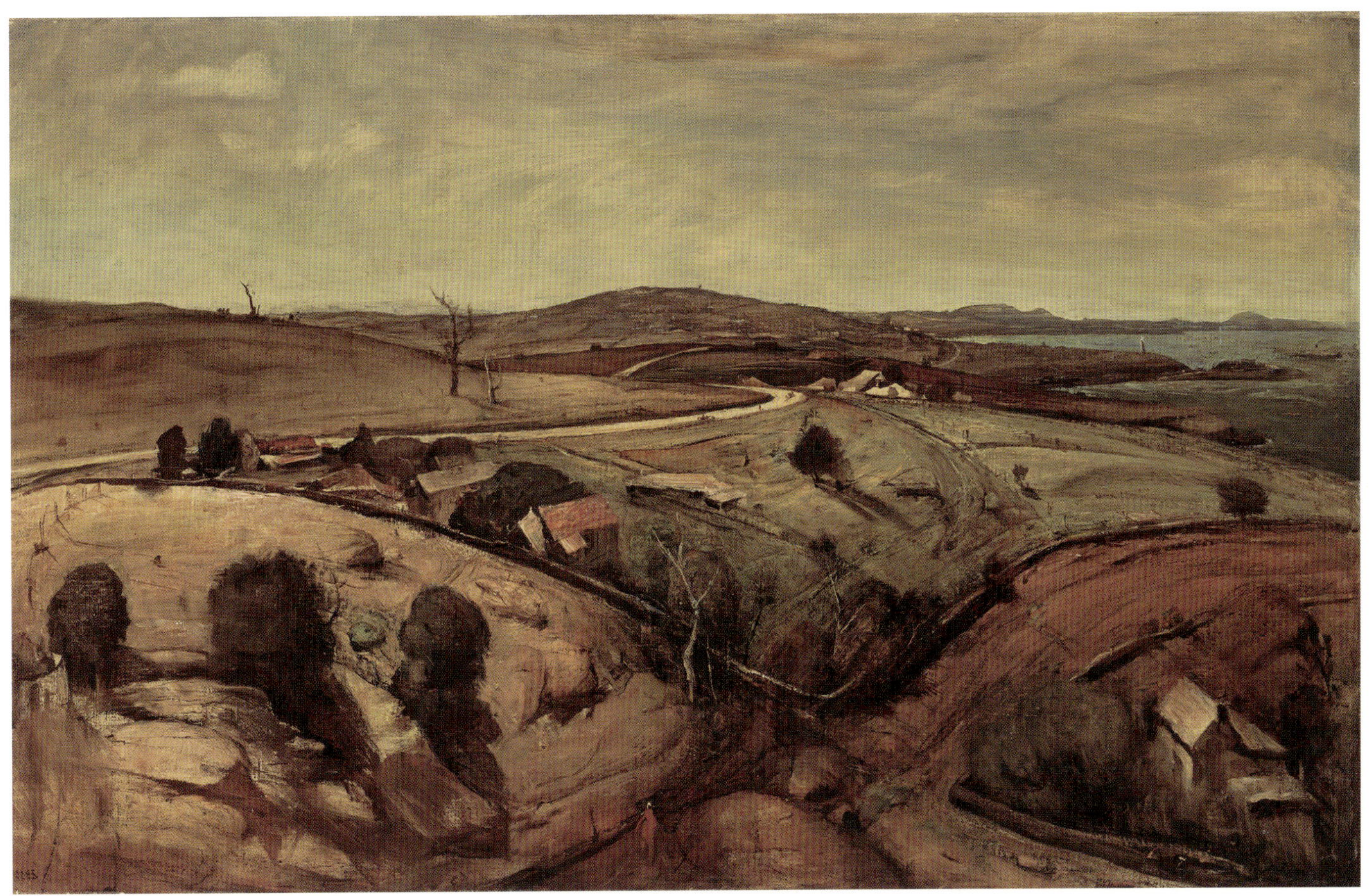

Russell Drysdale (1912–1981)
Golden Gully 1949
oil and ink on canvas mounted on composition board
66.0 x 101.4 cm
Purchased 1976

> Hill End with cultivated and intelligent detachment achieves its real and significant beauty to an artist, its sense of history, its charm, of form and dignity, its life of contrast that its roots in the past give it in this day and age.
> Russell Drysdale 1948[1]

In *Golden Gully* Russell Drysdale created a painting that combines elements of history, observation and imagination. The work was inspired by Drysdale's visits to the abandoned gold-rush town of Hill End in the Bathurst region of New South Wales. He first visited Hill End with his friend, the artist Donald Friend, in 1947. They were attracted to the history of the town and its isolation. Shortly after their first visit Friend purchased a cottage in Hill End, which became an important gathering place for a small group of Australian artists.

At the height of the gold rush in 1872 Hill End was the largest inland settlement in the colony of New South Wales and had a diverse population of more than 30 000 people. By the end of 1874 the land had been exhaustively mined and Hill End was abandoned and largely forgotten.[2] When Drysdale visited the area he found a landscape rich in subject matter and made a number of sketches, paintings and photographs. In *Golden Gully* he explores the relationship between the town and the environment. He depicts the layers of earth like a skin that has been peeled back to expose an inner structure. The eroded gully frames the view of a cross-section of the earth, leading to the entrance to two underground mines. Above this a thin crust separates the gully and the town, suggesting a fragile balance between human settlement and the environment.

1 Russell Drysdale, writing to Donald Friend, April 1948, quoted in Gavin Wilson, *The artists of Hill End: art, life & landscape*, Sydney: Art Gallery of New South Wales, 1995, p. 69.
2 Wilson, pp. 15–16.

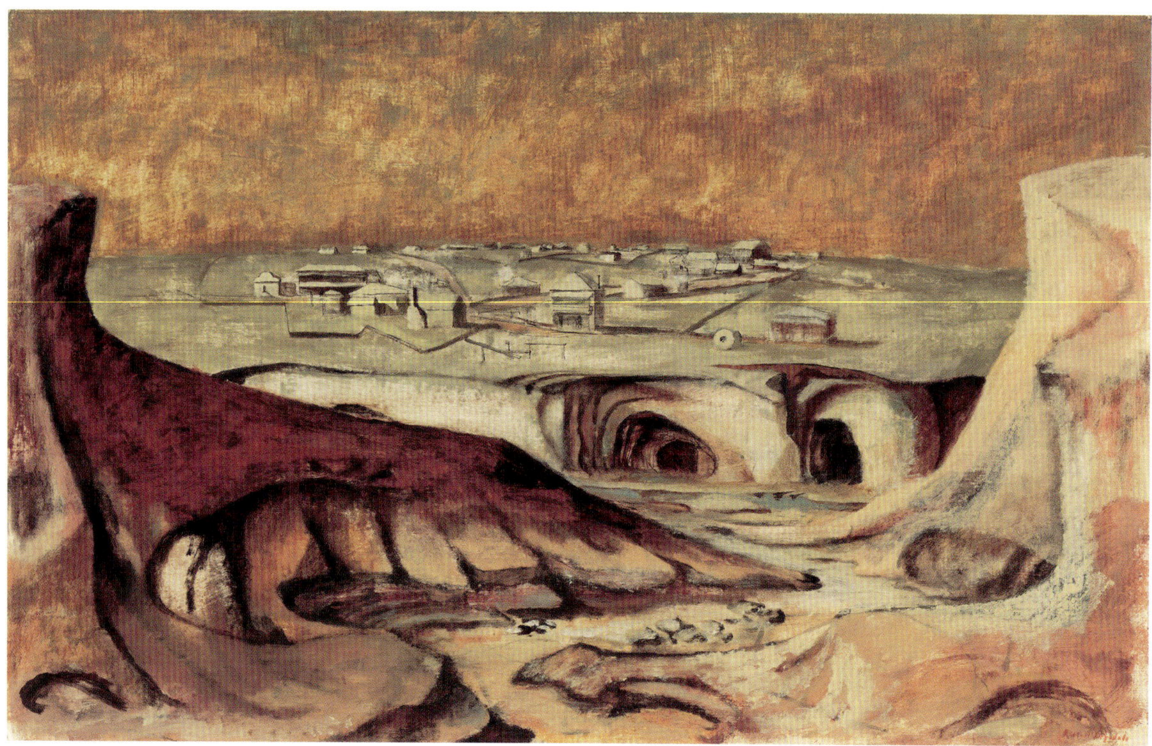

Russell Drysdale (1912–1981)
Emus in a landscape 1950
oil on canvas 101.6 x 127.0 cm
Purchased 1970

> … it is continually exciting, these curious and strange rhythms which one discovers in a vast landscape, the juxtaposition of figures, of objects, all these things are exciting. Add to that again the peculiarity of the particular land in which we live here, and you get a quality of strangeness that you do not find, I think, anywhere else.
> RUSSELL DRYSDALE 1960[1]

In 1944 Russell Drysdale was commissioned by the *Sydney Morning Herald* to accompany journalist Keith Newman to western New South Wales to document the effects of the drought. This experience significantly changed the way Drysdale looked at the Australian landscape. The photographs and sketches he made on the trip informed much of his work in the following years.

In *Emus in a landscape* Drysdale has explored the strange and surreal qualities of the Australian outback. The native birds move quietly through the landscape, passing a precariously arranged structure of wood and corrugated iron. This sculptured mass of refuse represents the remains of a previous settlement. It could be an abandoned dwelling or a wrecked ship on a dried inland sea. In *Emus in a landscape* Drysdale has created a sliding space between reality and imagination, fact and myth, and has captured the vast space and timelessness of the Outback.

1 Russell Drysdale, interview by Hazel de Berg, 1960, Canberra: National Library of Australia [deB 27].

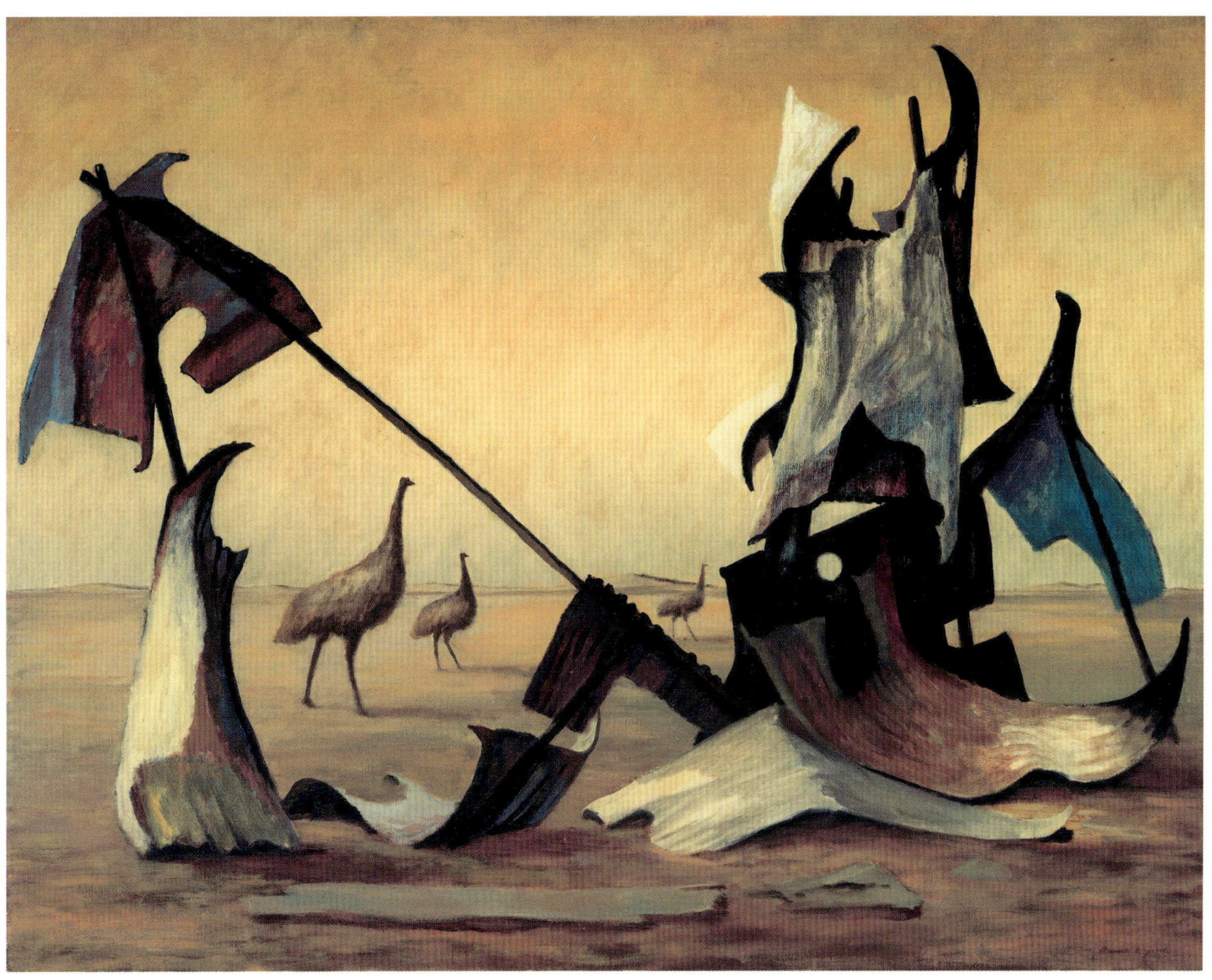

Russell Drysdale (1912–1981)
Boy running, Cooktown c. 1952
oil on canvas 51.0 x 77.0 cm
Purchased 1959

In 1951 Russell Drysdale spent a number of months travelling throughout northern Queensland and the Cape York Peninsula. In response to this trip he painted *Boy running, Cooktown.* This painting combines a number of characteristic Drysdale motifs: a long street leading to a vanishing point on the horizon, a building with veranda in profile and a dramatic sky balanced by a vast foreground.

There is an inherent drama in this image of a young Indigenous boy running across the street, his action rupturing the stillness of the picture. Drysdale depicts the boy in dynamic movement, yet he seems suspended in time and space. His activity in the isolated street begs the question: where is he running?

In his paintings of Australia's remote towns and settlements Drysdale conveyed a sense of life lived in connection with the land. He explored the spatial, environmental and personal elements that contribute to our experience of place. As in so many of Australia's remote country towns, the main street in this painting includes the iconic structure of a war memorial. In contrast to the youthful potential of the boy, the memorial is a reminder of history and the loss of many young Australians in wartime.

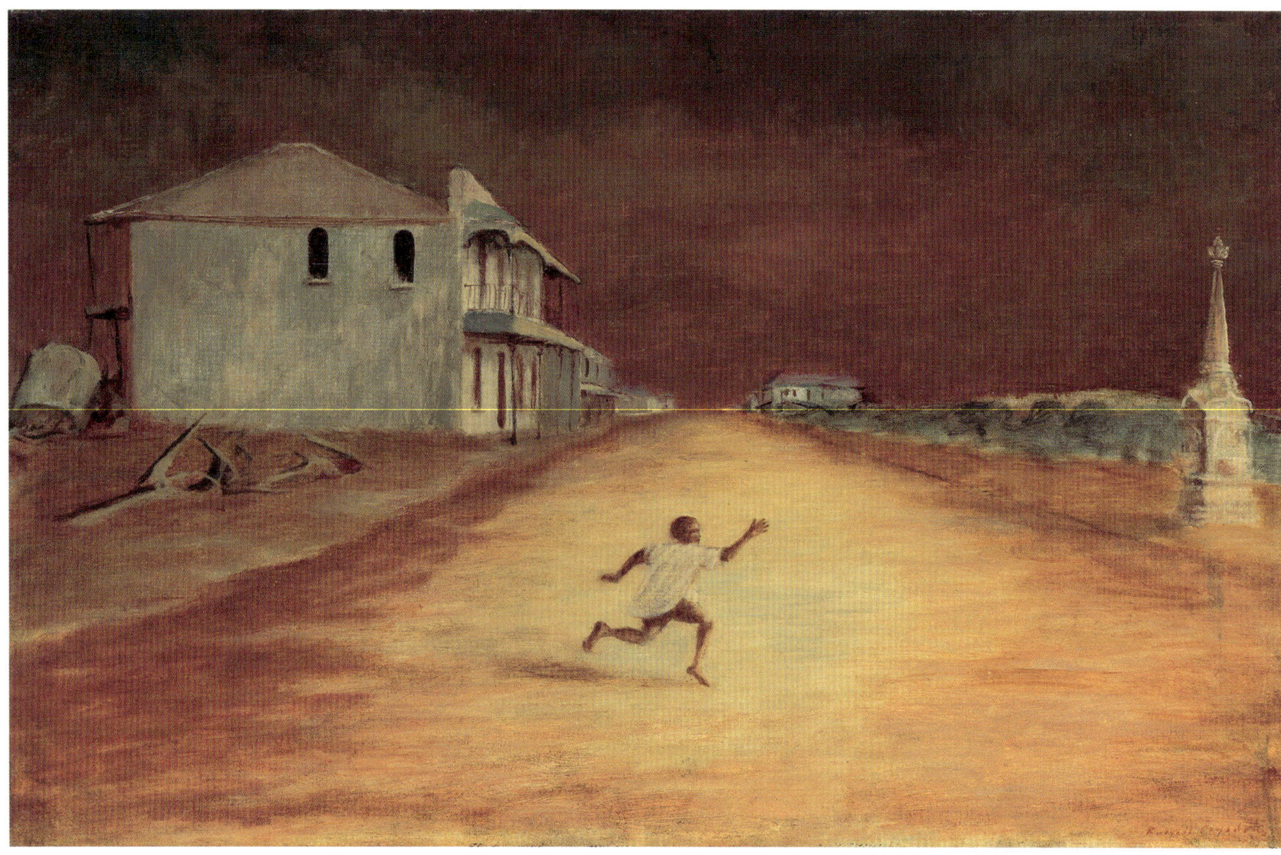

Sidney Nolan (1917–1992)
Ku-ring-gai Chase 1948
synthetic polymer paint on composition board 91.0 x 102.0 cm
Purchased 1976

In late 1947, following a number of months travelling throughout Queensland, Sidney Nolan settled in Sydney. In March 1948 he married Cynthia Hansen (née Reed), a writer and the sister of his patron John Reed. The marriage between Nolan and Cynthia caused a painful rift with John and his wife Sunday and, after an unsuccessful visit from the newlyweds in March 1948, Nolan would never see his first and most important patrons again. The Nolans settled in Wahroonga, a leafy suburb in the municipality of Ku-ring-gai about 20 kilometres north of Sydney on the edge of the Ku-ring-gai Chase National Park.

Ku-ring-gai Chase is a startling image of a hazy, smouldering bushfire. There had been an early start to the summer season of bushfires in 1947, the *Sydney Morning Herald* reporting in late October that:

> … last summer's late rains brought out a bountiful growth of tussock and grass as well as a record season of wildflowers. An almost continuous run of westerly winds to date has dried out the forest to a condition like tinder. It requires only a spark to start a fire, and with the prevailing winds behind it a small blaze would soon become an inferno.[1]

Nolan's skilful handling of paint, swift brushwork and freshness of colour conveys the ferocity of this scene: the heat and dust of the wind, the crackling of leaves and grasses and the smell of burning bush. There is a heightened tension in the picture; uneasiness as to whether the fire is receding or approaching, a knowledge that with a change in conditions the situation could rapidly alter. In *Ku-ring-gai Chase* the advantages of living in rural suburbia seem reversed as the threat of danger encroaches.

An inscription on the back of the work suggests that Nolan gave the painting to Cynthia as a gift on 22 May 1948. A message in pencil (visible only with infrared screening) reads 'Cynthia XXX Sidney'. In this powerful painting it is possible that Nolan is also exploring his personal reaction to events taking place in his own life, the fire serving as a metaphor for notions of passion, destruction and new beginnings.

1 'Danger of forest fires', *Sydney Morning Herald*, 27 October 1947, p. 2.

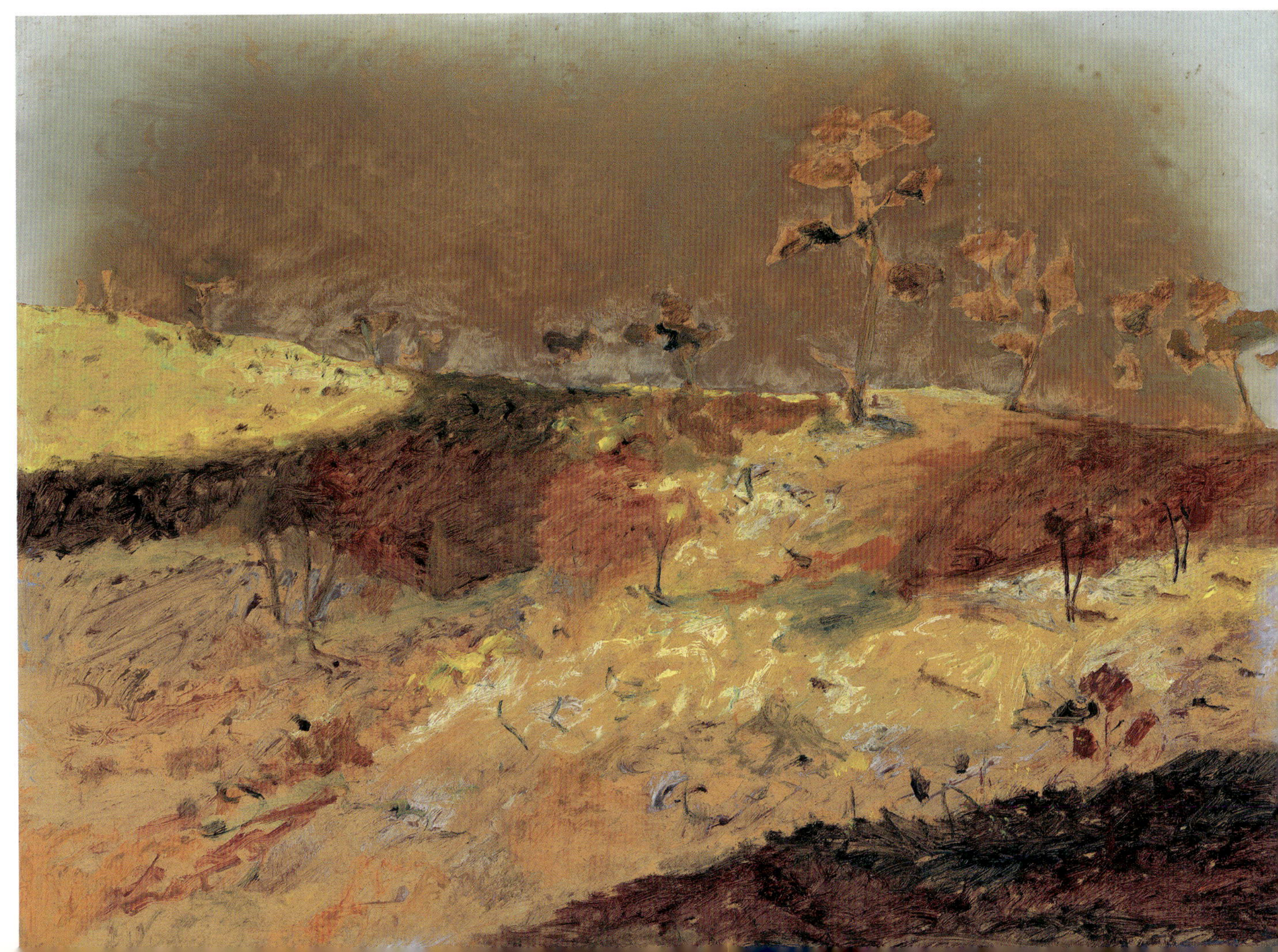

Sidney Nolan (1917–1992)
Inland Australia 1950
oil and enamel paint on composition board
91.5 x 121.0 cm
Purchased 1961

> We leaned over in our seats and straining down, our foreheads pressed against the glass windows, found our own land and heard its voice alone.
> CYNTHIA NOLAN 1962[1]

Between 1947 and 1950 Sidney Nolan spent months travelling through remote areas of Australia. Using money he had made from a successful exhibition of Queensland Outback paintings held at the David Jones Gallery in Sydney in March 1949, Nolan, accompanied by his wife Cynthia and stepdaughter Jinx, travelled through Central Australia, the Northern Territory, Western Australia and South Australia. This trip, from June to September 1949, inspired a body of work, including a series of paintings that depict inland Australia from an aerial perspective.

Inland Australia is an extraordinary image of the heart of the continent, possibly of the Durack Range. The undulating shapes and intense colour of the red earth evoke an 'otherworldly' sensation – a feeling of the land's inherent grandeur, timelessness and mystery. Nolan painted the work quickly, with the composition board lying flat on a table. Using sweeping brushstrokes he has pushed the paint around the surface of the work. In some areas the paint has been wiped back, exposing the white undercoat of the composition board.

Nolan won the inaugural Dunlop Australian Art prize of £250 for *Inland Australia*.[2] He described the work as 'a composite impression of the country from the air'.[3] Using photographs he took from the plane as a visual aid, *Inland Australia* is an example of Nolan's technique of fusing elements from existing locations with a landscape remembered from experience.

1 Cynthia Nolan, *Outback*, London: Shenval Press, 1962, p. 206.
2 Arnold Shore, 'Dunlop prize won by Sidney Nolan', *The Argus*, Tuesday 6 June 1950, p. 7.
3 'Sydney artist wins big prize with landscape', *Sydney Morning Herald*, Tuesday 6 June 1950, p. 1.

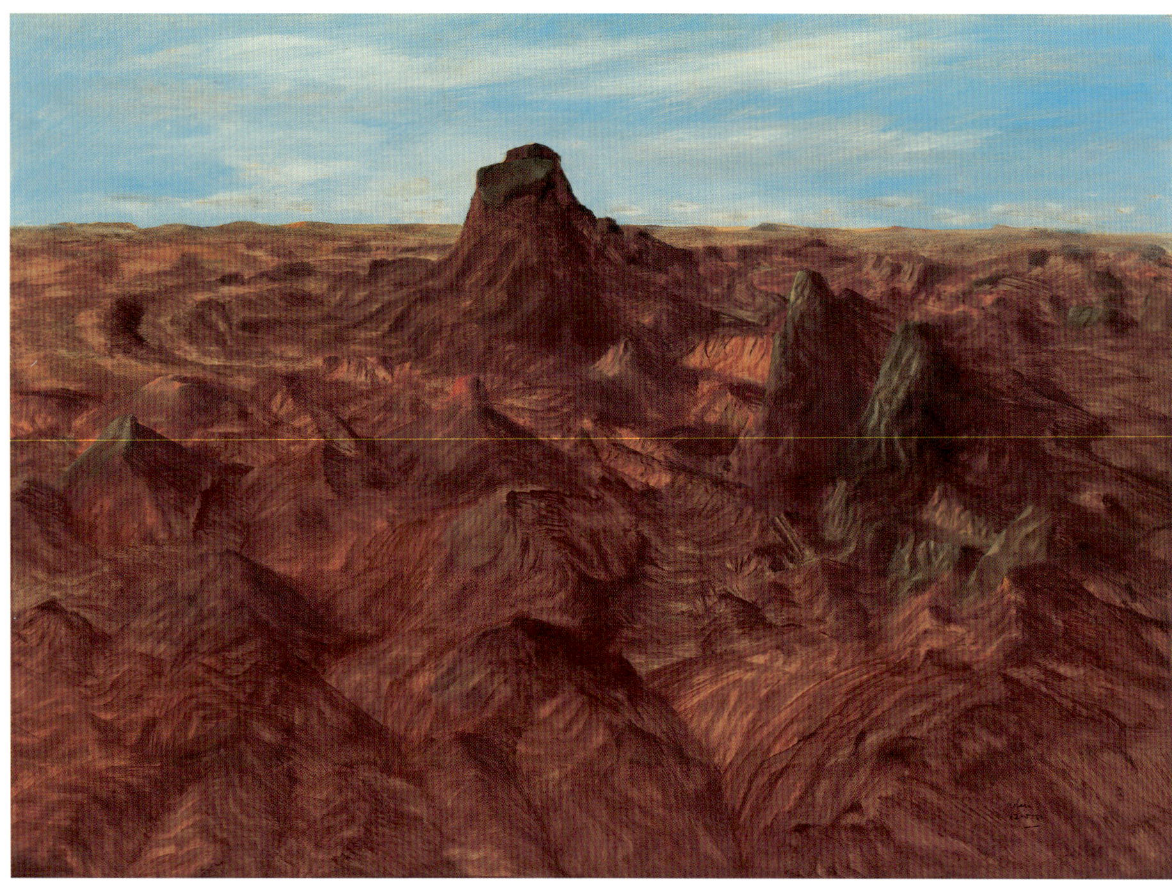

Sidney Nolan (1917–1992)
Burke at Cooper's Creek 1950
oil and enamel paint on composition board
121.5 x 152.0 cm
A gift to the people of Australia by Mr and Mrs Benno Schmidt of New York City and Esperance, Western Australia through the American Friends of the Australian National Gallery 1987

Fuelled by a keen interest in travel, Nolan's personal experiences of the land are closely linked to the development of mythology within his work. The Burke and Wills paintings from 1949–50 emerged after a journey to Central Australia in 1949. Robert O'Hara Burke and William John Wills were explorers who died in an attempt to make the first organised crossing of Australia from south to north in 1860–61.

In *Burke at Cooper's Creek* the ghostly appearance of the ill-fated Burke compounds the notions of isolation, displacement and tragedy relating to the expedition. On leaving the Cooper's Creek depot on 16 December 1860, Burke told his party that if he had not returned within three months he could be considered perished. Four months later he returned to the empty site, only nine hours after the rest of the party had departed. He died from exhaustion, south of the camp.[1] Writing about the series some years later, Nolan said that:

> … wanting to paint Burke and Wills really comes from a need to freshen history and to make these remote happenings really belong to us now … There seem to be three elements in the paintings: the actuality of the landscape, which for Australians is intensified to the point of a dream; the strange conjunction of a man on a camel, from which he surveys the landscape as if he were walking on giant stilts; and always the birds, which make everything vivid … I doubt that I will ever forget my emotions when first flying over Central Australia and realising how much we painters and poets owe to our predecessors the explorers, with their frail bodies and superb willpower.[2]

1 Felicity Johnston, 'Sidney Nolan', in Anne Gray (ed.), *The way we were 1940–1950s from the University of Western Australia Art Collection*, Perth: Lawrence Wilson Art Gallery, 1997 p. 24.

2 Sidney Nolan, letter to Geoffrey Dutton, London, 28 April 1967, Cynthia Nolan Papers. See Geoffrey Smith, *Sidney Nolan: desert and drought*, Melbourne: National Gallery of Victoria, 2003, p. 66.

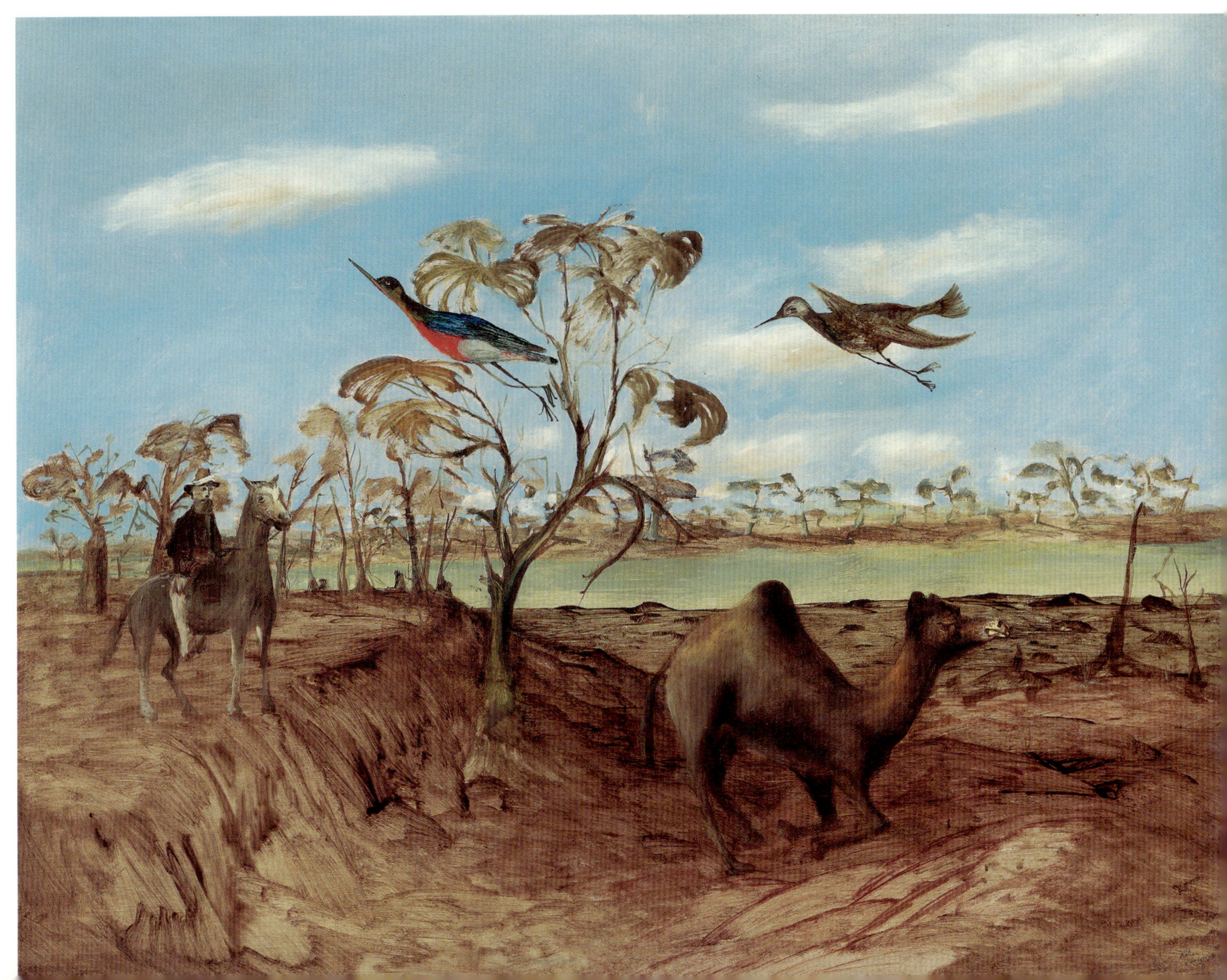

Albert Tucker (1914–1999)
Sunbathers 1944
oil on cardboard 59.2 x 86.0 cm
Purchased 1981

In *Sunbathers* Albert Tucker projected his feelings of unease and anxiety during the Second World War onto his local landscape, Melbourne's St Kilda beach. The ideas of recreation and play associated with the beach are replaced in this work by Tucker's protoplasmic forms of swollen, blistered flesh. He painted *Sunbathers* during a period when 'everything seemed to be seething with ideas and energy and experience'.[1] In his painterly approach Tucker revealed his knowledge of German Expressionism, Surrealism and Picasso which he adapted to express his personal feelings.

In *Sunbathers* two figures appear as discarded lumps of flesh occupying the beach at night. Tucker reduced the human body to a bulbous landscape of headless, conical limbs. The skin appears to glow from within and the figures cast shadows in opposite directions. In this surreal landscape Tucker has reduced the beach into the basic elements of sand, sea and sky – all of which are depicted using heightened, symbolic colour. The dark band of sky evokes the tense evening 'black-outs' Melbourne experienced during the war.

Tucker was interested in the night-time activities of the city and between 1943 and 1947 painted a body of work that he called *Images of modern evil*. These paintings are powerful social commentaries that explore the dark and gritty side of urban wartime life.

1 Albert Tucker, interview by James Gleeson, 2 May 1979, Canberra: National Gallery of Australia Research Library, transcript, p. 12.

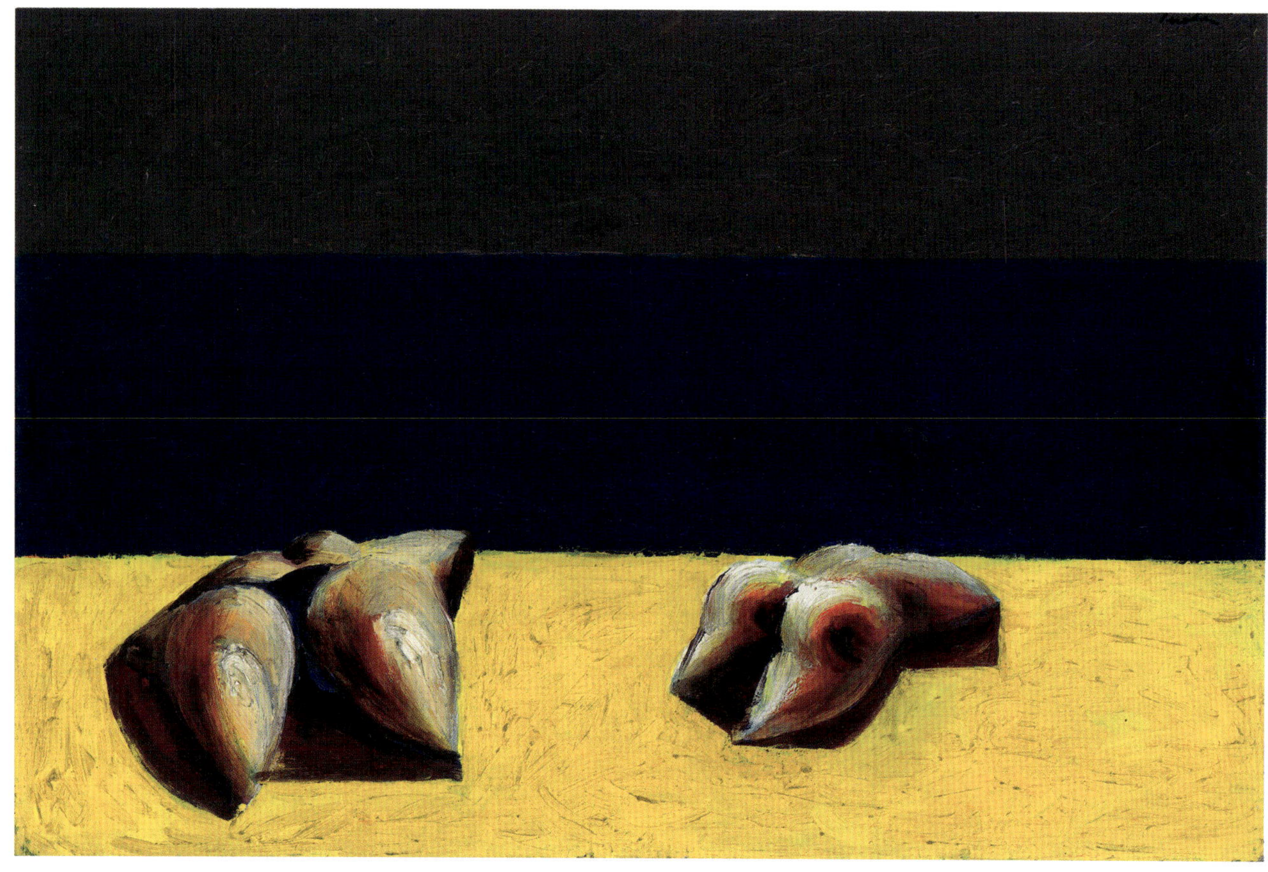

Jeffrey Smart (b. 1921)
Wallaroo 1951
oil on plywood 68.4 x 107 cm
Purchased 1959

Inspired by the South Australian copper-mining town, *Wallaroo* is an atmospheric and mysterious painting. Located on the Spencer Gulf coast, Jeffrey Smart visited Wallaroo in 1951 and made a number of watercolour studies of the town's buildings, beach, mining sites and breakwater. Returning to his studio, Smart 'began mixing all the sketches together, trying them this way and that, seeing how they could agree in a large composition – a painting in oils'.[1]

In *Wallaroo* two young men carry a boat ashore, one figure stepping out of the water and swinging his arm out to balance himself. The entire composition is an exercise in balance – the stretch of sand meeting the curve of the breakwater, the height of the chimney balancing the weight of the figures. Each element is carefully placed to direct the eye around the painting. There is an eerie stillness to the image, created by the long shadows and abandoned environment. The rusty ochres and greys of the earth and sky contrast with the bright strip of sand and the building. In discussing the painting Smart said:

> I tried all sorts of skies, ones with huge clouds, those with strata clouds, a stormy sky and so on. Finally I settled for one which graduated, light at the horizon and becoming darker near the top. But then it looked too dull. It wasn't interesting enough. So a moon – which you often see at evening, was brought in, just to make a note against the plain surface.[2]

1 Jeffrey Smart, 'An edited version from the artist's explanation of how he painted *Wallaroo*. ABC Children's Hour 1956', published in Edmund Capon, *Jeffrey Smart*, Sydney: Art Gallery of New South Wales, 1999, p. 78.
2 Capon, p. 79.

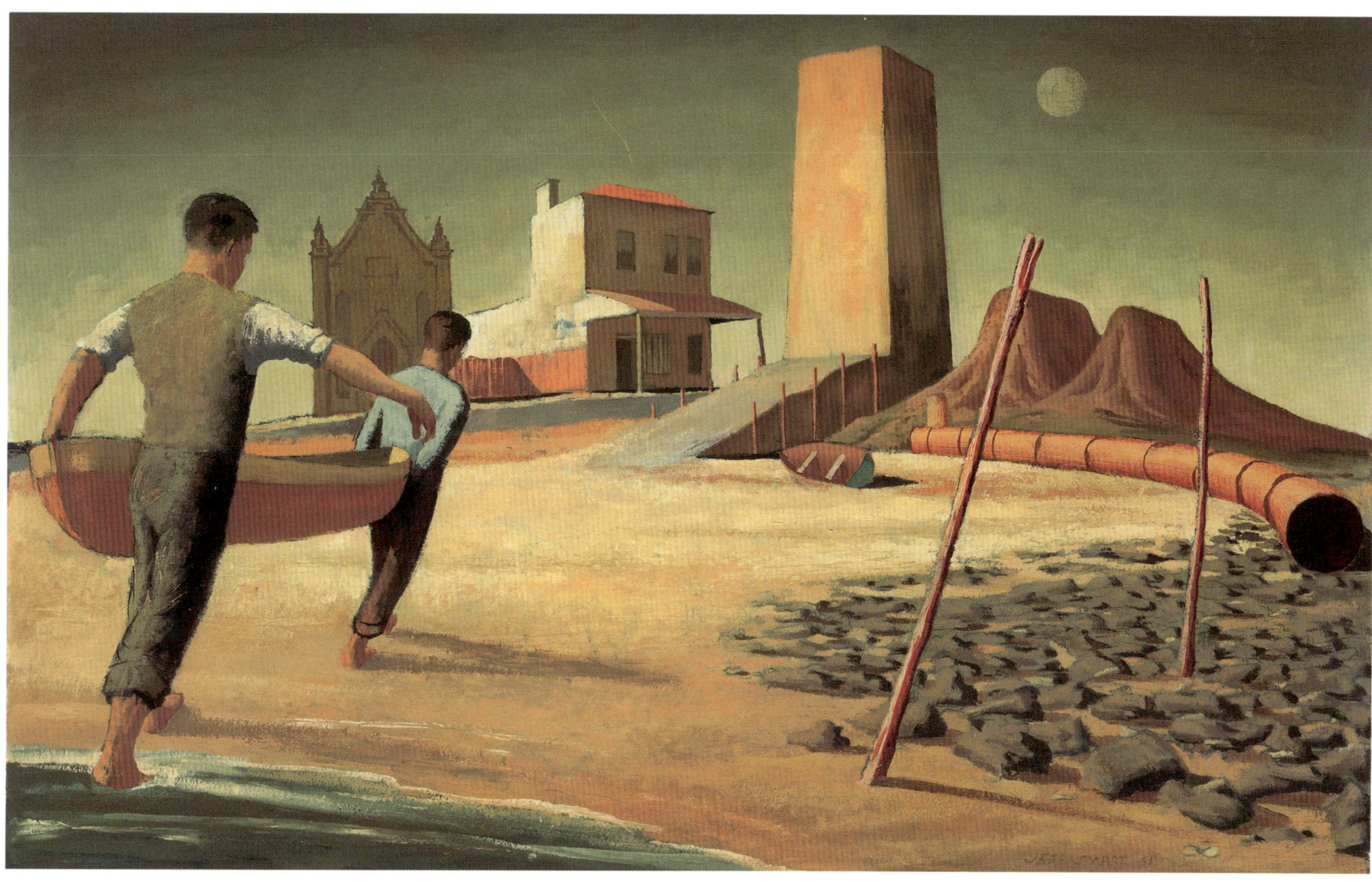

Hans Heysen (1877–1968)
In the Flinders – Far North 1951
oil on canvas 102.0 x 141.0 cm
Purchased 1959

For almost three decades the landscape of the Flinders Ranges in South Australia provided inspiration for Hans Heysen. Known for his imagery of Australian gum trees, the artist was forty-nine when he first visited the Flinders Ranges. The scenery of this country had a deep impact on Heysen, and between November 1926 and April 1949 he made many painting trips to the region.

In the Flinders – Far North is an example of Heysen combining the two great motifs of his oeuvre in one composition: the Australian gum tree and the view of the Flinders Ranges. The mightiness of the gum dominates this work, set deep in the arid amber and lilac landscape of the Ranges. The work was commissioned by the Commonwealth Government to celebrate the fiftieth anniversary of Federation and was displayed in the Australian Embassy in Paris for many years.[1]

In discussing the impact of the Flinders Ranges on his work and the contrast it provided with the landscape of his hometown of Ambleside (also known as Hahndorf), South Australia, Heysen said:

> … I go to the north, to the Flinders, where I find an entirely new landscape, quite divorced from anything that surrounds me here at Ambleside, and it gives me the fresh impulse to create the bare bones of our landscape in South Australia. It is an old country, very old, and it is that very age you feel in your surroundings, that spaciousness and those rugged peculiar shapes in the hills, that fascinate one, and the dry quality of the colour and the infinity of the vast distances have a fascination which this country surrounded by foliage and trees doesn't give you. You feel freer.[2]

1 Colin Thiele, *Heysen of Hahndorf*, Australia: Rigby Limited, 1968, pp. 264–65. See also Alisa Bunbury, *Arid Arcadia: art of the Flinders Ranges*, Adelaide: Art Gallery of South Australia, 2002.

2 Hans Heysen, interview by Hazel de Berg, 1960, Canberra: National Library of Australia [deB 27].

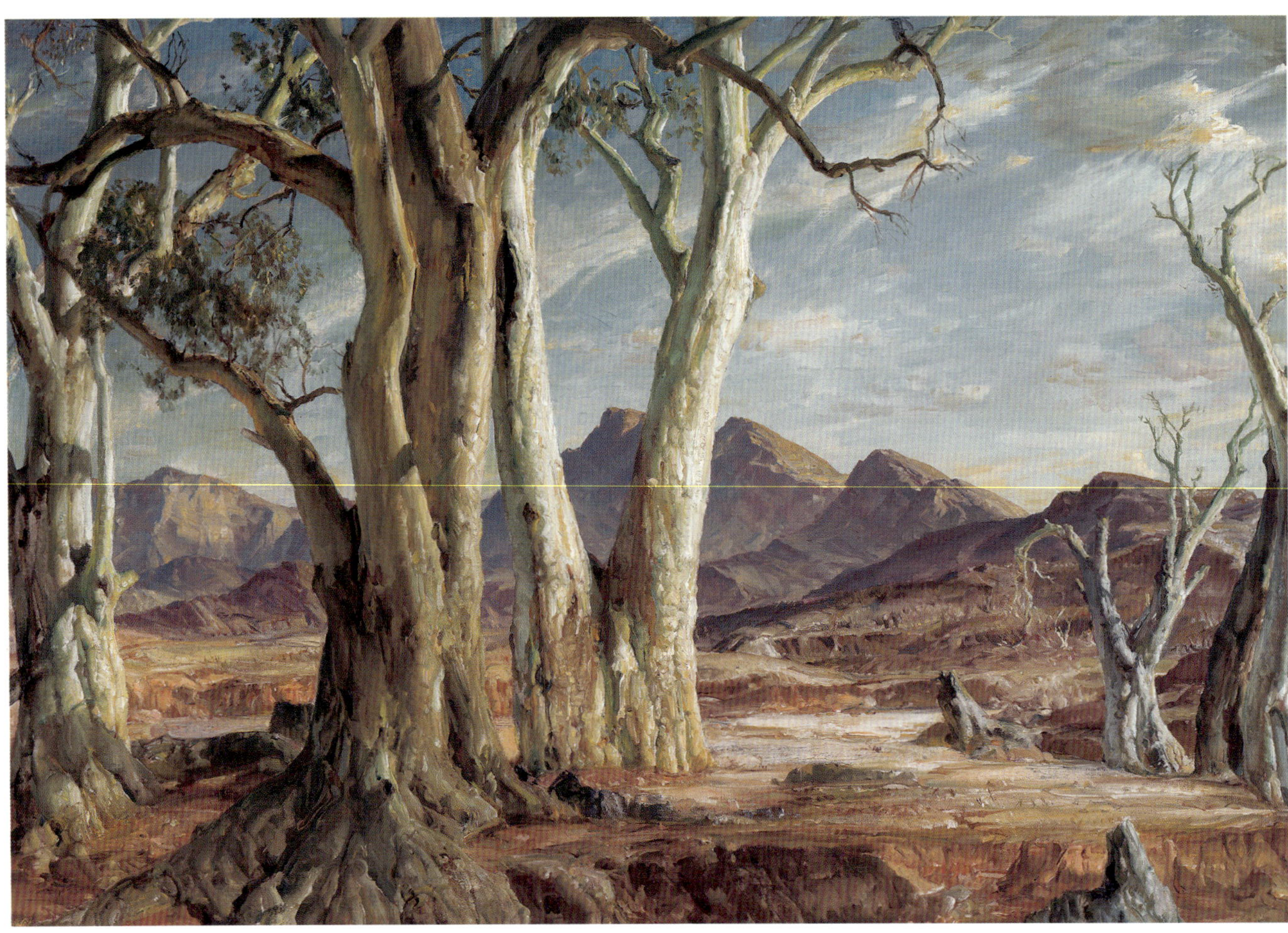

Horace Trenerry (1899–1958)
The ploughed field 1947
oil on canvas on cardboard 48.0 x 65.5 cm
Bequest of Dr Mildred Mocatta 1984

The ploughed field is an expressive response to the Aldinga and McLaren Vale region south of Adelaide where Horace Trenerry lived from 1934. Having left Adelaide during the Great Depression, Trenerry lived and worked in Willunga in relative isolation and poverty until 1951. In the early 1920s he lived briefly in Sydney where he studied at the Julian Ashton Art School. During this period he painted alongside Elioth Gruner who instilled in Trenerry a love of painting outdoors and an interest in depicting the effects of light on the Australian landscape. Returning to South Australia from Sydney in the late 1920s Trenerry developed a friendship with Hans Heysen who encouraged the younger artist to travel and visit the Flinders Ranges. Trenerry engaged with the painting styles of Gruner and Heysen, yet responded to the landscape with his own instinctive and highly sensitive approach.

In *The ploughed field* Trenerry used a restricted palette, tightly structured composition and dynamic painterly surface typical of his work. He defined the expanse of the field with short, layered, vertical brushstrokes (depicting the crops) over long horizontal lines. Bands of pink, orange and red suggest the rich, fertile earth of the region. The trees, sky and distant buildings are represented by dabs, dots, scrapes and square strokes of paint. Trenerry often mixed oil paint with powdered paint, a technique that created the opaque and chalky effect characteristic of his work.[1]

1 Lou Klepac, 'Hans Heysen, Elioth Gruner, Horace Trenerry', in Barry Pearce (ed.), *Parallel visions: works from the Australian collection*, Sydney: Art Gallery of New South Wales, 2002, p. 36.

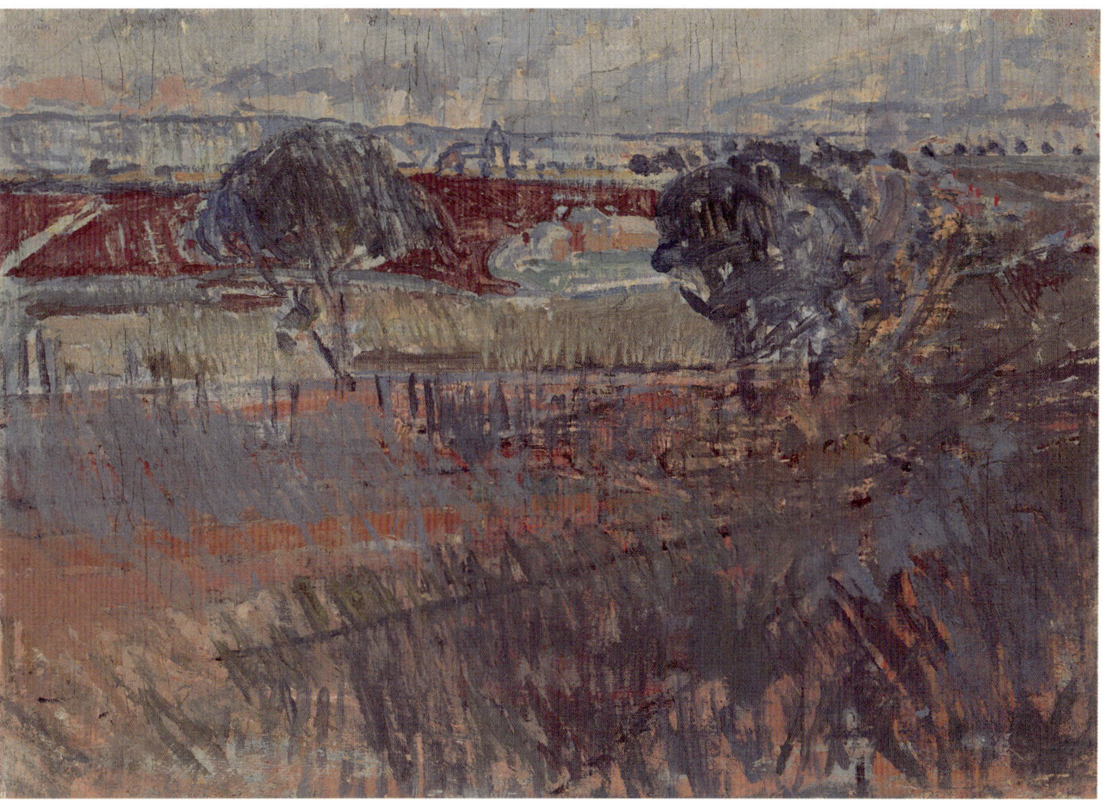

Elise Blumann (1897–1990)
Storm on the Swan 1946
oil on paper mounted on cardboard on composition board
57.0 x 67.0 cm
Purchased 1978

Elise Blumann painted Perth's Swan River and the native melaleuca trees of the region many times. Escaping the Nazi regime that devastated much of Europe, German-born Blumann came to Perth with her husband and two children in 1938. Educated at the Berlin Academy of Arts and the Royal Art School Berlin, Blumann was familiar with the modern art of the German Expressionists, Matisse, Picasso, Kandinsky and Chagall. In Australia Blumann's painting was unconventional, however her peers regarded her as a valued member of Perth's artistic community.

In *Storm on the Swan* Blumann uses broad sweeping gestures – strong horizontal and diagonal brushwork – to capture the power of a storm. Wind and rain beat against the limbs of the trees which appear to almost float in space. This dynamic and sensitive composition displays Blumann's modern approach to her art and her desire to capture the 'essential spirit' of nature.[1] Areas of the painting's surface are blank, while others are scratched with the end of her brush to indicate sharp, fast, rain. This is a vigorous, physical and quickly executed work, a powerful response to the speed in which a storm can approach and pass.

1 John Scott & Richard Woldendorp, *Landscapes of Western Australia*, Claremont, Western Australia: Aeolian Press, 1986, p. 17.

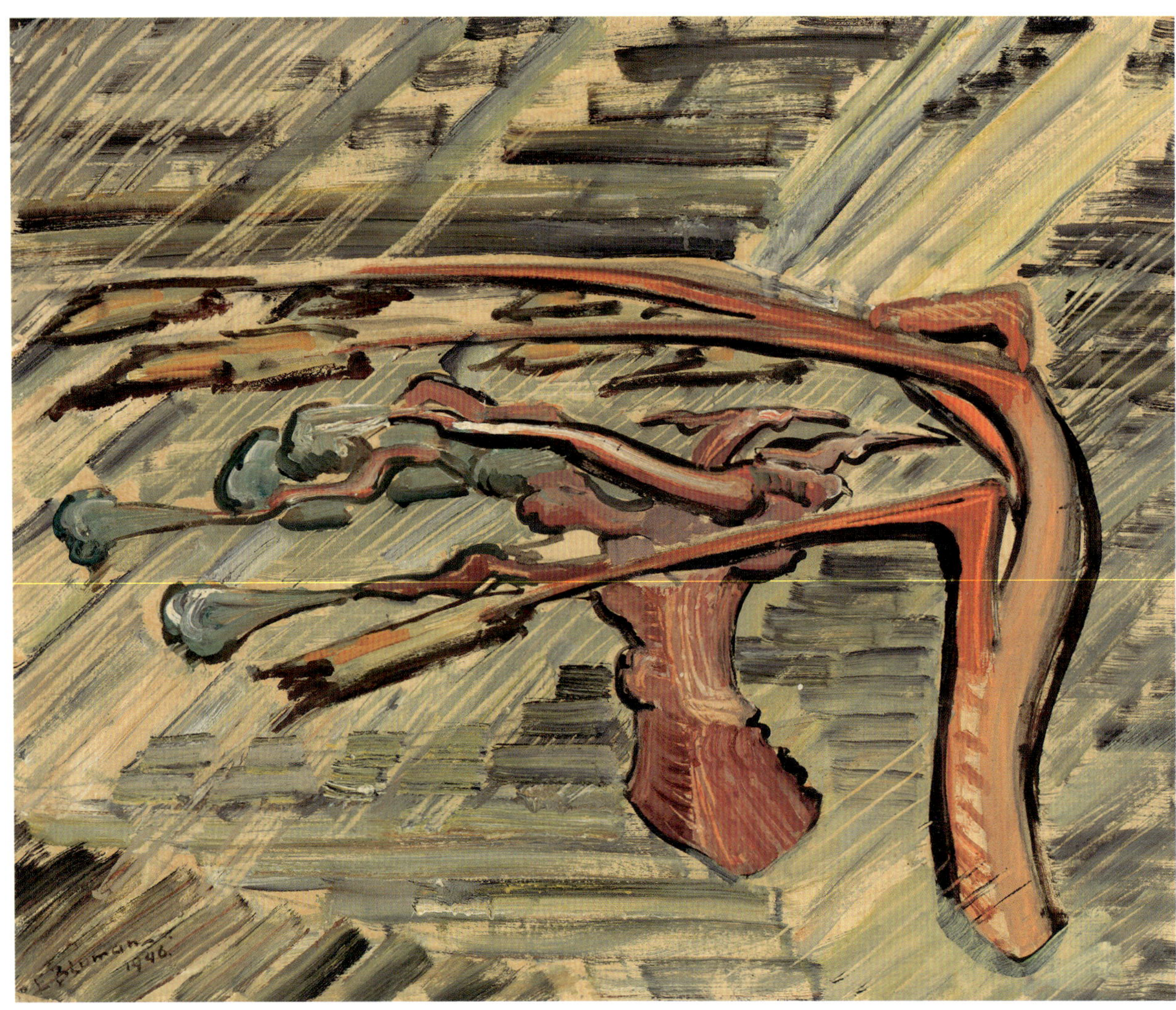

Guy Grey-Smith (1916–1981)
Perth from Kings Park 1949
oil on canvas 50.5 x 65.6 cm
Gift of the artist's son Mark Grey-Smith 1991

> … all my paintings are derived directly, really directly from nature, they are realistic in so far as they have a truth to me, if it is only a truth of feeling, not visual truth, but a truth of feeling.
> GUY GREY-SMITH 1965[1]

In *Perth from Kings Park* we peer through gum trees and across the Swan River to the city of Perth. When this work was painted in 1949 Perth had a population of 296 000 – a small city that rapidly expanded after a growth in migration at the end of the Second World War. Guy Grey-Smith also returned to Perth after the war, during which he had served in the Royal Air Force and had been interred in a German prisoner-of-war camp. It was during wartime that Grey-Smith began sketching and making watercolours. He later studied at the Chelsea School of Art in London before returning to Australia in 1948.

Grey-Smith determinedly championed artistic and cultural activities in Perth. He worked as a painter, printmaker and potter and it was in the landscape of Western Australia that he found his greatest inspiration, seeking out its rejuvenating, spiritual qualities. *Perth from Kings Park* is a kaleidoscopic view of colour and light, with prisms and planes intersecting to shape the scene. Searching for his own visual language, Grey-Smith used colour to explore spiritual states and reduced form to the basic shapes of triangles, prisms, cubes and spheres.

1 Guy Grey-Smith, interview by Helen Grey-Smith, 29 May 1965, National Library of Australia, Canberra, p. 4.

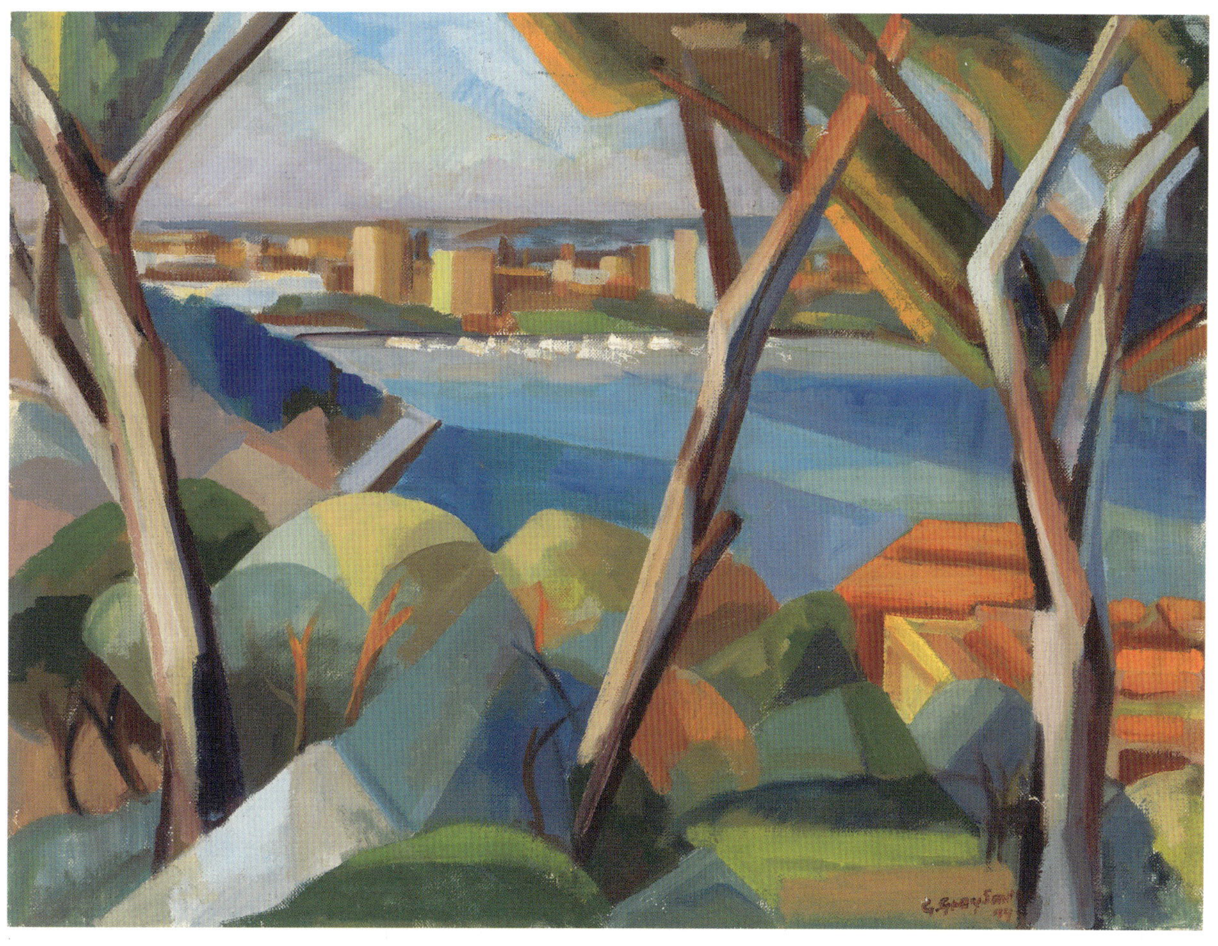

Howard Taylor (1918–2001)
Trees 1950
egg tempera on hardboard 40.5 x 50.8 cm
Gift of Esther Constable in memory of her husband
Dr Roy K. Constable, Perth 1987

Trees is one of a number of works in egg tempera that Howard Taylor painted from around 1950. The work is a disciplined study of line, light and shape combined to create an overall shimmering effect. In this work Taylor explored the ephemeral qualities of light and colour and the rich and subtle surfaces he observed in the Australian bush. He said that: 'painting the Australian landscape involved a big change for me, and another change was that I soon got more involved in tempera painting … if you paint in tempera you become engaged in a highly disciplined technique … you've got to plan right from the beginning.'[1]

In *Trees* the composition is divided into distinct planes, the horizontal bands set against a vertical cluster of trees. Positioned in the centre of the work is the apex of a circle. This circle is filled with light from an unknown source. Around its perimeter are eight trees, the trunks of which create long shadows stretching to the bottom right-hand corner of the composition. The tree foliage resembles a three-dimensional structure, carefully constructed by lines and subtle tonal variations. The shape of a figure 8 defines this arrangement, symbolic of infinity and the cyclical patterns of nature. *Trees* is a dense picture, yet the overall effect is one of lightness. The meticulous repetition of line suggests both the complexity and ethereal delicacy of the natural world.

1 Howard Taylor, interview by James Murdoch in 1986 for the Australia Council Archival Art Series. See Gary Dufour & Allan Watson (eds), *Howard Taylor: phenomena*, Perth: Art Gallery of Western Australia & Sydney: Museum of Contemporary Art, 2003, p. 61.

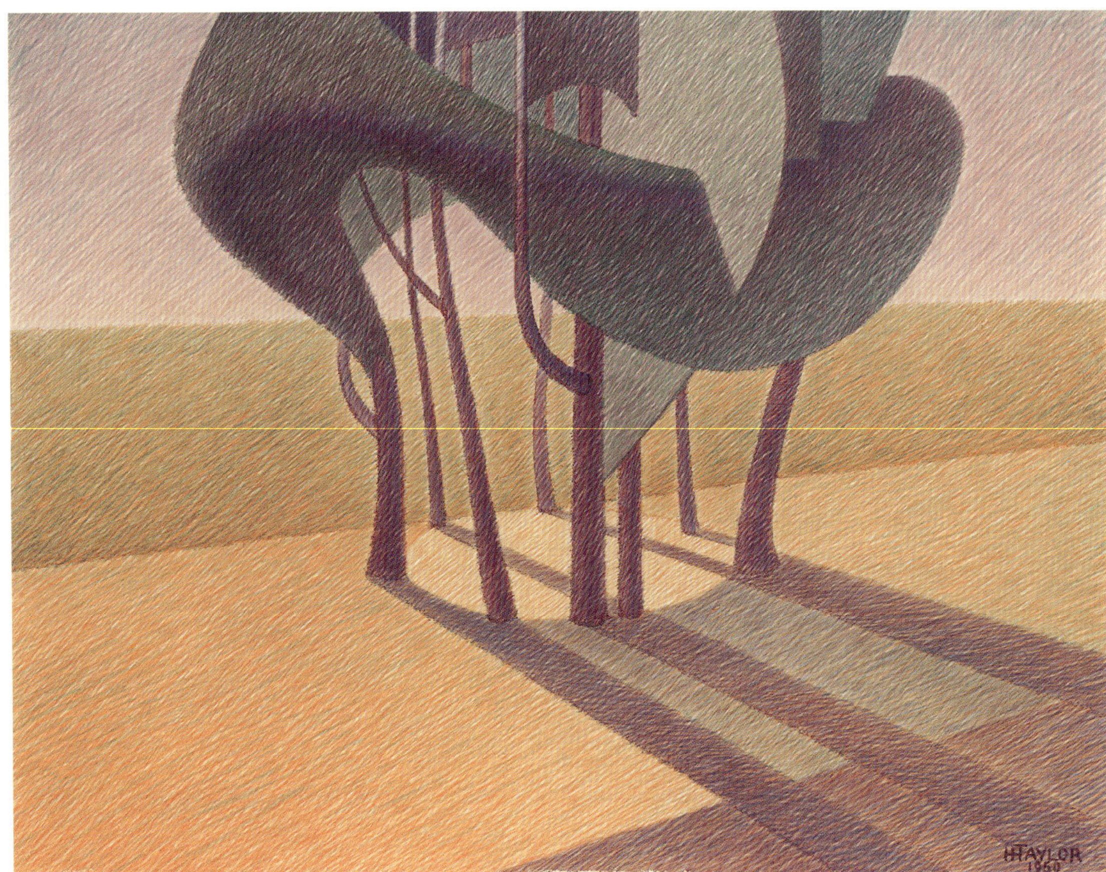

Ray Crooke (b. 1922)
'Kingfisher', Thursday Island 1950
egg tempera and oil on composition board 25.0 x 35.6 cm
Purchased 2006

> I find a strange island sometimes where ghosts of ancient glories linger, where the winds and the flowers are sweet and the people are still gentle and smiling, where man is conscious of his grandeur and is content to live simply in harmony with the forces around and within him. Yet if we found this island we would destroy it in a month.
> RAY CROOKE 1949[1]

'Kingfisher', Thursday Island marks the beginning of Ray Crooke's longstanding interest in painting the people and landscapes of Far North Queensland and the Pacific. The work was painted after Crooke's 1949 visit to the Torres Strait where he stayed for several months on Thursday Island (*Waiben*) working as a cook, labourer and trochus-shell diver.

Crooke first visited the Torres Strait and Thursday Island in 1943 as a soldier with the Australian Army. The artist enlisted in 1940 and during the war travelled extensively throughout Far North Queensland and the Pacific. For his first stay on Thursday Island soldiers were billeted in the abandoned Federal Hotel that was built around 1903. This building is identifiable in *'Kingfisher', Thursday Island* by its arched veranda and red roof.

An abandoned lugger sailing vessel dominates the image: a connection between land and sea, humans and the environment, past and present. From the 1860s the region was a centre for the risky activities of pearl and trochus-shell fishing, however the industry fell into decline after the Second World War.[2] Lugger sailing vessels, such as the one depicted in this painting, were used by fishermen to explore the tropical waters of the Darnley Deeps.

1 Ray Crooke, journal entry, quoted in Ray Crooke & Peter Denham, *Island journal*, Brisbane: Bede Publishing, 2000, p. 28.
2 Regina Ganter, *Mixed relations: Asian-Aboriginal contact in North Australia*, Perth: University of Western Australia Press, 2006, pp. 62–66.

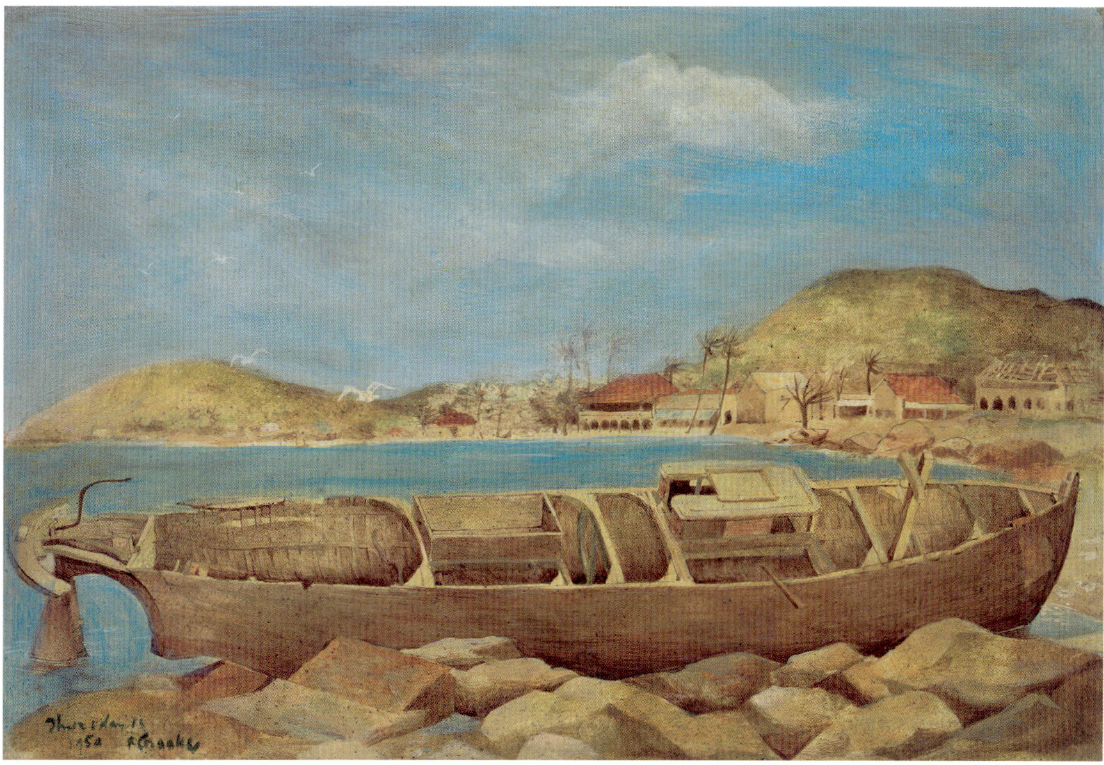

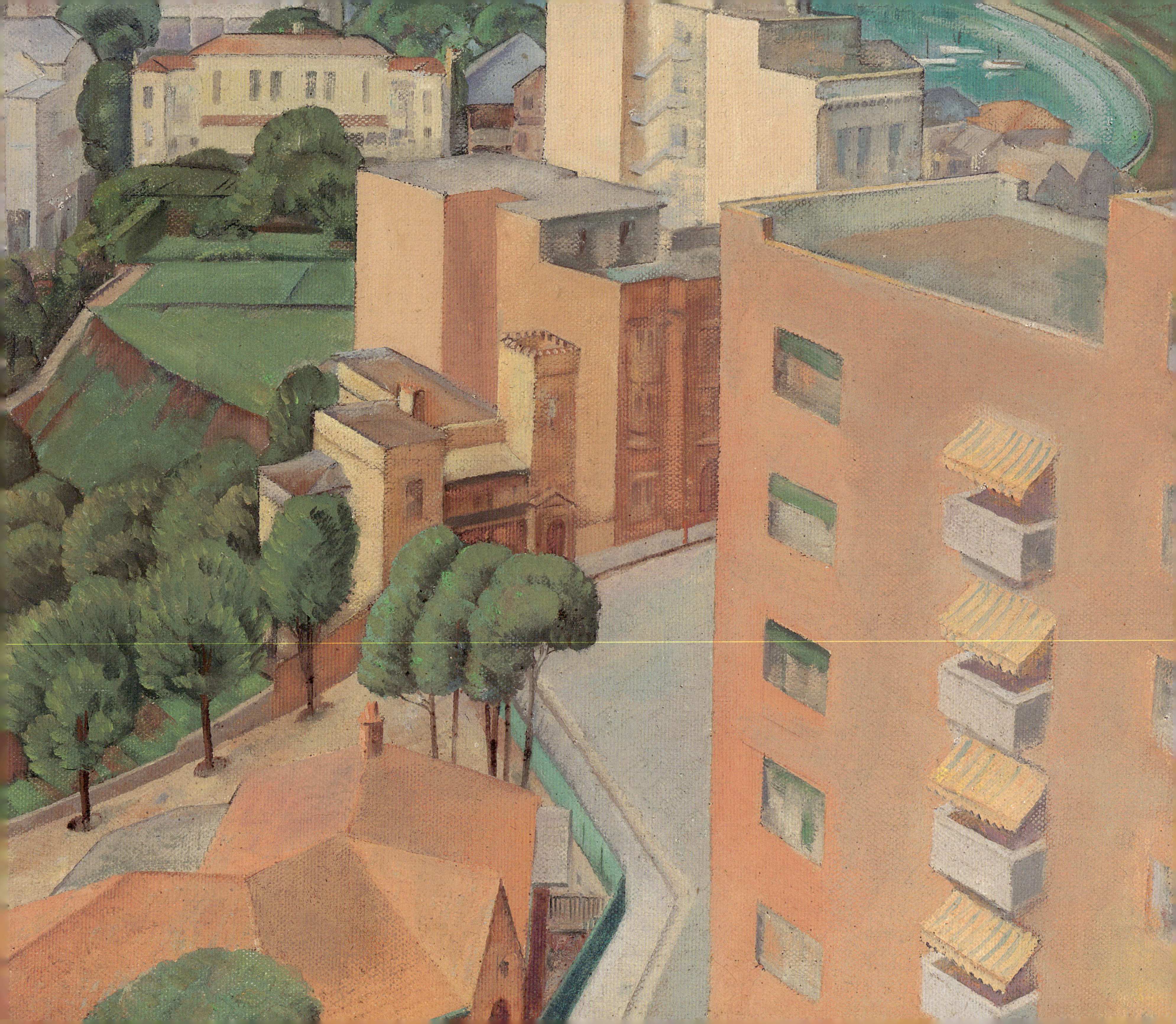

Map of Australia

indicating the location of capital cities and the places depicted in paintings included in the publication.

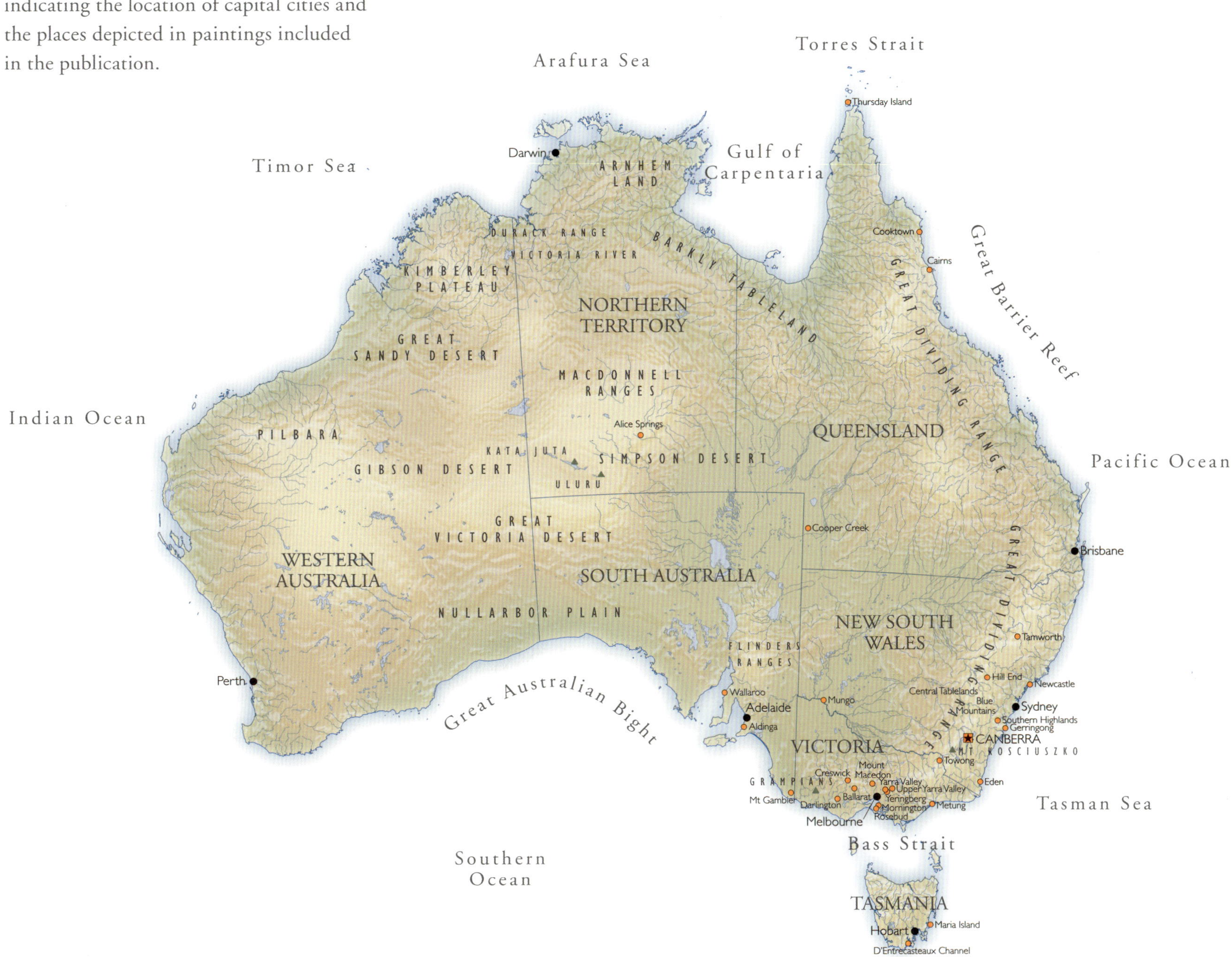

Timeline

60 000 BC Indigenous Australians are estimated to have arrived on the continent.

1606 First undisputed sighting by Europeans of Australian mainland, at Cape York Peninsula. During the seventeenth century other Dutch navigators chart the whole of the north and west coasts of the continent, and the south coast as far as Ceduna. They name the land New Holland.

1642 Dutch explorer Abel Tasman sights the west coast of Tasmania, which he names Anthony van Diemen's Land.

1770 Captain James Cook charts the east coast of New Holland, names it New South Wales, and claims it for Great Britain.

1788 The First Fleet, of British convict and military colonists, arrives and the first European settlement in Australia is established on 26 January at Sydney Cove.

Minimum estimate of Australian Indigenous population 314 500.

1803 A second convict settlement is established at Van Diemen's Land, now Hobart.

1813 Crossing of the Blue Mountains by settlers opens up inland pastoralism.

1824 British Admiralty agrees that New Holland be officially known as Australia. The name had been occasionally used since 1625, was popularised in 1814 by navigator Matthew Flinders, and recommended in 1817 by colonial governor Lachlan Macquarie.

1825 Van Diemen's Land is proclaimed a separate colony from New South Wales.

1829 Colony of Western Australia is founded, formally making the entire continent a British territory.

1835 Melbourne is settled and in 1836 is named and declared the capital of the Port Phillip District of New South Wales.

Conrad Martens arrives in Sydney from London.

1836 Province of South Australia is founded on 28 December.

W. C. Piguenit is born in Hobart.

1840 Transportation of convicts to New South Wales is officially abolished. Convicts are still sent to Norfolk Island and Van Diemen's Land.

1846 Knut Bull, convicted while visiting London from Norway, is transported to Norfolk Island and then to Van Diemen's Land.

1851 Port Phillip District separates from New South Wales and on 1 July becomes the colony of Victoria.

Gold is discovered in New South Wales and soon afterwards at Ballarat and Bendigo in Victoria.

1852 Lured by the gold rush, Eugene von Guérard arrives in Victoria, but in 1854 abandons gold digging and returns to painting in Melbourne.

Henry Rielly arrives in Melbourne from London, aged seven.

1853 Transportation of convicts to Van Diemen's Land ceases.

1854 Nicholas Chevalier arrives in Melbourne from London.

1855 A. C. Gregory leads the North Australian Exploring Expedition to investigate the sources of the Victoria River, in what is now the Northern Territory but was then part of New Soauth Wales. Thomas Baines comes from England for two years to be the official expedition artist, and also the storekeeper.

Frederick McCubbin is born in Melbourne.

1856 The name Tasmania, after the Dutch navigator Abel Tasman, is officially adopted, replacing Van Diemen's Land.

1859 Queensland becomes a separate colony from New South Wales on 10 December.

1861 A Museum of Art is established at the Public Library of Victoria, a picture gallery first opens there in 1864, and in 1869 is renamed the National Gallery of Victoria.

1863 New South Wales hands over its north-western lands beyond Queensland and they become the Northern Territory of South Australia.

1865 Louis Buvelot arrives in Melbourne from Switzerland.

1867 Arthur Streeton is born at Mount Duneed, Victoria.

1868 Last convicts transported to Australia arrive at Fremantle, Western Australia.

1869 Tom Roberts arrives in Melbourne from England, aged thirteen.

Nicholas Chevalier leaves Melbourne and settles in London.

1870 National Gallery of Victoria Art School is established. Eugene von Guérard is appointed Master of the school and also Curator of the National Gallery of Victoria.

Percy Lindsay is born at Creswick, Victoria.

1871 Sydney Long is born at Goulburn, New South Wales.

1872 First message is transmitted on 23 June on the Overland Telegraph, connecting Adelaide via Darwin to Java; Australia is now in near-immediate contact with the rest of the world.

1875 Margaret Preston is born in Adelaide.

1876 Art Gallery of New South Wales collections, begun in 1874 with a grant to an artists' society, first open to the public in a former dance hall.

Haughton Forrest arrives in Hobart from England.

1878 Harry Garlick is born at Orange, New South Wales.

Conrad Martens dies in Sydney.

1880 W. C. Piguenit moves from Hobart to Sydney.

1881 Art Gallery of South Australia collections, established in 1879, first open to the public in a room in the Public Library of South Australia.

Tom Roberts travels to Europe to study, returning to Melbourne in 1885.

1882 Eugene von Guérard leaves Melbourne and settles in Europe.

1883 Walter Withers arrives in Melbourne from England.

Elioth Gruner arrives in Sydney from New Zealand, not quite one-year-old.

1884 Ballarat Fine Art Gallery collection is established.

Charles Conder arrives in Sydney from England, aged fifteen.

Hans Heysen arrives in Adelaide from Germany, aged six.

1885 Tom Roberts, back from London, takes Frederick McCubbin and others on outdoor landscape painting excursions on the outskirts of Melbourne; in 1886 they establish a tented artists' camp further out at Box Hill.

English journalist George Sala, visiting Australia, calls it the 'Land of the Golden Fleece', wool being its principal source of wealth, and coins the phrase 'Marvellous Melbourne'.

Henry Rielly moves from Melbourne to Queensland.

1886 Frederick McCubbin is appointed Acting Master of the National Gallery of Victoria Art School and Instructor of its School of Design.

1887 Clarice Beckett is born at Casterton, Victoria.

Bendigo Art Gallery is established.

1888 Charles Conder moves from Sydney to Melbourne. Arthur Streeton is given the use of a farmhouse at Eaglemont, above the suburban railway station of Heidelberg, and there establishes another 'camp' for outdoor landscape painting.

1889 Early in the year, Tom Roberts and Charles Conder join Arthur Streeton at Eaglemont.

9 x 5 Impression exhibition in Melbourne includes works by Arthur Streeton, Tom Roberts, Charles Conder and Frederick McCubbin.

Max Meldrum arrives in Melbourne from Scotland, aged fourteen.

Tasmanian Museum and Art Gallery is established. Some of its present-day art collections had earlier been included in natural-history collections open to the public from 1848.

1890 Melbourne land-boom crash, and one of Australia's worst economic depressions begins.

Charles Conder departs Melbourne permanently for Europe.

1891 Queen Victoria Museum & Art Gallery is opened at Launceston; its first collections are transferred from a Mechanics' Institute museum established in 1844.

Tom Roberts shifts his base from Melbourne to Sydney and lives in depression-period tents at Sirius Cove in Mosman, where Arthur Streeton joins him in December 1892.

Rah Fizelle is born at Baw Baw, near Goulburn, New South Wales.

A. E. Newbury is born in Melbourne.

1892 Grace Cossington Smith is born in Sydney.

Julian Ashton begins classes at the Royal Art Society of New South Wales; establishes his own Académie Julian in 1896, which is renamed Sydney Art School in 1907 and Julian Ashton Art School in 1942.

1894 Roy de Maistre is born at Bowral, New South Wales.

1895 Art Gallery of Western Australia is officially opened as part of the Perth Museum.

Queensland Art Gallery is opened, in the Brisbane Town Hall, Queen Street.

A severe drought begins, affects most of the continent, and lasts until 1903.

Lloyd Rees is born in Brisbane.

1896 Geelong Gallery is established but exhibits only loans; collections start in 1900.

Australia's first cinema opens in Pitt Street, Sydney.

1897 Walter Withers is awarded the inaugural Wynne Prize, for Australian landscape painting, by the Art Gallery of New South Wales.

Art Gallery of South Australia receives bequest of £25 000 from Sir Thomas Elder, the first significant bequest to a major art museum in Australia.

Arthur Streeton departs for London, where he is based until 1920.

1899 Horace Trenerry is born in Adelaide.

Hans Heysen travels to Europe to study, returning to Adelaide in 1903.

Max Meldrum wins National Gallery School Travelling Scholarship; returns to Melbourne from France in 1911.

1901 The six colonies of Australia become a federation, known as the Commonwealth of Australia. Melbourne is the temporary capital of Australia until 1927.

Queen Victoria dies.

National population over 3.8 million.

Minimum estimates of Australia's Indigenous population 94 564.

1902 Edward VII is crowned king of the British Empire.

1903 Tom Roberts departs for London where he is based until 1923.

1904 Eric Thake is born in Melbourne.

National Gallery of Victoria receives the Felton Bequest, from the businessman Alfred Felton, the largest acquisition fund for an art museum in Australia.

Dorothea Mackellar writes the poem *My country*, published with the title *Core of my heart* in the London *Spectator*, in 1908.

1905 Henry Rielly dies in Brisbane.

1907 Frederick McCubbin visits Europe.

1908 The Yass–Canberra area is selected as the site for the federal capital of Australia.

1910 Sam Atyeo is born in Melbourne.

Harry Garlick dies in Sydney.

1911 Australian Capital Territory is proclaimed, but is known as Federal Capital Territory until 1938.

Administration of Northern Territory is transferred from South Australia to the Commonwealth Government.

Australian National Art Collection is founded.

1912 Russell Drysdale is born in England of Australian parents; he settles permanently in Australia in 1923.

Margaret Preston leaves Adelaide for Europe, returning to Sydney in 1920.

Roland Wakelin moves to Sydney from Wellington, New Zealand.

1914 First World War begins.

W. C. Piguenit dies in Sydney.

Walter Withers dies in Melbourne.

Albert Tucker is born in Melbourne.

1915 ANZAC military forces lead British and French invasion of Turkey and land on Gallipoli Peninsula on 25 April.

1916 The Meldrum School of Painting is established in Melbourne; it operates until 1926.

Sydney Ure Smith establishes the magazine *Art in Australia* which runs until 1942.

Guy Grey-Smith is born at Wagin, Western Australia.

1917 South Australia closes forty-nine Lutheran schools and officially replaces more than forty German place names with British names; Queensland renames thirteen places, other states fewer.

Sidney Nolan is born in Melbourne.

Frederick McCubbin dies in Melbourne.

1918 First World War concludes.

National population over 5.3 million.

Howard Taylor is born at Hamilton, Victoria.

1919 Spanish flu epidemic kills nearly 12 000 people in Australia.

Roy de Maistre and Roland Wakelin hold exhibition of 'colour-music' paintings in Sydney.

1920 Arthur Boyd is born in Melbourne.

1921 Jeffrey Smart is born in Adelaide.

1922 Country Women's Association is established in New South Wales and Queensland. By 1936 there is a branch in each Australian state and territory.

Ray Crooke is born in Melbourne.

1925 Haughton Forrest dies in Hobart.

1926 Hans Heysen makes his first trip to the Flinders Ranges, 500 kilometres north of Adelaide.

1927 Federal Government moves from Melbourne to Canberra on 9 May.

1929 The economic crash known as the Great Depression begins.

Roy de Maistre leaves Sydney and settles in London; he had been in Europe from 1923–26 on a travelling scholarship.

1931 Rah Fizelle returns to Sydney from Europe, where he had been since 1927.

Tom Roberts dies at Kallista, Victoria.

1932 The Great Depression peaks, with nearly one in three men unemployed.

The Sydney Harbour Bridge is completed.

George Bell and Arnold Shore establish the Bell-Shore art school in Melbourne, which operates until 1936; Bell continues alone until 1939.

Grace Crowley and Rah Fizelle establish the modernist Crowley-Fizelle art school in Sydney, which operates until 1937.

1934 William Moore's *The story of Australian art: from the earliest known art of the continent to the art of to-day* is published.

1935 Clarice Beckett dies in Melbourne.

1938 A Contemporary Art Society is established in Melbourne; branches open in Sydney in 1939 and Adelaide in 1942.

Elise Blumann arrives in Perth from Germany.

Russell Drysdale travels to Europe to study; he returns to Melbourne in 1939 and moves to Sydney in 1940.

1939 Second World War begins.

National population over 7 million.

The Melbourne *Herald*'s *Exhibition of French and British contemporary art* opens at the Art Gallery of South Australia. Includes works by European modernists such as Gauguin, van Gogh, Cézanne, Seurat, Picasso, Braque, Matisse, Bonnard and Dali. It travels to Melbourne Town Hall and David Jones department store in Sydney, reaching an audience of about 70 000 people.

Elioth Gruner dies in Sydney.

1941 *Angry Penguins* literary and artistic magazine is first issued, edited by poet Max Harris in Adelaide, soon assisted in Melbourne by John Reed; it presented the work of Albert Tucker, Sidney Nolan and others and continued until 1946.

A. E. Newbury dies in Melbourne.

Japanese raid on Pearl Harbor; war begins in the Pacific.

1942 Fall of Singapore to Japanese, February.

Air raids begin on Darwin in February; air raid on Broome, Western Australia, in March.

Between July 1942 and January 1943 battles are fought between Australian and Japanese forces along the Kokoda Track in Papua New Guinea.

1943 Ray Crooke visits Thursday Island in the Torres Strait as a soldier with the Australian Imperial Force (AIF).

Arthur Streeton dies at Olinda, Victoria.

1944 Russell Drysdale accompanies the *Sydney Morning Herald* to record drought devastation in western New South Wales.

1945 Second World War concludes.

Bernard Smith's *Place, taste and tradition*: *a study of Australian art since 1788* is published.

1947 Albert Tucker leaves Melbourne for Europe.

Sidney Nolan moves from Melbourne to Sydney.

1948 Guy Grey-Smith returns to Perth from war service and study in Europe.

1949 Howard Taylor returns to Perth from war service and study in Europe.

1950 Sidney Nolan leaves Sydney for his first visit to Europe.

National population over 8.3 million.

Acknowledgments

Ocean to Outback: Australian landscape painting 1850–1950 has been sponsored by the recently formed National Gallery of Australia Council Exhibitions Fund. This fund is a bold and generous twenty-fifth anniversary initiative of the Gallery's Council, and aims to ensure that people across Australia have access to the treasures of the National Collection including this Australian landscape exhibition and publication.

Since its inception, Visions of Australia has been a strong supporter of the National Gallery's Travelling Exhibition program, having funded fifteen exhibitions. More than 100 venues have enjoyed exhibitions through this valuable partnership.

I would like to thank the many people who have helped me assemble this major travelling exhibition from the National Gallery of Australia. Firstly, Beatrice Gralton, Curatorial Coordinator, who did so much of the legwork for the exhibition and wrote the catalogue entries for every painting. Belinda Cotton and Dominique Nagy must be thanked for organising the extensive tour to every state and territory. Anna Gray, Deborah Hart and Elena Taylor from Australian Art provided useful advice on the exhibition and editing notes towards the catalogue entries. David Wise has cleaned, restored and prepared a great many paintings for the tour and was helped by Sheridan Roberts and Allan Byrne. John Jones gave advice and supervised much of the reframing, assisted by Greg Howard. The editing of my text, exhibition checklist and timeline was done by Daniel Thomas. Kirsty Morrison, Paige Amor and Jeanie Watson from Publications, Emilia Rossi from Exhibition Design, Erica Persak, Rebecca Nielsen and Ted Nugent from Registration, Jael Muspratt from Conservation, Craig O'Sullivan from Security, Peter Naumann and Adriane Boag from Education and photographers Brenton McGeachie and Steve Nebauer have all made valuable contributions in their respective fields. I would also like to thank my executive assistant Hester Gascoigne.

The venues that have exhibited *Ocean to Outback* must be thanked for their enthusiasm towards the project and contribution to the Gallery's twenty-fifth anniversary celebrations. The ongoing relationships with these venues throughout Australia reflect a twenty-year association with the Gallery's Travelling Exhibition Program, bringing the National Collection to their respective communities.

Ron Radford AM
Director
National Gallery of Australia

Index

Numbers in **bold** refer to reproductions

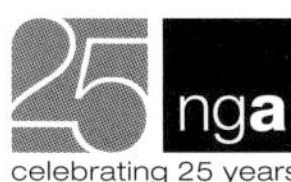

national gallery of **australia**
travelling exhibitions

Produced by the Publications Department
of the National Gallery of Australia

nga.gov.au/OceanToOutback

The National Gallery of Australia is an Australian Government Agency.

Editor: Claire Armstrong
Designer: Stephen Smedley, Tonto Design
Cartographer: Suzanne Keating
Printer: National Capital Printing

Cataloguing-in-publication data

Radford, Ron, 1949- .
Ocean to Outback : Australian landscape painting 1850–1950

1st ed.
Bibliography.
Includes index.
ISBN 9780642541451 (pbk.).

1. National Gallery of Australia - Exhibitions. 2. Art, Australian - Exhibitions. 3. Art, Australian - History. I. National Gallery of Australia. II. Title.

709.94

Published on the occasion of the exhibition:
Ocean to Outback: Australian landscape painting 1850–1950

The National Gallery of Australia's 25th Anniversary Travelling Exhibition

Tamworth Regional Gallery, NSW, 4 August – 22 September 2007
Tasmanian Museum and Art Gallery, Hobart, Tas., 5 October – 25 November 2007
Riddoch Art Gallery, Mt Gambier, SA, 8 December 2007 – 20 January 2008
Ballarat Fine Art Gallery, Vic., 2 February – 30 March 2008
Lawrence Wilson Art Gallery, Perth, WA, 13 April – 1 June 2008
Cairns Regional Gallery, Qld, 21 June – 27 July 2008
Araluen Arts Centre, Alice Springs, NT, 9 August – 19 October 2008
Newcastle Region Art Gallery, NSW, 8 November 2008 – 18 January 2009
Canberra Museum and Gallery, ACT, 31 January – 3 May 2009

The exhibition was organised by the National Gallery of Australia, Canberra

The exhibition was curated in Canberra by:
Ron Radford, Director, National Gallery of Australia
Beatrice Gralton, Associate Curator Australian Painting and Sculpture, National Gallery of Australia.

FRONT COVER
Russell Drysdale (1912–1981)
Emus in a landscape 1950
oil on canvas 101.6 x 127.0 cm
Purchased 1970
© Estate of Russell Drysdale

BACK COVER
Knut Bull (1811–1889)
The wreck of the 'George the Third' 1850 (detail)
oil on canvas 84.5 x 123.0 cm
Purchased with funds from the Nerissa Johnson Bequest 2001

PAGE 112
Rah Fizelle (1891–1964)
Elizabeth Bay 1931 or 1932 (detail)
oil on canvas mounted on composition board
45.0 x 38.0 cm
Purchased 1971